Marriage Ain't No Picnic

a love story
by Carol Hrehovcik

MARRIAGE AIN'T NO PICNIC

"I'm nobody! Who are you?
Are you nobody, too?"
Emily Dickinson

"Who is this woman and why should I be interested in her marriage?"

"What does she have to say that I haven't read or heard a thousand times before?"

If you are asking yourself these questions, I say "good for you." These are fair questions. The simple answer is I am a survivor of forty-two years of marriage to the same man. Even you must admit this is a rare accomplishment today. When statistics show one out of every two marriages end in divorce, I wonder. I still ask questions of other couples because I want to know their secret.

The unexpected part of my story is I have no secret. What I offer instead is a story I hope will give you faith in *yourself.* There is no easy answer to what makes a good marriage because marriage is hard work. It takes commitment and resolve of two people to make a marriage. But it is much more than just work.

I talked with an older woman who has been married almost fifty years and asked her secret. "Choose your battles," she said, "and know when to keep your mouth shut." Good advice I thought, but that is only one answer.

The trick is to work at it always. You can never rest from working at your marriage. Just as you accept the fact that you are a parent forever, you must believe this marriage is also forever. It helps when you say to yourself "in good times and bad, when I'm not even sure I especially like this person, I'll stay married." (Please take note: I am not encouraging people who are in abusive marriages to stay. That is a special circumstance requiring expert help.)

It is so easy to leave a marriage, to quit as if it were a bad job you didn't like. And sometimes it is that – a bad job, a lousy job. Oh, but when it is good, it is very, very good, and also like that little girl, when it is bad, it is indeed horrid.

This then is our story, or more accurately, my story. I have written a daily journal most of my married life and for some time before that. I wrote these journals for myself, for my own self-expression and sometimes self-fulfillment. I needed to write what I was feeling and what I was thinking, hoping it would help me to understand myself and perhaps my husband. I wrote also for my children. I hoped, as most parents do, they wouldn't make the same mistakes we made. Now, all these years later I have learned another lesson: Our children must live their lives, learn from their own mistakes, and celebrate their personal victories.

So I offer this book, no, I dedicate this book to anyone who has the curiosity, the courage, and the desire to stay married. Read it for yourself, not because I am rich or famous or remarkable in any way. Read it because I am just like you; doing the best I can, wanting to do it all better and believe that after all Love really is the answer.

In the end I hope you'll say to yourself: "If she can do it, so can I." And you know what? You can.

INTRODUCTION

My husband Stephen and I have been married for forty-two years and this is the story of our marriage.

When anyone asks me how we have stayed together this long, I tell them frankly, "Because we were both too stubborn to quit."

Stephen says, "Because we have always loved each other."

Speaking for myself, that has not always been true. There were many times when I didn't like the man, and yes, I even hated him on occasion. I believe in all the years we've been married. I have felt every feeling you could possibly feel toward another human being. But you know what? We're still together.

I wish I could have skipped some times, changed many situations, but I can tell you our marriage has never been dull. There were days I used to wish for "dull." Somewhere inside me I still believe that life and marriage don't have to be as hard as some of us make it.

A friend asked me not very long ago why I was writing

this book. She asked in a very matter of fact manner, "Why would anyone want to read this book?"

Since I had obviously asked myself the very same question, I surprised myself with my quick reply, "How many years have you and Sam been married?"

"Forty years."

"Tell me, do people often ask you how you and Sam have managed to stay married for so long?"

She replied, "Always."

"Exactly. That is why I'm writing this book, and this is why I believe people will read it. I think most of us are curious to know how someone stays married for more than five years. We think perhaps they have a secret. The knowledge that someone else has done it often gives us the courage to work at our own marriage." She seemed satisfied with this answer, and frankly so was I.

Originally, I started out merely to leave a written legacy for my children. I thought the story of the families, and, in particular, their own childhood, would help them understand not only where they came from, but also who they are. As I continued writing our story, it seemed to me we are not very unique or special. With one exception: we're still together because we worked through all our problems, got help when we needed it, and simply refused to give up.

For whatever reasons we chose to stay together, whether it was for the children or a fear of abandonment, Stephen and I are happier than we've ever been. We enjoy our life both as individuals and as a couple. For us, the best part of our marriage is now. Any of you who are wondering if the struggle to stay together is a journey you want to make, I can tell you only from my own experience the rewards will be there.

Perhaps you are one of the lucky ones and have had a wonderful marriage from the very beginning, knowing you were both so much in love and committed to stay together forever. I know there are marriages like this. It may even be your second marriage in which you found this love and success. I point to the example of my brother and his second wife who have such a marriage.

But for many of us the choice is not so clear. Should we stay or should we go? I could not have predicted how good our marriage would become. In our sixties now, we are enjoying and cherishing all our time together and discovering love all over again.

At long last, the title of this book, *To Love and to Cherish*, is a reality. I don't pretend to have the answers for you, after all this is not a how-to book. In fact, this is more a "how-not-to" book.

Yet, I believe for those of you who pick it up and choose to read it, you will find hope for yourself and your spouse and a renewed faith in your future together.

Remember: "If she can do it, so can I."

CHAPTER ONE

Two Different Worlds

Since this is the story of a marriage, you'd expect it to begin when Stephen and I met. But I believe, and many of you already know this, the true beginning of any marriage is long before you meet. It starts with the people themselves and who they are when they meet.

I was born in a small town in Pennsylvania in 1937. My parents lived there in Amish country for three years before they moved to what became their final home in Haverhill, Massachusetts. I grew up there, about 30 miles north of Boston and not very far from the seacoast. My roots and my heart will always be in New England and close to the ocean.

Stephen was born in Canada in 1938, and two years later he and his family moved to the United States. Linden, New Jersey would be his home for most of his adolescent years. He was close enough to New York to form a lifelong love affair with the city. Our backgrounds were vastly different, and yet because of the times in which we were raised, also very similar.

My parents were born in Rochester, New York, first generation Americans of Italian heritage. They met and married there in 1931 at the height of the Great Depression. During the Depression my father was fortunate to get a job in Carlisle, Pennsylvania, where he worked in a shoe factory as a machinist. Because of his skill and his trade at the time, he was one of the lucky few to have a job all through the Depression.

As good fortune as this was for my parents, it meant leaving their families behind and starting a new life on their own. Now we think nothing of packing up and moving away; in the 1930s, life was not as mobile as it is today. Transportation was by car or railway. Still, my mother, along with my brother, Louis, followed her husband to this unfamiliar and strange new home. I often think what an adventure this must have been for all of them! In later years, my mother talked of this experience as one of the happiest times of her life.

Three years later my parents were on the move again. My father followed where his work led him, and in 1939 it led him to the Queen City of shoes – Haverhill, Massachusetts. After settling into the apartment my father was lucky enough to rent, my mother declared she "would never move again." And she didn't!

Far away, in a land I knew nothing about, danger threatened the safety of our time. The threat of another world war was being argued and discussed everywhere – on the radio, in the papers, at home and at work. I was two years old and oblivious to all of it. I played with my dolls, with my brother, with new friends. In other words, I was doing a child's job: I played and imagined and explored, and like most kids, I got into trouble.

My brother is four years older than I, and one day I decided to meet him at his school. My mother and I had walked there often, and I was sure I knew the way, so off I went. I was excited to be on my own and thought how surprised and pleased my brother would be to see me. Whenever I made this journey with my mother it didn't seem very far, but as I walked and walked nothing looked familiar to me. Having a child's sense of time, which is no time at all, I knew I should have been there by now. I was lost.

Two women who lived in a big yellow house (only a block away as it turns out) saw me looking scared and confused, and probably crying. They came to help me and were very kind. They called the police, and a nice policeman took me in his car and brought me home to a frantic mother and neighbors.

I thought this was a grand adventure! I mean I was safe. I met some lovely ladies in a big, rich house, I got a ride in a police car, and I was not hurt in any way. But was my mother happy? No. She spanked me very hard and put me right in my crib. I was confused. What had I done wrong? Why wasn't she happy to see me and why didn't she hug me and love me and tell me she was relieved I was safe? I cried and cried both out of confusion and pain; that was a bad spanking. I know I didn't go exploring again for quite a while.

I do not tell this story merely to ramble on about some childhood escapade, nor do I plan to talk at any length about my childhood, as this is the story of a marriage not about my growing up. Yet this story illustrates a part of my personality that is significant to the tale.

In later years, when you begin to reflect on your life and your path, you may ask yourself many basic questions, such as

"Who am I?" "Where have I been?" and "Where am I going?" At times like this you may return to your childhood self, for it is there you were your truest self. Also, the kind of parenting you had may have formed you to become the kind of parent you are.

You either replicate, repeat what you know, or you may do as I did, rebel against the kind of parenting I had and do just the opposite. In my case I always wanted a kind, gentle, loving mother. I say mother most particularly, since she was the one who had the most profound influence on me. She was a mother who was at home all day, as was usual in those days. I did have one friend growing up whose mother had a job. Only one! This must be very hard for younger people to imagine, and yet that is the way it was.

My father went out the door every morning to work. Sometimes he was able to come home for lunch, but generally he left in the morning and we didn't see him again until supper time. And it was supper time for us, not dinner; we had dinner only Sundays and holidays. I wish I could tell you mother was a fabulous, wonderful cook. Well, she wasn't a bad cook, but she wasn't a great cook either. My mother didn't like to cook, and she didn't like anyone messing up her kitchen, which meant all my brother and I could do was set the table, clean the table, and do the dishes. And like most brothers, Louis always managed to go to the bathroom when it was time to do the dishes. As my mother wanted things done in her way and on her timetable, I often ended up doing the dishes alone.

One of the important guides of growing up in the early forties were the rules for dressing. All the young boys at the time wore knickers: "loosely fitting short breeches gathered

12

at the knee." A boy only got to wear long pants when he was considered a man, sometime around twelve years old. I am not sure whether the parents decided, "All right, now he's a man," or if there was another general rule.

I asked my brother if he remembered how old he was when he got his first pair of long pants, and he replied vaguely that it was before high school. I have found that men, in general, do not have many specific recollections of their childhoods.

This naturally takes our story to Stephen. When asked his earliest memory of childhood, Stephen has finally come up with a few memories prior to junior high school. As time has passed, he's begun to remember some small incidents that shaped him. Mostly he talks about being "afraid" of his father. As a consequence of this fear, Stephen would hide and be quiet just to escape his father's anger. Of course, this didn't help him in the long run as it only made his father lose all respect for him.

Stephen's mother...one of the stories he tells about her is how he would sit on the pedal under the sewing machine while she sewed. He does remember fondly how she cut her homemade noodles with skill and speed. And, of course, he remembers her praying "often." Mostly Stephen remembers his sister, and frequently will say "my mother" when he means "my sister." Since his father's death, he also says "my father" when he means "my brother." This interchange sister/mother brother/father gives you some clue about Stephen's growing up years.

I remember in college one of my psychology professors said, "You marry the family." The other girls and I scoffed at him. How right he turned out to be! And yet, if I had met

Stephen's family first, would I have thought again about marrying him? No, I would have believed "he's different," and he is, thankfully. But oh, the price we paid for the knowledge that we have now.

Needless to say, we are doing our best to be good in-laws. That is to say we mind our own business and respect our children's choices and their need for privacy. We respond to their need to do things on their own and always say "How wonderful!" even when we may think it is not quite so wonderful.

How do we choose the ones we choose? Why do we select one as if he were the only one? Is there really only one person in the whole world we could love, marry and live with for the rest of our lives? Logically we know this doesn't make any sense. Yet most of us look for our "one" out there in the big "somewhere." Books have been written suggesting many theories. Personally, I have no affinity for any of them.

I don't believe we all marry our fathers or our mothers. I don't know whether we marry someone because of a person or a thing we missed as a child, or because we have wonderful memories of Uncle Bill and as a result have a weakness for blue eyes. Why are we attracted to tall, short, lanky, ambitious, kind, gentle or rugged types? That is another book.

However, I do believe it's important to know why you picked the one you did. What makes this person more lovable to you than any other? At the same time, you can't help but wonder at the "chance" of your meeting and choosing this one person. Coincidences exist that lead me to the questions: Is it Fate? Is it God? Is it Karma?

For instance, our "coincidence" is that both my father and

Stephen's father were orphaned at an early age. Both men lost their fathers when they were about nine years old, thus making each of them head of the family. My grandfather died of the influenza epidemic when my father was nine years old, and, so, my grandmother said to him, "Well, you are the man of the house now. You will take care of me and your brothers."

Stephen's grandfather was kicked by a horse and died from the accident. They were living in Czechoslovakia, and his grandmother said to Stephen's father, "Now you are the head of the family and the man of the house." Whereupon the grandmother cried and cried and according to the story didn't stop for years. Finally, in exasperation, Stephen's father told her she was never to cry again.

This is a significant story because my mother-in-law never, ever cried. One of the few times we talked she told me almost proudly, in her very broken English, "I don't cry. I never cry." This is not something you tell a girl with a Sicilian heritage!

I think I was supposed to be impressed. Instead I thought this was really strange and not normal. After all, I thought, everyone cries sometimes, but not my mother-in law. More puzzling still was the fact that she didn't laugh either. As time went on in our marriage, I discovered my husband shared these qualities with his mother, no crying and not a lot of laughing. This was especially confusing to me as Stephen was a very funny man. I was to discover many years later the difference between funny and fun.

I believe this background, these early years are truly the beginning of our marriage. At this time, I must talk about Stephen's heritage.

Stephen's parents were both born in Eastern Europe,

in Czechoslovakia. I was always glad Stephen was born in Canada, for good speller that I am, I still struggle when I have to spell Czechoslovakia. Of course, that country has changed its name many times since then.

His brother and sister were born in Czechoslovakia as well, and this fact alone may be one of the reasons my husband always felt like an outsider, even in his own family. English was the second language and Slovak was spoken in his family's home even at the time we were married in 1965. To say his family, particularly his mother, did not assimilate into the American culture is not an overstatement.

Stephen became a naturalized citizen when he was in college, shortly after the rest of the family had become citizens. Because his brother and sister were four and seven years older than he, Stephen is considered a first generation American. As such he faced all the torments of wanting to keep the peace and heritage with his family but also yearned to be like everyone else, an American.

I was luckier than Stephen as I had no such conflict. I was a second generation American and taught to be proud to be an American.

All my grandparents came to America from a small town outside of Palermo, Sicily. They were teenagers when they first arrived. But it was my grandmother on my mother's side who always insisted English be spoken in her house, especially when there was company. "We are Americans," she was proud to say. That is the way I was brought up.

I had my Italian heritage, but I was American through and through and never thought a thing about it. Being a child is so wonderful, so free from prejudice and hate. I know it existed, but just like the song says, "You have to be taught." I was taught the opposite lesson by my mother, and that was to take each person, one at a time, individually. This is how I have always looked at the world and the people in it…one at a time. I brought my children up the same way. Thanks, Mom.

Whereas my family was American and happy to be here and a part of this grand land, Stephen's father had always intended to go back to his homeland, reclaim his family's farm and live out his life as a major landowner in the old country. However, the timing couldn't have been worse since it was just at the time Hitler was busy taking over Eastern Europe and marching steadily to take over the rest.

What has this to do with the story of a marriage? I wish I had known some of this family history when Stephen and I met, and before we were married. But again, would I have made a different choice? No. I was on a course and so was he, and as it happens with most couples, fate steps in and takes us on turns that lead us toward each other.

Stephen was the youngest child of immigrant parents, torn between two worlds. Carol (that's me), was, and sometimes is still innocent, oblivious, naïve. I thought everyone wanted to be happy. There was work and there was play and life was good. Or so I thought.

Our childhoods have many similarities but many major differences. The first and foremost is Stephen's family was very religious. Mine was not so much. We both grew up in the Catholic faith. I, a Roman Catholic, believed this was the only kind of Catholic.

Stephen grew up in the Byzantine Catholic faith, a fact of which I was totally unaware until after we were married. I never even knew such a sect existed. I told you I was naïve!

I must confess though, we both know and can sing many of the same songs. He remembers pictures on the inside of Hoodsie cups, and he'd collect them just as I did. Of course, you had to lick the top to see whose picture you got. Stephen and his friends played Kick the Can, Giant Step, Hide n'Seek, King of the Mountain, Marbles, Dodge ball and the same games I was playing in my neighborhood in Bradford with my friends.

I broke my leg when I was six, and he had his appendix out about the same time. I loved school and reading and writing and even arithmetic. I was smart and proud of it. We had a girls' entrance on one side of the school and a boys' entrance on the other. The girls played Dodge, Jump Rope, Hopscotch and Red Rover. "Red Rover, Red Rover, send Judy over," and Judy would run and try to break through the holding hands of the other team.

Sometimes we'd sneak a peek at the boys' side before the teacher caught us and told us to get away. Somehow it seemed like the boys didn't care about us at all; I learned in the fifth grade that wasn't true. Do you know I still dream about that school every now and then? The Cogswell School in Bradford. Not only is it in the very same location, but it continues to be used as an elementary school. I'm sure there is no longer a separate entrance for the boys and the girls.

Stephen's experience with school was not quite as positive as mine. I know he liked school and was always curious, but his family expected more from him. Work and church were more important to his parents than school. There were no books or magazines to read in his family's house, not even a comic book. No English was spoken at home.

Stephen struggled in school with reading and Language Arts. Today with the innovation in our school programs, such as English as a Second Language, Stephen would have flourished. Yet he was fortunate to be blessed with a great native intelligence, a curiosity about everything in the world and beyond, and a desire to read every word ever printed, including those on cereal boxes!

As a child I thought life was mostly fun and games, with some occasional work thrown in. Of course, we had chores to do, and my mother was a fanatic housekeeper! She had two very simple rules: "Do it MY way, and do it NOW!"

Everything had a place, (and it better be in that place, or else) and it had to be dusted, polished, and waxed. There were no compromises with either her time schedule or the way you were supposed to do your chore. There was only one way: her way.

When I was first married, having been brought up this way, I kept my house the way my mother did. That was the only way I knew: perfect. For example, in the beginning I would dust every day, then it got to be every other day, then maybe twice a week. Soon I decided that it was acceptable for me to dust every other week, and now I dust whenever the dust bothers me – and believe me, dust doesn't bother me that much!

Every Friday after school when we'd arrive home my mother would be on her hands and knees washing and waxing the floor, hollering at us: "Don't come in!" Why did she wait till we got home from school? I can tell you: because my mother spent most of her day reading. To say that mother was a voracious reader is an understatement. She read a book a day, at least.

We were always going to the library or to Mitchell's Department Store which had a lending library of the latest books. Other times we'd go across the street to Peabody's, another department store which also had a lending library of new books not yet available at the public library. I remember these trips as great journeys of exploration and imagination. These were also the times my mother was happy.

I loved my mother, but I would not describe her as a happy woman. She read to escape, pure and simple, but she read and instilled in my brother and me a love of reading. I'd often come home from school and she wouldn't even know I was home because she was reading. For a while, just to rebel, I wouldn't read for fun because I resented my mother for ignoring me to read. In my mind I still see mother in her rocking chair in the living room with a book in her hand, totally unaware of anyone or anything.

In those days it seemed as though the only way to get her attention was to throw something on my bed. My mother had an unfailing instinct to know if you'd broken her number one rule. She did not allow clothes, books, or any "thing" to be placed on the bed. We had to change when we came home from school. This was another inalterable rule: there were school clothes and play clothes.

Basically, I would say my life was fairly simple and ordinary growing up. Yes, there were a lot of rules but in a way these same rules made my life secure.

Stephen doesn't have many good memories of elementary school. Both his parents worked at that time; he remembers his sister taking care of him. Stephen's sister, Anne, took care of everyone, including Stephen's mother. From the stories Anne has told us, it seemed she wasn't allowed much of a childhood. She was a mother to Stephen and to her own mother. I'm not sure who parented his brother Mike, perhaps he parented himself. When Stephen's mother was home, she was more than likely praying, saying her rosary, and if I had lived with my father-in-law I'd have been praying too!

I don't ever remember seeing my mother pray. I know my father said the rosary and my mother had a rosary. My grandmothers were religious, but my parents didn't go to church regularly, and yet they expected Louis and me to go. Well, of course I didn't want to go, it interfered with my playing, but it was all right with me if some of my friends went too.

One of my most defiant moments took place when it was time for me to make my First Communion. You know that time when you are six or seven and you really have no idea what "sin" is. Not only did I not understand, I also didn't care.

Let me tell you about the "mean" Sister Bianca. It was she who ABSOLUTELY, irrevocably turned me off the Catholic religion for all of my life. I imagine many of you older Catholics out there have a similar "Sister" story.

Sister threatened that if I skipped Sunday School just one more time, I wouldn't be allowed to make my First Communion. Too bad for her she didn't know this was perfectly all right with me. I thought, "Oh, good, now I'm free to play with my friends after school on Mondays." After all, who knew what fun I must be missing?

However, when I told my mother, thinking, somehow, she

wouldn't mind, since after all she didn't even go to church, she was really mad. I mean she was *really* mad! Then it got to be a question of who was I more afraid of, my mother or Sister Bianca? No contest! I was more afraid of my mother.

So back to Catechism class I went, resenting and hating every minute, mind wandering, wanting to be outside, wondering what games my friends were playing and what I was missing. I got my knuckles slapped more than once, and other humiliations only the black-vested nuns could impose.

I didn't deserve the punishment! I was a good girl, and they were trying to make me feel wicked. I was seven years old. What did I know about sin? And now they were telling me I had to go and tell some stranger, a priest, just how bad I was and all the bad thoughts I had, which at that time mostly centered around Sister and my mother!

Perhaps some of you remember marching over to the church for that very first confession, trying to remember all the words to "Bless me father for I have sinned," and in your dear little head not believing for a moment you had. I was a regular little girl, and I had regular little girl thoughts and feelings. If these things were so bad, why did God give them to us in the first place? None of it made sense to me, and I confess it still doesn't.

Stephen, on the other hand, believed all he was taught in the Catholic Church, both by priests and nuns and his family. He never questioned anything until he was much older. While I was going to the movies on Saturday, he was being a good boy, obeying the laws of the church and his father.

Religion became one of our biggest problems. One of our first fights was whether or not to take our newborn son to church on Sunday. Needless to say for which side I was advocating! As with most fights, no one won, but Josh, our first, seemed to fall asleep just when it was time to leave for church. Imagine that!

Religion, sex, in-laws, money – most couples argue about these things during their marriage. Stephen and I argued about *all* of them, only to discover many years later that we weren't arguing about these things at all. I would say the most valuable knowledge we got from all our various counseling was this: whatever you are fighting about, it's something else. When after so many years of having the same arguments over and over, we made this discovery, we learned how to break the cycle. It was many years into our marriage before we knew how to be honest with each other.

Has this happened to you? Do you find yourself in an argument with your partner when you reach the point that you know exactly what the other person is going to say? Then, in spite of yourself, you say the same thing that got you into trouble in the first place. Others make it sound so easy. They tell you communication is key, it's important to be honest, just ask for what you want. Ha ha.

Ask for what I want? Unheard of, unless it was for a new dress for school. To ask someone directly for what I wanted took me many years to learn. Do you ask your special someone to pay attention to you, to hold your hand, to hug you or simply to love you, or better yet to love you simply? Perhaps you learned this lesson early. But for Stephen and me it would take many years to learn to ask for what we wanted. We are still learning.

Still, don't you find it easier to go back to the same old

patterns of behavior, even when you know they don't work? This is one of the kinds of "work" I was talking about earlier. Be patient with each other. Learning a new behavior takes time after all.

Stephen and I came from different ethnic and religious backgrounds. Our childhoods had some similarities, but more impressive differences. It's funny, too, don't you think, just because you love someone and he loves you, you believe you feel and think the same about everything, or at least all the important things. What's so impressive to me now are the opportunities younger people have to discuss these important issues before they get married. Issues such as money, work, children, sex; Stephen and I never discussed these things. We simply believed we felt the same about everything and there was no need to talk about it. We were so wrong.

We became teenagers in the 50s and were part of what is now referred to as the "silent generation." I believe we grew up in the best of times and personally I was never aware of being very "silent," and neither were most of my friends. We were allowed to be kids, doing what kids are supposed to do: play, daydream, work hard in school, obey and rebel against your parents, be polite and not be rude to other people, especially older people.

I particularly liked being a girl. Even though as girls we didn't have the opportunities young women have today, we did know what it meant to be a girl. We also knew when we rebelled, and we did, just what it was we were rebelling against. I am so happy and proud of young women today and the women of my generation as well, for we are all growing and learning together.

Girls today have so many choices, so many options and opportunities. Perhaps that is one reason why everyone seems so confused. Teenagers will always rebel, for that is their job, but it helps to know what it is you are rebelling against. My kids always said we didn't give them too much to rebel against, because we always tried to be fair and respectful of their need to be independent and their own person. They found ways to rebel, nevertheless.

I am ahead of my story, but you see, the story of a marriage is not just the story of two people, but the story of their families, their communities and the society in which they were raised. If you've done any reading you know the society of the 50s is very different from our society today. Not that one is better than another, for there are virtues to be admired in all societies and times. At the same time there are many aspects of both not to be admired and certainly not to be repeated. Would we take back any of the rights women and minorities have struggled so hard to get? No, of course not.

My generation may have yearned for more opportunities and more freedom, but at the same time it was a comfort to know there were rules, boundaries and guidelines. Then, of course, it was also fun to break the rules, push the boundaries and bend the guidelines. Stephen and I grew up in this framework of a simpler and more rigid society. That's just the way it was.

I remember my childhood with mostly warmth and affection. It wasn't perfect or idyllic, but whose ever is? I felt safe; I wasn't always sure that I was loved, especially by my mother, but I had a lot of friends and life was okay with me. From the little Stephen has shared with me, I have come to realize how little I know about his growing up years.

I don't believe as a child Stephen felt safe. He may have known he had a home and food and clothing, but I know he missed what I did: warmth and affection. One story he shared with me was the time he was about ten years old and he got a new wallet. In it was the card to fill out your name and address and who to call in case of emergency. Wouldn't it be natural to assume at that young age you'd put down your parents? Stephen felt he would be bothering them, mostly his father, so he left that part blank.

Another story he tells is the time his father told him he had to drown a litter of kittens, and to his regret, even to this day, he did it. You see it would never have occurred to this dear, sensitive, kind little boy to disobey his father. One thing I absolutely know about my husband is he would never intentionally hurt anyone or anything.

Puberty is a particularly awkward time for boys and girls, and at the time we were growing up it was more than awkward; it was never discussed. My mother would turn red whenever anyone said the word "sex." She never told me about menstruation. I learned about that from the girl on the third floor.

When I was eleven and got my period, with great embarrassment and hesitation I approached my mother. "I'm bleeding," I said. I thought I had some horrible disease. Perhaps the girl on the third floor, the only one who had talked to me about this occurrence, didn't explain the bleeding part to me.

My mother put down her book and said, "Oh, well, go get a napkin." So, I went and got a dinner napkin. "Not that kind," she said, "the other ones." What was she talking about? What other ones? She'd never mentioned anything in the slightest way to me about this mystery, but suddenly I was supposed to have this burst of knowledge about the whole ordeal. Finally, she got out of her chair and showed me what she was talking about. Then she handed me one of those little pamphlets: "What Girls Need to Know About Menstruation." There was no discussion. There was no question and answer period. Read this little book. Ha!

Poor Stephen, on the other hand, has an even more painful memory of puberty. He recalls his father laughing at him when Stephen asked, "What's happening to my chest?"

"Ha, ha, ha." His father laughed and announced to the family, "Stephen is turning into a girl. Stephen has breasts."

Would Stephen or I like to return to those "thrilling days of yesteryear?" When I started to grow pubic hair, I had no idea if this was normal or not, but I sure wasn't going to ask anyone about it, not even my friends. Was I turning into a boy? They'd laugh at me.

Do you think Stephen and I were made for each other?

It was very common in those years to share a bed or bedroom with your siblings. Privacy was scarce or unheard of. With the exception of one girl, all my friends shared a bedroom. Or as my brother and I did, one of us slept on the couch that opened to a bed. We'd alternate; one week Louis would get to sleep in the bedroom and the next week I'd sleep there. Another friend shared a bedroom with two sisters and a brother.

I would have enjoyed my own room, and I definitely would have preferred to sleep on the bed all the time, but that simply was the way it was. Since most of my friends had similar arrangements, I never thought it was a big deal.

But, oh, we did love to go over to Gail's, the girl with her own room. Perhaps because she was an only child or maybe because her mother worked, Gail's room was a place where we could go and hang out. She even had a bulletin board on her closet door, and she didn't have to share her closet with anyone else! Her mother made most of Gail's clothes, and Gail was always complaining about how she absolutely hated to stand still. Gail always looked so pretty; I wished my mother would sew for me. Mother didn't sew and neither do I. I tried, but I just wasn't good at it. Guess who sews in our family? You got it; Stephen sews.

Stephen moved several times while he was a young boy, and he says he remembers different events based on whatever house the family was living in at the time. He frequently shared a room and a bed with his brother; sometimes the room was in the cellar. The most significant story about Stephen (prior to junior high that is) occurred when he was about seven years old.

Like all neighborhoods in those days, there was a grocery store where everyone went most often. The proprietors of course knew all the neighbors and their children by name. Stephen liked going to this grocery store and liked the owners. One day he asked them if he could work there. He was a little boy, and shy as you can imagine he would be, so they politely said, "Oh, sure."

My poor Stephen took them seriously, went home to his parents and told them he was going to work for the neighborhood store. His parents could see he was earnest, so his mother gave him an apron, and off he went. The owners of course were shocked to see him and quickly but kindly sent him home. Stephen says he was confused and devastated. When he got home and told his parents what had happened, his parents were surprised that he had gone to the store and really expected to work. They dismissed the incident and him.

Stephen questioned why his parents let him go. Why did they bother to give him an apron? One of his parents ought to have explained to him that he was too young to work and that perhaps the people at the store were only being kind, and maybe he could help out a little bit once in a while. Stephen felt abandoned, although of course he didn't know the word for it then. But, somehow, he knew he wasn't safe.

We are talking about a very sensitive and earnest little boy. This little boy would grow up to be a sensitive, insensitive, earnest, devout, rebellious, unforgiving, kind and gentle, stubborn and self-righteous young man. The man who would one day be my husband.

Did I know any of this history when we met? When we married? How many years was it before he shared this story with me? This is a story he believes is very significant to his relationship with his family.

A mind, a subconscious mind, I believe, is like a treasure chest. Sometimes you explore it and pull out a jewel, and other times you find only snakes and demons. The inclination is to put the lid on that chest and lock it up and throw away the key. I could have done that, and there were times I not only considered it, but believed that divorcing Stephen was the only answer to my sanity. Had I thrown away the key and the chest I would have thrown away one of the greatest treasures in my life today.

Stephen and I unlocked, opened, and explored both of our treasure chests. We threw out the old, decaying, tarnished pieces of ourselves and polished, shined, and loved the precious parts of each of us that drew us together in the first place. This is love – beyond love – this is life, living and forgiving and mostly, this is the story of a marriage.

CHAPTER TWO

Not A Jane Austen Novel

World War II erupted and affected everyone's life. Of course, some more than others. Since I was a child, I thought it was like a game when the air raid warden, with his funny-looking hat, stopped by. He would remind us of the rules and the blackout. We had to pull down all our shades and there was a black curtain over the windows in the kitchen. They he would tell us everything was all right.

Whatever "war" meant I knew it was something important. When I walked down our street then, many of our neighbors had little flags with a star in the middle. I didn't know what it meant, but my mother told me each star in the window meant a man in the family was in the service and away at war.

I recall ration books, and my mother complaining about having to use lard instead of butter. One day the market in town advertised real butter, and I stood in line to buy it for the family. I remember using the ration books to go to the corner store and get coffee – freshly ground A&P coffee. It always smelled so good in there; I'm sure this memory is why

I enjoy my coffee so much. Today the smell of freshly brewed coffee evokes that memory still. I see Jerry, the proprietor, winding up the green shades he had closed the night before to protect and cover his merchandise.

My mother laughed at Louis, my brother, because whenever she sent him to the store for some groceries, he almost always forgot what he was supposed to buy. He would either come home to have her write a list for him, or call her from a neighbor's. Being a typical kid sister, I was always very proud of the fact this hardly ever happened to me. If you are a "kid" sister or brother, you know what I mean!

I haven't talked much about my father. I know he was working at two jobs during the war, so we mostly saw him at supper time and then he'd go off again to work. His shoe factory was making boots for the Army. I remember being glad that he didn't have to go away to war. I liked that he'd be home at night because even though I was afraid of my father, I always felt safe knowing he was close by.

The nicest memories I have of my father is how he would sit me on his knee and sing to me. I love and cherish those memories. He would usually sing "Daddy's Little Girl" and "Girl of My Dreams." I still remember the words to "Girl of my Dreams," although it is not a song you hear very often.

We didn't have a car during these wartime years as there was a shortage of rubber, and all the rubber was needed for the war effort. I remember hearing my parents talk about that, but as usual we'd walk across the bridge and end up getting a banana split at the ice cream shop, Pickett's.

We were lucky to have some friends who owned a farm; we'd take the bus there. This was another wonderful adventure for me. Their name was Campagna and because they were also Italian, my parents spoke Italian with them. Mrs. Campagna was the best cook I knew. There were always fresh pies waiting to be served. Because there were several daughters in the family, there was always somebody to pay attention to me. I liked that of course. One of the daughters played the piano, and I was very happy to listen. There was always so much to do and see at the Campagna's; this outing became a favorite of Louis' and mine.

I think it was a lovely time to grow up. And growing up was what we, Stephen in New Jersey and me in Massachusetts, were doing. I made my First Communion (at last), and later, in the fifth grade, I even made my Confirmation. By this time, I was not such a rebel about religion. Mostly making my Confirmation meant I got to wear nylons for the first time.

In junior high all the girls were anxious to be grown up and start wearing makeup, mostly lipstick. My parents didn't allow me to wear lipstick, but that didn't stop me from trying it out. My friends and I went to Woolworth's and bought some Tangee, one of the less expensive and popular brands of lipstick at the time. We couldn't wait to get to school so we could put it on and feel grownup at last; I remember the color as a rather bright orange. When the boys saw us in all our splendor, they laughed at us. Well if this was the reaction to our new glamour, maybe lipstick wasn't the answer after all.

Speaking of boys laughing at me, I have a memory that made a lasting impression on me and not in a good way. In the seventh grade I was pretty well shaped and begging my mother to buy me a bra. "What do you need a bra for?" she asked me. I, of course, thought it was obvious.

The boys would stand on the porch and the Greenleaf School and laugh and point at me; I can see them there still, and I even remember some of their names. Whenever I wore a sweater, my breasts would be bouncing up and down. It was very embarrassing. For years after that I almost never wore sweaters, only blouses and cardigan sweaters. I would try very hard to make my bust appear smaller.

I thought it was funny, too, as I was crying and wishing for a smaller bust, many of my friends were crying and wishing for a bigger one. Finally, but too late to save me from the humiliation I had already endured, my mother took me to be fitted for a bra. This gave me little comfort at the time as I felt I had been humiliated beyond repair. I knew everyone knew my "secret."

Graduation from the eighth grade meant I could wear my nylons and lipstick, although my father wasn't happy about the lipstick. I suppose wearing lipstick for a girl then was the equivalent of a boy getting his first pair of long pants. How times have changed. But you know what? Lipstick is still my favorite makeup. My daughter laughs at me because I have so many different colors and brands. Don't you think it's funny how much of who we are can be traced back to our childhood?

I was excited about high school and boys and confident this was going to be a great time. My big plan was to go to the movies in the afternoon. At that time there were four movie houses in Haverhill: the Lafayette, the Colonial, the Strand and the Paramount. It was a time of double features, serials on Saturdays, fresh popped popcorn, balconies and new movies twice a week. You could come and go at any time during the shows, and often I would watch a movie more than once. I think the movies for us were what television is for kids today. Except, of course, we had to go out of the house, walk to town, pay our money and be quiet. The ushers were very strict and woe to you if the manager had to come down the aisle!

I knew by this time I wanted to be a writer. Ever since my mother first taught me to write I was excited by the sight of words on a page. I thought how wonderful it was to be able to actually see your thoughts and feelings on a piece of paper. As I grew up, I would write stories and read them aloud to all my friends. I loved the world of my imagination.

High school didn't turn out to be the dream I anticipated. I had wonderful classes and always good grades, except in Chemistry. I had several of the best teachers of my life in high school, many even better than some of my college professors. I have always believed I had a first-class education. Of course, in the public school especially, it helps to be smart. I was smart and that made me confident, until the last two years of high school.

I began to doubt my ability to be a good writer. No matter what I wrote or how hard I worked at it, Mr. Harriman, my English teacher for the last two years of high school and the head of the English department, kept giving me C's and B's. I couldn't understand, but he was so demanding and made me work so hard that when I finally would get an A I knew I had earned it. Yet to my surprise and delight he chose me to write the words to our graduation song. Another student wrote the music and the high school chorus sang it at our graduation.

The big lack in my life was that I never had a boyfriend in high school. All my friends had boyfriends, but not me.

My father said "I don't know why you don't have a boyfriend. Your looks aren't so bad." Not so bad. Thanks, Dad.

No one ever told me I was pretty, not my mother or my father or heaven forbid, my brother. Sure, boys would say I had a nice smile, or nice teeth or pretty hair, but a girl always wants to think she's pretty. Stephen was the first person to tell me I was pretty. I was twenty-seven years old, so naturally I didn't believe him. After all, if your own father doesn't think you're pretty, how could anybody else?

High school graduation was a major turning point in my life. I had applied and been accepted to Boston University's School of Communication. I had set my sights on a career in television. In 1955, television was still new, and the field was open to many exciting and challenging possibilities.

I hadn't counted on being awarded a full scholarship to another school, a prestigious junior college which just happened to be four blocks from my home! I said, "Thanks but, no thanks, I want to go to school in Boston." I wanted to ride the train with my friends. I wanted to make new friends and get away from home. I knew I couldn't live in Boston, but just being there would be all right with me. I knew I had to get away from home, and more importantly away from my parents. This was a fact. More than just a desire, I had an absolute need to get away from home. This overwhelming feeling to break away from my parents is significant to our story.

Alas, my dreams were about to be shattered. The scholarship to Bradford Junior College, "The oldest women's institution for higher learning in the east," was so good that both the dean of women at the high school and my parents convinced me I would be a fool to pass it up. The dean encouraged me because she knew I would get a first-class education there (and she was right) and also because, "it would look good" on my resume. My parents encouraged me because of the money it would save them and also for not wanting to let go of me.

Like the good little girl I had learned to be at the time, the decision was made for me to attend Bradford Junior College, taking the courses and credits that would transfer to Boston University where then I would go as a full-fledged junior. "All right," I'm thinking, "What's two years when you are 17 years old?" The end of the world. Yet it is everything and nothing at the same time.

I loved and hated BJC. I loved the education I got there, the professors, the knowledge, love and enthusiasm that was passed on to me in the classroom. Whole new worlds were opened there to me. Worlds of art and music and poetry and literature and sociology, psychology and philosophy. I never realized there was so much to learn, to know, to enjoy, to think about. I especially loved philosophy, and I always thought if I could figure out a way to make a dollar as a philosopher, that is what I would have become.

Speaking of philosophy, it was here at Bradford I found out there was a name for the way I felt about God and what I believed. Pantheism. This philosophy suited me perfectly, and I was happy to have found an identity for my values and beliefs. Pantheism is the belief that identifies the universe with God, God and nature as one.

What I hated about Bradford was the snobbery and the wealth that almost all the girls enjoyed. I had never felt deficiencies in anything, except my looks, but now I felt very inferior and left out. I didn't like this feeling at all. I spoke with the dean of students about these feelings, trying to get some help. He told me, "All the girls who come to Bradford are used to being chiefs when they were in high school. But in college, some of you must learn to be the Indians, that's just the way it is."

'Hey wait a minute,' I thought. 'I want to be a chief, damn it. Thanks all the same.' But that was not to be.

So, I went ahead and did what I did best. I was an excellent student, a good learner, a willing and eager scholar. I give major credit for this ability to my high school. I never for a moment felt inferior in the classroom. For there I learned it doesn't matter if you go to the most prestigious prep school in the world, and almost all the girls at Bradford had come from that background, what matters most is your desire to learn. If you have a willingness to learn, then an education will be yours. So, thank you Haverhill High School and Miss Huntington, my math teacher, Mr. Pearson who taught history, and Mr. Johnson, who encouraged me to pursue a career in speech and communication, and to my most wonderful Mr. Harriman. I knew my high school had prepared me well and even better than some of the girls in my class at B.J.C. As happens with most freshmen classes, the fallout rate was steep that year.

Outside of the classroom I didn't belong at all. I joined the drama club and quickly ran afoul of the senior "thespian." This experience took away all my love for acting. Part of my scholarship included working in the snack bar twelve hours a week. All right, I was used to working. A snack bar had nothing on a shoe factory. The only problem was that while my scholarship called for twelve hours of work a week, all the other girls on scholarship seemed to be working four hours. 'Hey, wait a minute again. There must be some mistake.' No, there was no mistake.

Since most of the girls came from well-to-do families, many were used to having cooks and maids and so on, and when they came into the snack bar several of them thought I was just part of the hired help and treated me that way. Well, didn't I just pour a little less "tah-mah-to" juice for her, or maybe I burned someone's grilled cheese, and perhaps I didn't give another one so much chocolate syrup. Yes, I would have my petty revenges. At the same time there were other sweet girls, and I would treat them extra nice as well.

The best part of working in the snack bar, aside from learning all these great grilling tricks and getting free brownies (like I needed free brownies even then) were the two ladies I worked with, Mrs. Kelley and Mrs. Edgerly. I admired them both and learned a lot from them, just about being human and women.

Happy at last with graduation in sight and Boston in my future, traditions would soon be behind me. "It's a tradition here at Bradford..." Everything was a tradition "here at Bradford," even some that President Bell couldn't acknowledge. I'm sure being president in an all-girls junior college, she was aware of some of the girls' own traditions; there couldn't have been much that she hadn't seen before. Several girls kept a car off campus, this was against the rules. There was liquor in the dorms (naturally) and everyone, it seemed to me, was losing her virginity every weekend at the "frat house." I was so far out of it that I only knew about these escapades by eavesdropping. No one shared their stories with me. Even though my Catholic faith was not about being a saint, I still believed there were only two kinds of girls: good girls and the other kind, and that kind was bad.

I also knew you could get pregnant, although diaphragms were the birth control of choice at Bradford. Worse than getting pregnant or almost as bad was the fear that the boy wouldn't respect you and then you'd end up losing him anyhow. At least that was what my mother kept telling me. "You want a boy to respect you." She would say. Let me tell you, I had a lot of respect. Not many boyfriends, but a heck of a lot of "respect!"

It was finally May 1957, and I was about to graduate from Bradford Junior College. I could see a rosy future in front of me. I was going to break free at last, from Bradford, from my family, from feeling poor and inferior. My credits had all been transferred and Boston University had accepted me as a full-fledged junior. I would begin classes there in the fall. Hooray! Free at last!

Uh, oh. Once again, my plans were not meant to be.

There was a fire at the Dispenza's that would change the course of my young life. Mother and I were reading in separate rooms when we heard a boom, a very loud boom. I ignored it, it will go away, I thought. Mother, dear, brave heart, actually dropped her book, and went to see. "What the hell was that?"

"Son of a bitch," I heard my mother from downstairs. "Call the fire department. The furnace has exploded." Actually, it was the gas incinerator. Our phone didn't work, so I went to look for my mother. I opened the cellar door, but I couldn't see anything – not my hand in front of me, not the steps, not the light switch, not a damn thing.

My mother was still down there.

Now she and I may have had our differences, but she was my mother after all, and I did love her and the thought of her burning up in our cellar was horrifying to me. "Son of a bitch," I heard again. I smiled, relieved to hear my mother very much alive. "Go next door and call the fire department," she shouts to me.

I do not remember this, but our next-door neighbor, Mrs. Madden, loved to tell this story. "Carol is so polite. She came and knocked on my door, waited for me to answer and then said, 'Excuse me, Mrs. Madden, but can I use your phone to call the fire department? Our house is on fire.'"

Fortunately, everyone from the other two apartments got safely out of the house and no one was hurt. However, the house was not livable for more than three months. The very bad news for me was that because of the damage to the house and because there was not enough insurance to pay for all the repairs, I cannot go to Boston University. If I wanted to continue to go to school, I had to attend the State Teachers College in Lowell. That's where Louis was going to school. This was all they could afford now, they told me. My brother wanted to be a teacher, so that was a fine choice for him. In all my life there were three things I never wanted to be: a nun, a nurse, or a teacher.

At this time, I had an opportunity to live with a friend in New York City who was working as a secretary in a television studio. I thought that since my plans to go to Boston were thwarted once more, I could go to New York and follow my original dream – work on Broadway, take singing lessons, and perhaps be another Mary Martin.

When I told my parents my decision, my father responded with a threat. "If you leave here now, you can never come back to this house again, and you can just forget that you are our daughter. We just won't have a daughter anymore." My mother was unusually silent, so I assumed she felt the same.

I would love to tell you that I was such a rebel at nineteen in 1957, and that I left for New York anyhow. I would be so proud to say that I flaunted convention and my father's threats and followed my heart and my dreams, but alas, I was afraid. I was afraid if I failed, I would have nowhere to go, no home, no family and no one to say, "Hey, it's okay, you tried."

No, instead I lived at home and commuted with my brother to Lowell Teachers' College for the next three years. However, after some time of being quite miserable and thinking my life would never be my own, I learned to enjoy myself and my time at Lowell. I made new lasting friendships, and most importantly, it was here that I first fell in love, madly and truly, and of course, most unhappily. I wrote a lot of poetry at Lowell.

His name was Roger and I cherish the memory of our relationship to this day. My brother introduced us, telling me that Roger was the only other guy in school with brains to match his (Louis). I didn't think much about Roger one way or another until my next year at Lowell. I'd see him in the library often. He was doing research or reading or sometimes, like me, listening to music. But what really brought us closer together was when we discovered we were each reading books about sex and hiding them in the back of our three ring binders! I know I was too embarrassed to let anyone know what I was really reading. I felt at the time I must be the only virgin in the entire country.

You can imagine my shock to discover there was someone else as innocent as me, and it was a guy. Wow! I am sure young people find this not only hard to understand, but probably incomprehensible as well. By this time, I was just twenty-one and so was Roger. I thought all boys had sex while they were in high school. What did I know? Were boys to be believed? Can you believe them now?

I didn't fall in love with him then, in fact it wasn't until the next year. One day in the cafeteria something more than coffee passed between us, some electricity, a shock to both of us as we quite literally bumped into each other. We looked into each other's eyes and knew something had happened and changed between us. We went out later in his car to discover just what it was. It was a major sexual ignition that led us from reading about it to experimenting with just how far we could go without "going all the way." He was Catholic too, and he had the guilt thing going, and I was still holding onto my "respect." This above all.

My lack of an affair and the sexual torment with Roger went on for the rest of college and after that for nearly three years. We'd both see other people, and he was very involved with another girl from school. He lost his virginity long before I did. When we met several years later and finally gave into our feelings for each other, it was too late to rekindle any flame, but a nice way to say goodbye.

In the spring of 1960, Louis and I graduated from Lowell Teacher's College. Even though my heart would never be in teaching, I liked working with the kids and I liked the teaching part. I also discovered I was good at it. I recall my final interview with the head of the education department at Lowell. She said that my particular class was one of the biggest ever filled with people who really didn't want to be teachers, people like me, she added. She went on to lament about our sorry lot and told me my student teacher advisor had written at the top of my evaluation that I didn't pay enough attention to bulletin boards.

I was not impressed. After nearly six months of working in the classroom in various and challenging circumstances, this remark about bulletin boards was the opening comment. There was no mention made until later in the evaluation how I got along with the children, or the famous "rapport" they liked to talk about in those days. No, it was all about bulletin boards. This was a hint of what was to come in my elementary teaching career; those damn bulletin boards would continue to haunt me. I discovered in elementary grades especially, if your bulletin boards looked good and were changed often, the administration thought you were doing a great job.

Of course, it seemed to me if you spent so much time making your bulletin boards look that good, when were you teaching? I always thought the bulletin boards were best used to exhibit the kids work anyhow, not mine. Since I wasn't artistic to begin with, I was operating under some handicap.

Think of it though. We were supposed to teach everything to everyone, all classes, all levels, all subjects. I still don't think anyone is that good. We would talk about the children's strengths and weaknesses, the need to treat each child as an individual. Only the children? Not the teachers? Not me? When did I stop being an individual, I wondered. No, the teaching profession and I were not compatible.

My brother was married by this time and had a wife and baby daughter to support. I was happy to graduate and made plans once again to move away from home. Alas, not yet. I made another compromise with my life. I had envisioned myself breaking away at last and was interviewing with schools from all over the New England area, I was particularly interested in Connecticut.

When my parents heard this plan, they were outraged. It was time to "pay them back" they said. For what? For putting me through school, they replied. I thought I did most of that myself, and what about those two years at Bradford on full scholarship? But since I ate there and lived there and worked only in the summertime at the shoe factory (even though I handed over most of my check to my father) it didn't matter.

I backed down and accepted a job at an elementary school in my hometown. Once again, I felt spineless. My only excuse is that it was a different time and I had such a sense of loyalty to my parents and yes, I imagine I felt some guilt as well. Hey, even though I was not 100% Catholic in my heart, that guilt stuff still affects you.

I tried a different job that summer, as a counselor in a Girl Scout camp in Maine. It was, of course, in the woods, and I mean in the woods. As my parents were driving me "Down East" and then down the long, dirt road leading to the camp, my father looked around and said to me, "You'll be back home in a week." Usually that was enough to make me more determined to do the opposite.

The counselors were all young girls like myself, and several of them had worked there before. First they wanted to give me a nickname. One thing I have always liked about my name is that I have no nickname. Then another girl handed me a hatchet "to clear the site for my tent."

I called my parents the next day.

After my futile attempt at being a summer camp counselor, I bargained with my father about money so I could take the summer off. My father loves to tell this story about my brief camping excursion and laughs to retell how he knew me better than I knew myself. If you are a parent, you know what a superior feeling this can be.

That was the best summer of my life. The summer of 1960 I went to the beach, I played golf with some friends (not very well and definitely not very seriously), I did a lot of shopping for my "school clothes" and attended several parties. Basically, this was the first summer I was free to play, relax and prepare form my first year of teaching. I thought maybe life wasn't going to be so bad after all.

Meanwhile in Florida, at the University of Miami, Stephen graduated in 1960 and was on his way to Korea. He had spent his first two years at Rutgers University, but when his parents moved to Florida, Stephen went along and entered the University of Miami. It was here that he decided he wanted to be an actor. He majored in theater with a minor in art and likes to recount his proudest achievement at Miami. For his performance in the Drama department's production of "Hotel Paradiso," he won the "Best Actor" award.

As a participant in R.O.T.C. Stephen was commissioned a second Lieutenant in the Army and left in August, 1960 for his tour of duty in Korea. Stephen's recollection of his days in the service have always been summed up by this one sentence: "I'm glad there was no war."

How did he get the Korean assignment? This is how he tells the story. "The duty officer asked me how I'd feel about going to Korea. I said all right. I never asked if I could go somewhere else or if I had another choice, I just said, sure, why not."

Why not indeed? At the time I met him, which would be four years later, he still maintained this laissez faire attitude, at least that's what I called it. He always called it his "lily of the field" philosophy. This kept my future groom from making any decisions, and so he couldn't be wrong, could he? No, indeed for "Consider the lilies of the field, how they grow; they toil not, neither do they spin: And yet I say unto you, that even Solomon in all his glory was not arrayed like one of these." Just as the Bible says, Stephen believed God would provide.

I found this idea amusing at first, because of course I didn't take him seriously. Everyone knows you have to work, right? "God helps those who help themselves." This was closer to my philosophy; I was not afraid of taking the proverbial bull by the horns if there was a problem to solve.

In 1960 both Stephen and I were molding and forming our personalities as we searched for our individual identities. He was on his way to Korea because it never occurred to him to ask for another assignment. Mr. "Lily of the field." Out of a sense of both loyalty and duty, I remained in my hometown for another two years. Stephen spent those two years in the Army and I spent the same two years teaching the second grade in Haverhill, Mass.

While I was still pining away for Roger, all my friends

were getting married. I was in so many weddings in those two years. The joke, "always a bridesmaid, never a bride" was no joke to me. I stopped counting the bridesmaid's dresses and the weddings after nine. By then my ego was totally dashed and my self-esteem was at an all-time low – if I'd been aware there was such a thing!

I guess my father was right and I'm "not that bad," but not pretty enough apparently, or something else was missing. I kept wondering, "What's wrong with me that I can't find someone to love and who'll love me back?" My father said I should play hard to get; my mother told me I'm too smart; my brother said boys find me too "aggressive."

I always told my mother she had Louis and me mixed up. I should have been the boy and Louis, who was always a very gentle person, should have been the girl. In the 1950s, personality traits were very defined for boys and girls. Boys were supposed to be aggressive, ambitious, and strong. Girls were supposed to be supplicating and sweet and just smart enough, but not smarter than boys. Needless to say, I was not sweet, but with my parents at least, I sure was supplicant, and I liked being smart.

One clear memory I have of the kind, gentle man known as my brother is when Louis was in a fight with one of the boys in the neighborhood. I say "fight," but what was happening was Louis was being hit and wouldn't hit back. I ran for my mother, who rushed out of the house and down the street. Instead of breaking the boys apart, she stood by and screamed at Louis, "Hit him, hit him." Knowing my mother, she probably yelled a few other choice remarks either in Italian or in the sailor's language she knew so well. I only remember her yelling, "Hit him, hit him back."

Later Louis would get the lecture on what it means to be a boy and a man. I guess it took more than getting out of knickers. I was glad I was a girl and didn't have to worry about somebody hitting me or my mother getting mad at me for not hitting back. I don't know if that is the reason or not, but I do know I don't like to see people hitting each other or even being mean to someone.

I know one of the first attractions I felt for Stephen was his gentle quality, a quality that later would become a source of many of our quarrels.

CHAPTER THREE

Guilt: Don't Leave Home Without It

I wanted desperately to leave my parents' house and be on my own. After being set back in this effort two previous times, I was successful at last in 1962. It would be many years before I forgave myself for not having the courage to break away and to stop calling myself a coward. Ah, Fate, she plays her hand even though we do not know or understand. Only in looking back can we see where the turns in the road occur and how the choices we make or don't make, take us forward on our journey through life.

Years later when Stephen and I talked about our childhoods, we realized how much we each needed to break away from our families. For me I knew it would be the only way to survive. For both my soul and my spirit, I had to be free from my parents. I was aware of this on a conscious level.

Stephen, on the other hand, believes his move away from his family was made on a more subconscious level. Whether conscious or not, we were both able to establish our own identities at last and separate from our families. After much therapy and counseling, the reasons behind this drive for self-survival became clear to us.

Even as I write "1962" I am amazed that it is more than forty years ago. First of all, it seems as if that part of our lives never happened. Then of course it was another lifetime.

To break away, to go, yes, my friends, I was finally able to "leave home without it" – the guilt that is. I was almost twenty-five years old, still single, with what seemed to be no prospect of marriage in sight. The irony of my situation was funny because I used to say I would never get married before I was twenty-five. I knew there was too much I wanted to do and too many places I wanted to see. I needed to have my fun before I settled down. However, as 25 approached, I was ready for marriage, but discouraged, because "where was he?" There was still much I wanted to see and do, yet I knew I was "missing" something.

My two years of teaching in Haverhill were good years. I was making almost $4000 a year and I had my summers off. I thought I was rich. It has never taken a lot of money to make me feel "rich." When you had 25 cents a week to spend for three years, almost anything more seems like a lot. I was lucky a cup of coffee in the school cafeteria only cost a nickel, so I could manage a cup of coffee a day. Then I got really smart as I discovered for that same nickel, I could get a cup of tea and then go back for hot water. I had two cups of tea for a nickel.

There were two things I wanted to do with my first paycheck. One was to go to my favorite dress shop and buy something I really loved without asking the price. I cannot even begin to describe the pure pleasure, thrill, excitement I felt when I did that. I even remember the dress. It was a silver wool dress with a fringe around the skirt, long sleeves, a scoop neck and a wool belt that matched. I still had that dress when I met Stephen four years later. He never liked it.

The second thing I did was buy my parents a really nice anniversary present. All those years of scraping by, meager paychecks in the summer from shoe shops that I hated, now I could buy things for them. "This is great," I thought. "You work, you make money, you spend money."

"The way life should be." More philosophy. My life was so simple in those days, and call me naïve, if you must, but I enjoyed making money and I loved spending it as well. I was never in debt though, and I always paid my bills on time, and I must say I was one of the best-dressed women on the faculty. I even had matching lingerie. What fun it is to recollect and see in my mind's eye the special little outfits I had. My mother taught me well to love clothes and always dressed me special as a little girl. I dressed me special as a big girl. Yes, clothes and I were a happy couple indeed.

I always say I had the clothes; I did the traveling and pretty much did all I wanted to before I got married. I wanted to be sure that when I did get married, I wouldn't feel I missed anything. I did miss one thing. I wanted a sports car. Oh sure, I had a car, but not the car of my dreams. I haven't given up on that dream yet.

After two years of teaching in my hometown, I was really ready to make a move. I knew now I no longer felt bound to stay home and "pay back" anymore. I felt my duty and loyalty had gone far enough and now it was time to live for myself. My uncle had already called me an old maid. I was twenty-four years old and it was 1962. I didn't think I was an old maid and was angry that he thought I was.

I saw an ad in the Boston paper for interviews for overseas teaching jobs. Europe. Japan. "That should be far enough," I thought. Never believing I had the remotest chance to be chosen, I went to Boston for an interview, not quite as a lark, more out of curiosity and desperation.

Later that spring my father was having an operation for his ulcers which had gotten progressively worse over the years. This time the doctors would be removing more than half of his stomach and some of his intestines as well.

I knew I could never be a nurse and was so totally unprepared for the tubes and connections to my father's body after the operation. The surgeons had talked merely of how fast they got in and out and how well the surgery went that morning. No one said a word about what to expect in recovery, so when I went to his room and saw him all connected to the tubes and looking so pale, I was sick. The nurse threw me out.

During this time, I received the news I was chosen to go to Europe as a teacher for the Army. I would be leaving for Munich, Germany in August. I was so excited and afraid at the same time, yet I knew I had to go. "Son of a gun, I'm going to Germany!" This would be my first real adventure (if you don't count the two days in the Maine woods). My dilemma was how to tell my father, now in his hospital bed.

I must say my mother was very supportive of me at this time. Somehow, she understood I had to go and she helped me tell my father, who was not happy at all about my news. I felt, loyal little Carol that I was, I was betraying him somehow. However, I chose to do what I wanted to do for the first time. I felt very proud of myself, but damn it, yes, a little guilty too.

My mother and I were never very good friends and didn't get along for most of my life. I used to do many odd things to get her attention and to get her to love me. At this time, to her credit, she was understanding, supportive, and even kind to me.

I have very fond memories of my mother the summer I was getting ready to go to Germany. We did a lot of shopping together, and she bought me two beautiful suits which I wore all across Europe. I bought new luggage and was going to Boston for tests and shots and shopping. I'd be one of the best dressed teachers in all of Germany. My summer was spent preparing for the biggest adventure of my life. While my mother was being supportive and helpful, my father was angry and sullen. He felt as if I had deserted him.

I know my leaving and going off to Germany alone the summer of 1962 was the bravest and proudest thing I ever did. I look back on it now and feel very good about myself, a self I lost many years later and would struggle to recapture. Later years would be a search for my old self, my identity, for the Carol I had been and wanted to be again.

In August of 1962 as my parents were driving me to Logan Airport in Boston, I saw how sad and silent they were, and I knew they would miss me. My friends had given me a farewell party, and I wondered what the heck I was doing? Why was I leaving behind people who loved and cared about me?

As soon as we approached the airport and I saw the planes flying overhead, all my questions, all my doubts left me. I knew I was doing the best thing for me. I had no concern about my future, no fear of flying. I would be gone for a year and at the end of that year I could sign on for another year or return back home. At last I was on my way.

Munich, Germany, August 1962. The Berlin Wall had been erected, almost overnight, and so many of the men stationed in Germany had been "extended," that is they had to stay longer than their original duty time. Vietnam, on the other side of the world, was still a voluntary post. Many of the officers from Germany volunteered to go to Vietnam as advisors. This was a way of advancing their careers in a shorter span of time. Our country was involved at this time in an advisory capacity. That soon would change dramatically.

While I was in Germany, worrying about the Berlin Wall, and always, as usual, being unhappy in love, back at home Americans were faced with the Cuban missile crisis. What an ironic twist of fate. We were in Germany, consumed with the tensions of the Berlin Wall. Suddenly, it looked as though the folks at home could be blown up any minute. It was a tense time for Americans all over the world. What a great relief it was when Khrushchev finally pulled the Russian missiles out of Cuba. That was too close for comfort.

As much tension as these world affairs provided, more important to me was the state of my love life. Even though I kept believing I was always in love, I didn't give up my virginal ways. I imagine the few men I was involved with thought I was a tease. I was never that intentionally, I was naïve. Of course, I had to have "my respect" you know. And the guys over there thought all of us girls, whether we were teachers or with the special services, were there for one thing: to catch a man. I was a one-woman crusade to prove them wrong.

I certainly enjoyed seeing all the men in the officers' club, but my intentions were: (a) to get away from home, (b) to travel and see as much as I could, and (c) to have a good time. The only piece of advice I got before I left home was from the family doctor. "Have a good time," he said, "but don't come home pregnant." I had no intention of that and was quite shocked actually that he would say such a thing to me, little Miss Respect.

With the AIDS epidemic now, getting pregnant doesn't seem so bad, but once again, you must understand the times we lived in. It was a scandal and a shame to be pregnant and unmarried. Now it seems to be no big deal and not very unusual, except of course the life of a child is always a big deal.

I managed to accomplish my three goals and look back on this year as one of the highlights of my life. I was always in love, but the men I cared for always would leave me when they knew I wasn't going to "come across," as they used to say. I traveled a lot, made some wonderful friends and regret only we didn't keep in touch over the years.

While in Munich I learned how wonderful and valuable friendship is among women. Some of us wrote back and forth the first year or so, but then as most of these women were adventurers, we lost touch with one another. I remember and think of them all very fondly, and I hope life has been kind to them.

The other insight I got from my year in Germany was learning about myself. After this time, I knew it didn't matter where I was teaching because I would never be fulfilled as a teacher. Teaching is an honorable profession to be sure, but it wasn't for me.

I decided to leave Germany at the end of the year to get out of teaching all together and to live and work in Boston. Now that I had established myself as my own person, I was ready to take on another world.

I left Germany in the summer of 1963 with self-confidence I hadn't possessed the year before. I had a flair for the taste of the good things in life, friendships I was sure would continue, and now I was armed with a new goal and purpose. I would work in a publishing firm.

I loved words, I loved writing, and I knew I was creative, smart and willing to learn. With my new self-confidence I was sure I would get a job and was willing to start anywhere and work my way up. Yes, I was self-assured and confident, but not cocky. From my parents I also had a good dose of realistic expectations. But hey, I'd been to Europe and lived there for a year. I could conquer Boston, Massachusetts and the publishing world. Isn't it grand to be young?

I remember being young and never thinking I would grow old. For some reason I believed getting older is something that happens to other people, but it wasn't going to happen to me. I think it's a blessing to feel as if you will always be young and never consider getting older. I've seen it in my children, and because I remember, I'm glad for them.

I also remember when I started to feel old. "Surprise! Guess who's older today?" I'm sure you remember when this happened to you. Do you remember the time your body wouldn't do what your brain was telling it to do? I was playing tennis at the time. I was about forty-two and thinking, "Oh, this is great. Look at me getting to be a better player all the time."

"Merrily, merrily, merrily, life is but a dream…" A gal on the other side hit the ball on the far side of my court. "Run, Carol, run," my brain told me, but my body laughed back and said, "Oh no, I don't think so, not today, I'm too tired." My feet had a will of their own and seemed to be stuck in quicksand. I could hear the dialogue in my head; my brain and my body were arguing, and my body won. I knew then this was just the beginning. I had to accept this fact of life; I was no longer young. I wasn't old either, but hell I wasn't young anymore. Previously I had been able to kid myself, kid my brain and my body, but now they were in cahoots and here was another version of me, another Carol… "gently down the stream."

I am ahead of my story again, you'll forgive me as I reflect on these times. I can't keep that philosopher out of my head, still looking for a dollar.

Yes, I was home from Europe, summer of 1963 and ready for a new and brighter future. I was back among my family and friends and I knew who I was at last and where I wanted to go. I had a renewed sense of purpose and life was looking pretty good. I knew the value of friendship, and now that my priorities were all sorted, my path was clear. America had survived the missile crises; my virginity was intact. Life was indeed good.

I had even seen Henry Fonda at the airport when I arrived home. I was having coffee in the café when this very tall, extremely tanned and handsome man sat down only a few seats away from me. "Gee, he looks like Henry Fonda. It is Henry Fonda. He is much more handsome than he appears in the movies." But I didn't go over to him or ask for his autograph or anything, I only gazed from afar. I mention this only to tell you how sophisticated I had become. A proper Bostonian respects a person's privacy.

I began my job search, making the rounds of publishers, Houghton Mifflin, Little Brown, knowing my resume looked good and in time I was sure I would find a job in Boston. Yes, I was feeling good about myself and then as my son often says, "all hell broke loose."

My brother had married a girl he'd been seeing before he went into the service. I didn't like her very much, but hey, I wasn't going to marry her. Naturally, they had a baby, a little girl, Lorrie, the apple of my mother's eye to be sure. Well, I told you she always liked Louis more than she liked me. The year I was away in Europe, growing and exploring and having a good time, my brother's marriage was not only falling apart but had become a nightmare for him and my family. Poor Lorrie was the pawn. I was oblivious to it all and thinking only of myself, as I believed it was time to do.

Soon after I arrived home, I was scheduled to take Lorrie to get her shots for school. I hated to go up to that apartment, so I beeped the horn at the curb and waited for Louis' wife to bring Lorrie down. I didn't even try to pretend that I liked Connie anymore. I beeped and beeped and waited. One part of me I haven't shared with you yet is how much I hate waiting, for anything or anybody. There were so many lines in the service, we had to wait for everything, everywhere. After that I could not tolerate lines or waiting.

"Damn," I thought. "I'm going to have to go upstairs."

Knock, knock, no answer, no sound, but the door was

open. The apartment was even dirtier than I remembered it. There were cigarette butts everywhere, including burns on the cushions of the couch and chairs. As I went into the kitchen, I saw there was no stove, and no refrigerator. Louis was cooking on a hot plate. I was nearly sick to my stomach; how could my brother live this way? What would my parents think if they saw this? Where was everyone?

Finally, I looked in the bedroom, and in the crib, huddled in a corner, quiet and scared and shrunken by fear, was my niece, Lorrie, all alone. She had not cried out. She was there in the corner of this dirty crib, in a dirtier room, no clean clothes to be seen anywhere, just piles of dirty clothes everywhere. I picked her up quickly and got out of there as fast as I could. The time had come to confront my brother.

I got to the gas station where Louis was working for the summer. I had the baby in the car beside me. I told him what I had seen and that I was taking Lorrie home with me. "You can do whatever you want, but she is staying with us."

My brother shook his head and said finally, "I guess it's about time I left her."

That night we went back to his apartment to pack up what belongings he had. Connie, his wife, was still not there and I was afraid what might happen if she came home and saw us. My brother didn't seem as concerned about that; he made sure he had all his books. I remember almost laughing at all the books we took. We were out at last and so began the long process of separating and divorcing and trying to mend a little girl's confused heart.

Louis may have been breaking free, but my freedom now was a big question mark. I was continuing my job search in

Boston, but with this family crisis, my parents did not want me to get a job that would take me away from home. There was a teaching job available in the same school district where Louis was working in New Hampshire, and my mother strongly "suggested" I go for an interview and "help out."

I would have liked to leave them all behind and say, "Too bad, sorry, but I have my life to live." However, I was nothing if not loyal, so I thought, "I'll go for the interview and perhaps I won't get the job and then I can get on with my life." I was appeasing, trying to be fair and please everyone. The joke would be on me.

No one then knew about dysfunctional families. Oh sure, we knew some families were a little bit "odder" than others, but no one had a name for them at that time. When people talked about addictions it was more linked to drugs or gambling. The term "co-dependency" was many years away. Meanwhile I was living a co-dependent's story and I was not aware of it until many years later. Too late to turn back the clock or change events and decisions, but, oh, what a relief it was to, at last, know I wasn't crazy.

Meanwhile back in New Hampshire in the fall of 1963, I was rather amused by my interview with the superintendent of schools. He seemed to be more interested in the color of my lipstick than about my teaching credentials. "Do you always wear that color lipstick?" he asked me. I smiled and thought, "Oh, good. He doesn't like the color of my lipstick. I won't get the job."

Sadly for me, I got the job despite of the color of my lipstick (hey, maybe because of it). The irony of it all was that that year turned out to be one of my best years in teaching.

I liked the kids a lot and their families were very supportive and interested, and I even liked the atmosphere of the little country school. My brother and I rode to school together, and the rides were pleasant and lovely as the scenery was so pretty with each passing season.

I had only one problem that year. I didn't like the principal, and I didn't respect him. All right, I thought he was a jerk. I know this opinion was shared by almost all the other teachers on staff, at least the ones who dared to talk out loud.

He and I had a problem about the reading books in my classroom one day. I had a very bright class and I wanted them to be challenged and so I requested third and fourth grade material. He told me to give them more second grade books. I had gone through a similar situation while teaching for the Army. The supply sergeant would only give me first grade materials; "You teach first grade, so that's what you get." At least he had an excuse, he was in the Army and doing his job. But this principal? What was his excuse? I didn't have either patience or respect for him. He proved to me what I have always believed: the American public school system takes better care of its slow learners than it does its talented and gifted. I have a special prejudice in this regard.

However, I do see that I could have been more creative in getting around the system, silly me going through the proper channels. I remembered and treasured the children as individuals, but it seemed the administration was more interested in keeping a smooth ship, no waves, no ripples. I had been given advice, "don't make waves," during my first year of teaching, but I just couldn't stop rocking the boat. Was I in the wrong profession or what?

There was more irony down the road for me that year. Just when I figured I could tolerate this principal, and that, all in all I liked teaching there, I learned I was fired. No one warned me or gave me a clue. The other teachers all knew before I did. I had been fired the night before at a school board meeting. The reason given: "Insubordination." I also learned that of the ten teachers on staff, eight would be leaving at the end of the term. But I was the only one whose contract had not been renewed.

When I pointed this fact out to the superintendent in a subsequent interview with him, noting that perhaps the principal's lack of leadership was the reason behind such a mass exodus, he told me "this may be true, but we don't get rid of principals. After all, teachers are a dime a dozen." Imagine some superintendent saying that today! "Teachers are a dime a dozen." I knew then more than ever I didn't want any part of this so-called "profession." I was not prepared to deal with this kind of thinking. Nor was I prepared with an alternative plan for my future. Once more I had the excuse I needed to leave home, but what was I going to do now?

I didn't want to go back to Boston and pursue a job there, I needed to rebuild my confidence after this shame, and to me it was a shame because I didn't feel I deserved to be fired. Years later I would look back on it as a badge of courage or something like that, but at the time I was humiliated, angry, hurt and for once I didn't pretend to be anything else but what I was.

So, I did what so many other young people do who stumble in the so called "real world." I went to graduate school. I applied and was accepted in the drama department at both

Connecticut College and Catholic University. I decided on Catholic University.

Fate was already at work. Stephen was also preparing for a new future. After he was discharged from the Army, he lived in Chicago for a year. Unhappy with his work and life there, he applied and was accepted to Catholic University in Washington, D.C.

In August 1964 Stephen drove his brand-new Ford Falcon convertible to the campus at Catholic University. I flew in and arrived from the airport in a taxi.

CHAPTER FOUR

We Meet But No Angels Sing.

I was almost twenty-seven years old and off again to seek my future. Because of my bad luck with jobs and men, my plan was to get my master's degree and teach in a private high school or maybe a college. I thought if I were teaching something I loved, and not in a public school, I could be happy. I decided to forget about men, accept my lot in life as the merry aunt and take very good care of myself. I had no plans except to support myself and do something I loved and of course live away from my family. In my mind I had given them another year of my life, done my share in my heart and mind. Now I was going to take care of Carol, or so I thought.

Washington, D.C. in 1964 was still charming, exciting and wonderful. Although I was very disappointed when I first saw the University, I soon came to love it. Because I was unfamiliar with this area I decided to live in the dorm. The graduate ladies' dorm was a few blocks away from the campus. I didn't mind living in a dorm, even though I hated all the rules. Most of them seemed silly to me, but I knew I wouldn't be living there very long.

After getting somewhat settled in the dorm I made friends with Diane, another graduate student in the drama department. The next day with both anxiety and excitement, I went to register for my classes.

The drama department at Catholic University had a very prestigious reputation, but you wouldn't have known it by its location on the campus. Any time you went to a University function and said you were in the drama department, you were instantly classified as someone who was not to be taken seriously.

The building was located at the lower end of the campus, but it was a pleasant enough little building. Registration was held in the basement, which was not very inviting, and again I wondered what I had gotten myself into.

There weren't many of us that day as we sat or stood along the narrow passage. I was nervous and I was sure I was not the only one. Naturally we were all looking at each other, surreptitiously of course, sizing each other up as if it were an audition and there were only so many parts to go around.

I noticed the young man standing across from me. He was wearing loafers and white socks. "Who does he think he is, Gene Kelly? No one wears white socks with loafers." I was amused and looked up at the rest of him. He wore glasses, wasn't very tall, not bad looking, but he definitely was not my type. Then I remembered I wasn't interested in men anymore, although I did notice this guy had nice hands. His hands looked very strong.

"I suppose you're all wondering why I've asked you here today," he said to us, with a big grin on his face. Everyone laughed and the tension disappeared. Soon we were all talking, laughing, and sharing our excitement.

"So, he's funny," I thought, "that's nice."

Registration for classes was wonderful; to me it was like a dream come true. I was still surprised by the fact that all my courses were about theater. I chose not to take any acting classes that semester, and instead concentrated on playwriting and directing. History of theater was a required course for all first-year graduate students.

That night Diane and I went to a production of the University's touring company. The young man with the loafers and white socks joined us and told us his name, Steve. He said his last name, but because I wasn't interested, I didn't pay attention. Only a short time later, I would pay very close attention not only to his name, but everything about him.

Since Steve had a car, Diane asked him if he'd give us a ride home, and he said sure. I thought he probably liked her. She was blond and men do seem to prefer them, you know. I didn't care one way or another. Remember he wasn't my type – not with those white socks and loafers.

Steve and I were in two of the same classes; history and our last class of the day, playwriting. We started to talk after class and he asked me if I'd like to have supper with him. "Sure," I said. What fun and excitement it was to share our experiences and get to know one another. Besides he had a car and I could get a ride home. His car was an important asset to our relationship. Later my books became an equally important asset to our friendship.

Soon we were meeting for lunch in the cafeteria and later

for supper after our last class. Everything was Dutch treat of course, after all most of us were lucky we could afford to be in school. We'd join other friends from the theater department, and there was always much laughter, stimulating discussions, and a lot of fun. The first production of the season was being cast, "The Lady's Not for Burning." Steve and Diane auditioned while I was happy to observe.

My big decision was to volunteer to do costumes for this show. Not because I could sew, but because working on costumes was a requirement and I thought I'd get it over with sooner rather than later. That way I'd have it behind me and I wouldn't have to worry about it.

The costume director could not believe how utterly helpless and hopeless I was in the sewing department. But he was kind and took pity on me "Just do the hems. Use your elbow as a guide for how much thread to use." But more than his acceptance of my clumsiness was the kindness extended to me by Sister Mary Gordon, the only nun in the drama school. She was funny and so down to earth that she erased (almost) all the traces of the nuns I'd known and feared at Sacred Heart. Even though she wore the traditional habit, the long black cassock and the wimple, there was nothing traditional about Sister Mary Gordon.

During this time, I was dating Stephen, at least I think we were dating as we spent a lot of time together and were becoming closer. Our first real date, the one where he actually asked me out, was to see a movie, *It's a Mad, Mad, Mad, Mad World*. The significance of this is not only the fact of its being our first official date, but also the fact that I paid. I hold this over his head frequently because it is such a good story. More than that it came to represent one of the biggest problems in our marriage: money.

Not only did I pay for this date, but he didn't even kiss me good night! Oh, and I wanted him to kiss me. Later, he told me he did this on purpose. Well, it worked because now I was feeling more than friendship toward him. Whenever I saw him coming into the cafeteria, I would smile all over and my heart would beat faster and faster. I was so happy we shared our last class because then I knew we'd be together at the end of the day.

My feelings for him grew stronger each day. I thought about him and yearned for him, yet I was angry with myself at the same time. I felt myself falling in love with him and this was not part of my plan. My heart was saying one thing, but my head said quite another. The logical part of my brain told me he was wrong for me. Everything inside my head said, "Carol, this is not the man for you."

For another date he came to my dorm wearing the brightest yellow turtleneck I had ever seen, he had a guitar slung over his shoulder, and he was wearing those damn white socks and loafers. He looked like one of the Kingston Trio. He serenaded me and Diane with his not too vast repertoire of songs. I must add here that his repertoire has not increased in all these years. All right, maybe he's added one or two, but mostly he still plays "Sylvie."

Stephen was very different from any guy I had dated. I didn't like the way he dressed, and I thought he was not sophisticated enough for me. He almost never had any money to spend, and worse still, he wanted to be an actor. By now I was twenty-seven years old and believed when and if I ever fell in love again the man would have a career, sown his wild oats and be ready to settle down. I was interested in someone who liked to go to concerts and movies and listen to jazz. He'd have to dress well and treat a girl like a lady. And he certainly would have money enough to take me out for dinner and drinks and dancing. That was the kind of man I wanted to date.

Stephen was not the man of my dreams. He had few of the qualities I was looking for, but remember, I wasn't looking. I had a choice; I could have listened to my head. Yet, I had no choice as my heart went on without the rest of me. I was in love and falling more every day.

Finally, our attraction for each other became stronger and more powerful than our friendship. Our physical relationship began to take over. It just happened. There was not a moment I can say how or when exactly it happened. It wasn't like it was with Roger, and yet the chemistry built up, slowly and suddenly. We were the formula simmering over the Bunsen burner until at last we exploded. Boom!

When Stephen touched me, I felt a desire and a passion that was totally new to me. I was confused, excited, anxious and afraid. Where was my old companion "Respect?" I was not headstrong now; I was totally *heart* strong.

I regard making love with Stephen as my first time. At the age of twenty-seven I discovered sex. I felt great every time we had sex and foolish that I had missed all this fun. I thought it was fun and thrilling and exciting and wonderful. For me, sex was magic. For Stephen it was both magic and guilt. I had no idea a man would feel so guilty about having sex especially when I was having so much fun. However, Stephen didn't feel so guilty that he stopped seeing me or making love to me.

I decided I was going to make up for lost time. My new relationship with Stephen prompted me to move out of the dorm and into an apartment. Diane moved in with me, and I felt this would give Stephen and me the privacy we needed to have "safe sex." It sure beat having to do it in his car. All we had to worry about was Diane's schedule.

I was so deeply in love with Stephen at this point, and although he kept breaking up with me and feeling guilty, he couldn't stay away from me either. We still shared our classes, and he shared my books and gave me rides. We did almost all our graduate projects together. We worked side by side at the Folger Library and the Library of Congress and in the stacks at Catholic University.

When his brother was sick with throat cancer and Stephen had to go to New Jersey for two weeks I thought I would die without him. I looked for him everywhere, even when I knew he wasn't around. The busy-ness of school could not keep me from thinking of him and wanting him and missing him every minute. Finally, unexpectedly there was a knock on my door, and he was there. I wanted just to throw my arms around him but held back as we were trying to stay away from each other. We didn't have a lot of success, but we did try.

He was not for me, I thought, no matter how great our sexual attraction was to each other. He felt too guilty all the time for us to relax and have fun and be happy together. This affair was more than I had imagined and yet nothing that I had imagined. I didn't want to be in love with him and I knew he didn't want to be in love with me. One night I bought myself a bottle of whiskey to drink my fear away. I thought if

I got drunk enough maybe I wouldn't feel this love anymore. It didn't work.

One night the drama department was invited to a special party, but then there was always a party at school somewhere. Since this was so special, I got all dressed up in my simply elegant black silk dress and my suede sling back pumps. What fun it was to get all dressed up again. Stephen was due to pick me up and even though we'd been arguing and getting back together again, I was happy we were going to the party together, just like a regular, normal couple.

The bell rang and I eagerly opened the door. Stephen was standing there looking like an orphan who'd just gotten off the boat at Ellis Island and wasn't sure where he was or what he was supposed to do. He had on an enormous overcoat, at least two sizes too big for him, his loafers, and perhaps for this special night, colored socks. It didn't matter. He looked lost and abandoned, and I remember holding the door open, looking at him, looking at myself and thinking, 'This person is not for me. I need a man and he's a lost, little boy. Close the door, Carol, close that door or you'll be sorry."

I opened the door and let him in.

Chapter Five

Love Hurts

A s I was soon to discover, I'd be sorry any way. The year was 1964 and the biggest problem facing girls who were "sexually active" was the fear of getting pregnant. Because I had been a "good girl" all those years I didn't expect to get pregnant. For one thing I figured I was too old. Honestly! And I thought God and I had a deal: for all the years when I said, "No," I could now say, "Yes," with impunity. I was wrong.

I hoped if I ignored the fact that I had missed my period and then missing my second one, "it" would go away, like the flu. After all these years, I still can't believe how naive we both were. First of all, I figured since Stephen had been in the Army he would naturally know about protection. He, on the other hand, thought since I was the girl, I would take care of the precautions. Like what? I wondered later. We are talking about a time before the Pill, and I wasn't using a diaphragm. The choice was obvious to me. Stephen had to take care of it, but he never did. God, I was so stupid and foolish, the belief in the goodness of each of us, that somehow being good was going to protect us.

Finally, after two months of worry and disbelief, I found the courage to call a doctor and go by myself to see him. I was honest with him about being a single graduate student and I was lucky he was a kind and understanding man. When I called the next day to hear the results of my test, trying and wanting so hard to believe I wasn't pregnant, I almost convinced myself I had some psychological problem. I was wrong again; I was indeed pregnant.

How could this be? It wasn't as if Stephen and I were having sex all the time, I mean we could never manage to be alone that much. I guess I was just one of the lucky, fertile ones. Wow. Now what? Now what, indeed! Funny the things you think of, I thought of Dr. Grassi's advice when I had gone overseas: "Don't come home pregnant." Here I was at Catholic University for heaven's sake. This was not a course I had planned for graduate school.

By this time I told Stephen what was going on and how concerned I was. I called him now to tell him I was definitely pregnant. Although he was very sweet to me on the phone, I had a feeling he was somehow not going to be a big help to me. I was right.

Although I believed he truly loved me, he kept telling me and himself that he didn't love me at all. All his actions spoke otherwise. During the rest of the semester at school and my first trimester with the baby, I kept asking him to marry me and telling him he really loved me. For a while we would see each other still but try very hard not to touch, as if it really made a difference now.

I went home for Christmas and kept my secret to

myself. I was miserable the whole time. I decided to return to Washington before the new year. When I called to tell Stephen I was coming back, he told me he had a date for New Year's Eve. Well, there were a lot of tears shed that New Year's Eve. All in all, it didn't look as if 1965 was going to be a banner year for me. What was I going to do? Where would I go? I was all alone, well, not exactly. I began to investigate my options.

I began in the stacks at the University. I read all about unwed mothers and discovered many interesting facts. Most unwed mothers were teenagers, some in their early twenties, but nowhere did I find any record of twenty-seven-year-old women reporting to homes for unwed mothers. I felt as if I were too old to be in this predicament. But here I was, alone in the stacks at Catholic University, reading about unwed mothers and options available. At the same time I was laughing at myself, I was crying for myself. Many of the teenage mothers I read about went back and forth to these homes, "repeat offenders" so to speak.

All right I didn't find a home for myself then, so I called Catholic charities. I was Catholic, after all, in a Catholic graduate school program, in trouble, so I thought I qualified on all counts for help. It seemed logical.

Perhaps I encountered this particular woman on a bad day, but she was not very friendly. After I told her my problem, she was less friendly and not at all charitable. She managed even over the phone to make me feel like a very bad person. Was there any help for me?

Finally, I called one of my oldest and best friends and left Washington to visit with her and her husband on Long

Island. She took me to see her doctor and we discussed options. Abortion of course for me was out of the question. "The father won't marry you?" the doctor asked. I shook my head, no. By now I had given up hope that he ever would. "Well then, let's consider adoption." The doctor talked about this for a while, but when he got to the part about the delivery room and I wouldn't be allowed even to look at the baby, I knew this was not an option for me either. I couldn't just deliver the baby and let him go.

No, I decided, as I had perhaps known all along inside myself, I would keep my baby myself. I knew instinctively it was a boy, and so I would have some part of Stephen after all to love and to cherish. I would find a way to raise this child by myself. I could teach, get a small apartment, find a good babysitter (not my parents certainly), and make a life for both my baby and myself. Now that I made that decision, I knew I'd work it out. Alone.

Soon after I returned from Long Island, final exams began. I took my exams and hoped still that Stephen would change his mind and marry me. At the same time, I was making plans for the baby and me. Stephen rented an apartment with another graduate student, not far from where I was living at the time. While he made plans for his next semester, I was making plans to return to Massachusetts. I had to figure out a way to tell my parents about my situation. Oh, boy.

In February, another dear friend, Lynne, came to Washington with her fiancée Bob. When we met for lunch, I blurted out my sad story. Lynne was surprised but not shocked. Together we came up with a plan that would benefit us both. I could live with her and her young son in her house in Hampton, New Hampshire. Lynne was attending the university in Durham and I was confident I could find a teaching job somewhere in the area. After my baby was born, we would also share expenses and a babysitter. She had no immediate plans to get married, and I was not going to live with my parents under any circumstances. New Hampshire would be far enough yet close enough to maintain some level of communication.

I breathed a big sigh of relief, for although this wasn't my first choice, it was a sensible and workable solution for me. Once again, I must remind you the times were so different in 1965. No matter what anyone says about the 60s and the radical changes going on, illegitimate babies were not something even movie stars announced. When I look back, I feel almost silly for all the tears and troubles I made for myself.

A sin and a shame, that was the view of my situation in 1965. Today it is viewed as neither by most people. I was not proud, and probably ashamed of myself, but I loved Stephen so much and I loved our unborn baby because it was a part of him and a part of us. I knew I could be a good mother. It would be sad for the baby not to have a father, but to have love from me and my friends, (I wasn't too sure about my family) well, it would have to be enough. That's all, I'd make it work.

At the time I thought how sad it must be for Stephen with no one to talk to about any of this. He didn't have any friends to share the problem with and yet he seemed just fine. I wondered how he would feel when he knew he had a son, so sure was I it would be a son. How would Stephen feel when he knew the fact of his son, of there being a part of him somewhere in New England. Would he ever think of him or want to see him or ever be a part of his life? Did Stephen ask himself any of these questions? To see him at the time, making plans to return to school and living in a new apartment, I honestly don't think he ever got beyond himself and his own ambitions. We certainly never talked about it.

Lynne shared my story with her fiancée, Bob, and later the two of them came up with the idea of Bob's talking to Stephen. Maybe Bob could convince Stephen to marry me. The International Inn in Washington was a grand, new place and we made arrangements to have breakfast with Lynne and Bob the next morning. I stayed upstairs with Lynne while Bob took Stephen downstairs for coffee. I paced and paced and fretted. "Oh, he's going to be furious with me for telling you and tricking him this morning." I was sure my situation was going to go from bad to worse. How could it be worse? Lynne kept reassuring me. Now that I think of it, what was the worst that could happen anyhow? The wonderful part for me at this point was that I was no longer alone. I had my friends to share this troubled time with me and help me. Thank God for friends.

Stephen and Bob returned to the room and both were smiling. Stephen came over to me, gave me a kiss, and said, "Let's do it." What? "Get married. Bob's talked to me and it makes sense. We can go to Maryland and be married tomorrow." Take my breath away! In all my fantasies and imaginings about what might happen, I honestly didn't see this. Even if he didn't marry me, I had decided I'd use his name anyhow. I mean who'd ever make up a name like Hrehovcik? Especially in a small town in New Hampshire? But this was even better.

What excitement. We went downtown to get a wedding ring. The only store that was open was Sears. He bought me a beautiful wedding ring, Florentine gold, that was at least three sizes too big. As far as I was concerned it was perfect. It cost $22. What a bargain. That night we drove to Elkton, Maryland, found a room in a nearby motel, made fabulous love, and for the first time, Stephen didn't feel guilty.

We met Lynne and Bob in Elkton the next day so they could be our witnesses. Unfortunately, when we went to the town hall to pick up our wedding application, we learned it was no longer possible to get married the same day. There was a two-day waiting period. We needed to have blood tests, so we had to come back next week. I was disappointed on more than one level. First of all, I wanted Lynne and Bob there with us, and more importantly I was sure this would give Stephen a chance to change his mind again. "Now he'll never marry me." I thought he had been swept along with the excitement, but left alone he'd desert me again. Lynne and Bob headed back to New Hampshire and Stephen and I returned, unmarried, to Washington.

That entire weekend I expected to get a phone call telling me to forget it, that he'd changed his mind. Instead both of us were like two little kids with a big secret, bursting to tell someone and yet caught up in the excitement of our planned elopement. On Sunday night Hildegarde performed at the University theater Stephen and I were holding hands and giggling to ourselves and each other. We left for Maryland right after the performance. The most popular song on the radio was "Downtown" by Petula Clark and since we heard it all night long, on every radio station, it became our song. Not very romantic, I know, but even when we hear it now, we remember still the excitement and the enthusiasm we were both feeling that night.

When we arrived at the motel this night, Stephen called his sister to ask about her recovery from an operation she'd had. She asked him when he was going to get married. He didn't tell her, but how surprised and shocked she would have been if he had said "tomorrow."

I must tell you that our pre-wedding night was absolutely thrilling. Now that we were going to be married, Stephen was feeling no guilt at all, so we made love most of the night with fire, fun and total abandon. Our sexual relationship has always been the most stable part of our marriage, and in no small way I'm sure, has been part of the glue that kept us together all these years. It seems we were truly made for each other, at least in the bedroom. In fact, the only problem we didn't have in our marriage was sex.

With that little aside, let's go back to the wedding day. Elkton, Maryland was apparently the place to elope many years ago. Many times, I've come across the name in a book when fictional characters elope. I still smile when I see the name. As it turned out we could have gotten married in any town in Maryland, closer to Washington, but we knew about Elkton and were so swept away by the romance of it the thought of somewhere closer never occurred to either of us.

We walked up and down the streets of what was at one time the City of Weddings. There were many places and chapels with cute names, but you could see the heyday of Elkton had passed. We finally chose "the Little Wedding Chapel" where a minister and his wife officiated at our quiet, lonely, little ceremony. I was too happy to care about the ceremony. It wasn't the way I imagined it as a little girl reading the Brides' magazines in Mitchell's, but it was my wedding and the love was there. I had been in enough weddings to know by now it wasn't about the wedding day itself, but how you lived your married life together, ever after.

You see, I was able to delude myself that Stephen and I were getting married to be married, to stay together for better or worse. It didn't take long for me to learn that Stephen had no such intention. On the way home while I was bubbling and bursting with the ideas and dreams of a new bride, my reluctant groom told me, "We're not going to stay married. We're married in name only. You still have to go back to Massachusetts and I'm going to continue with graduate school. Now I'm thinking I may even go to New York and look for an acting job there. Marriage and you don't fit into any of my plans."

There was to be no future for the new Mr. and Mrs. Hrehovcik. Stephen made it very clear there was no place in his life for me, the baby, or our marriage. I cried the whole way home. The little happiness I'd felt that morning evaporated as we got closer to my apartment. I went upstairs and sobbed to my roommate as I told her how we had eloped but that we weren't going to stay together. Diane called Stephen to come over because I was crying so hard, she couldn't calm me down. He came over and was tender and sweet but there was no doubt he wasn't changing his mind.

The next morning, he called me to tell me that his roommate had gone out and I should come over. And, silly me, I did, and we made love all morning. He brought me home later and went to register for his classes for second semester. I went to my apartment to pack and call my parents. I told them I was married, I was pregnant, and I was coming home. Stephen had agreed to take me back to Massachusetts. It was all so silly and yet it was real, it was happening

It was nearly two weeks before we left for Massachusetts. All the while Stephen would call me every morning to come to his apartment as soon as his roommate went out. I'd run through the park each time hoping today would be the day he'd realize how much he loved me and needed me. Instead we had an 'incident' with the exterminator. It was both funny and humiliating.

One morning while we were having our usual fun in bed, there was a knock on the door. Stephen tiptoed to the window to see who it was. He'd forgotten the exterminator was coming that morning, so while the exterminator stood outside the door, Stephen hurried me into the shower to hide. Once again, like a fool, I humored him and hid there in the shower.

Fortunately, it wouldn't take long for the man to spray the small basement apartment, and he assured my husband that it was perfectly safe to be in the apartment while he did his work. Yes, but how about in the shower? Stephen busied himself getting dressed and making coffee and some eggs for himself. Once in a while he'd peek in at me to be sure I wasn't coming out and assure me it would only be another minute.

Naturally, patience not being one of my virtues, after several minutes went by, I felt like more of a fool than ever for agreeing to hide. I started to make my exit, or entrance as the case may be, but Stephen waved at me to stay there because "it won't take long now." I laughed at the absurdity of it all, it was like a play by Moliere, but it was happening to me. Then I reminded him I didn't need to hide because we were married after all. "But no one knows," he said.

When the exterminator finally left, I was liberated from the shower. I started to laugh, but then it hit me, this was not funny. Stephen was embarrassed and ashamed of me. He would indeed be bringing me home and I must make my own life apart from him. Any doubts I had, any hopes I may have yet fostered, were all shattered by this one incident. I would fight his decision no longer.

On the weekend of Washington's birthday, on a cold, clear, crisp D. C. morning, Stephen and I and a U-Haul hitched to his '63 Falcon convertible began our journey to New England and home for me. We spent the night with Rita and Charles in Long Island. I was surprised by their cool reception to both Stephen and me. Looking back, I see it was foolish of me to think they would react any other way. After all it was Rita who saw me at my most desperate time and helped me make my decision to keep the baby no matter what. I was a fool in everyone else's eyes but my own. I loved Stephen so much, despite the circumstances, I wanted everyone else to like him too.

The next day was agony for me as we got closer to my parents' house. I imagined what my father would say and do to Stephen once we arrived there. After all my father had thrown out every boy I dated, and that was for nothing! What would he do now to Stephen, and for a very good reason? It seemed as if Stephen wasn't concerned at all, but he'd never met my father. After all, since this made perfect sense to my husband, I guess he thought everyone else would see the logic of the situation. I tried to warn him about my father, and I wasn't only concerned for Stephen. I was afraid for myself, as I had always been afraid of my father. Even though I knew I had a safe haven to go to with Lynne, I was still afraid of my father's anger and temper.

It was dark by the time we pulled into the driveway. My brother was still living there with his daughter and I had hoped he'd be home to help soften the blow with my parents. After sitting outside in the dark and trying to work up my courage, Stephen said, "Let' go. It won't be so bad." Silly boy.

You remember my family's heritage is Sicilian, which means a couple of things. First, we always offer a visitor food or something to drink, second, after this show of hospitality, we let loose the cannons. Somehow, I found my father rather calm for him and my mother was more or less matter of fact. After we had some coffee, my father told me and my mother to go into the other room while he talked to Stephen. Talk, oh sure, here it comes.

But while mother sat with me on the couch and even held my hand, a warm gesture for her, I didn't hear any screaming or shouting or banging on the table. Instead as both mother and I strained to hear my father speak, I heard him say to Stephen, "You can't leave her here. You have to take her back with you. She's your responsibility now." And my favorite part, and oh, so like the father I grew up with, "You may find prettier girls, but you won't find one as nice."

Isn't it funny, I thought, my own father still doesn't think I'm pretty? Anyway, I was "nice." I'd never heard that before, from either of my parents. Mostly what I heard when I was growing up was the name calling, like "lazy, selfish, spoiled" and mother's all-time favorite "bitch." These were the kinds of reviews I was used to. No wonder I thought no one could possibly love me. I was ready to take what I could get.

After Stephen and my father talked, my brother came home and he and I and Stephen went downstairs to talk. Stephen still hadn't decided what he was going to do. One thing he knew for sure was he was going back to D. C. with or without me, and I dearly hoped it would be with me. We slept that night in my bed, but I felt embarrassed to be in bed with him in my parents' house. He was thinking and dozing and talking and I was praying and listening and hoping.

Early the next morning he turned to me and said, "I've decided. I'll never find anyone who loves me as much as you do. I love you, I know that now, so we'll go back to Washington together." Just like that he had changed his mind. It took me many years to feel secure with Stephen's love; I was always afraid he'd change his mind again. Then there were the dreams. In my dreams I was always looking for him and couldn't find him, I'd lost him.

The next day we backed the U-Haul out of my parents' driveway and headed back to Washington to begin our married life together.

CHAPTER SIX

Marriage and the Extended Family

On our way back to D. C. Stephen announced we would stop in New Jersey to tell his brother and his family our news. I knew I would be a surprise and a shock to them, and I begged Stephen to please call them before we arrived. "Let them have some warning and a few minutes at least to get used to the idea that you're married."

Oh, no, my husband insisted it would be more "fun" this way. Fun for whom? Not for me, certainly, and I was pretty sure this was not going to be a fun surprise for his family either. Even in the best of circumstances accepting a person into a family is difficult, and these certainly were not the best of circumstances. First of all, no one in his family knew I existed, and now he was announcing not only were we married but I was four months pregnant. There was no convincing him to call; he was going to have his moment and damn the torpedoes, full speed ahead.

Even with this prospect in view, we had a pleasant ride and arrived at his brother's door in Passaic, New Jersey early in the evening. While Stephen was grinning in anticipation of his big surprise, I stood back, timid and afraid, and hoped if I were quiet enough no one would notice me. Stephen's nephew opened the door, smiled and greeted him. "Uncle Steve," he announced.

Stephen grabbed my hand, pulled me beside him and said, "This is my wife, Carol."

That darling little boy, not quite nine years old, took my bag and said, "Hi, Aunt Carol, come on in. Everybody's home and the Grubiaks are here too."

Oh, my God, they are all home and they have company besides. I knew Stephen should have called. Oh, Lord, let me fall into a hole right now, crawl away and die...

"Hey, everyone, I want you to meet someone. This is my wife, Carol." Well, to say jaws dropped, mouths were agape, and eyes bulged would not do justice the response these poor people expressed. I couldn't blame them, and I wasn't hurt or angry.

Imagine how you would feel in this situation! What did Stephen expect? I hoped he was happy with his game because I was embarrassed and ashamed. I don't recall ever feeling so much humiliation in such a short time. Me, Carol, the headstrong, independent, aggressive woman who had so much pride, now didn't have even my own respect – and remember I had the respect of men from New England to Germany! At the same time, I couldn't blame Stephen, except I did. But there was more to come: more blame, more questions, and more doubt in a very few minutes.

I recall the kitchen was pink. Apparently, Mike and his wife, Lee, had just finished painting it. Why would anyone paint a kitchen pink? I wondered as I sat there and took in my surroundings while they made a fuss over my husband and put the kettle on for tea. This was a family of tea drinkers, and I came from a family of coffee lovers. Coffee for me was the comfort drink of choice. Here it would be tea.

All right, so we were sitting there having tea in this pink kitchen and all I wanted to do was leave, go home, wherever that may be now. I listened, sort of, to his brother make plans for us to get married in his church in Passaic...ha, not me, I thought. And then Stephen must get me an engagement ring, his brother tells him. Sure, on a graduate student's good looks. His brother then goes on some more, listing all the things Stephen must do now, the first one being to call "Mom and Pop." As I sat and sipped my tea, I listened and thought about how I didn't like this guy very much, he was bossy and controlling and why wasn't Stephen telling him we would take care of it, thanks anyway. Why was my husband sitting there not responding but merely nodding his head? There was no way I was coming back here to get married. Nobody was going to tell me what to do. Silly girl.

We spent the night there and I couldn't wait to leave. My only comfort was that Stephen's brother lived in New Jersey and we'd be living in Washington, D. C. Stephen finally called his parents, who were living in Florida at this time, and told them his news. I didn't understand a word he said because he spoke in Slovak. I couldn't imagine his parents were very happy though. Understatement.

When he called his sister in Pennsylvania, she asked him

if he was sure the baby was his. Even this I could understand, she didn't know anything about me or who I was or what I was like. It seemed like a logical question to me, and yet I felt hurt. At least I had written to my family and friends about Stephen, so they knew that he existed, and I loved him. These people didn't know who I was or that Stephen and I had met in August in graduate school. He never told anyone about me. Imagine how I felt about that. No, to them I was a stranger, a total surprise, and there was no celebration. No one was happy that night, especially me.

Finally, we left New Jersey and there was only one more person to surprise whose life would be upset, Stephen's roommate, Mike. He wasn't not happy either.

The people who were happy with our news – at last there was someone – were the rest of the students in our graduate class. They threw us a big party and for the first time I felt like a normal bride. This party was a kind, thoughtful gesture and a lot of fun. We were the darlings of the campus, at least in the theater department, for a short time.

Father Hartkeye was the dean of the drama department and we met with him to arrange a proper wedding ceremony. Our plan was to have him marry us in one of the small chapels in the cathedral. Oh no, there were more shocks and surprises.

Stephen is a Byzantine Catholic. What is a Byzantine Catholic? Isn't Catholic, Catholic? No. And because it is Stephen's religion the Church said (at this time) we had to be married in his church. This was a cruel blow to me and a big disappointment. Now there would be no wedding with our friends to witness and bless us on our way.

So, we decide to try the Byzantine Church in Washington.

We'd attended mass there and felt confident we could make arrangements there. But then we encountered another problem. What? More problems?

Father Gregory couldn't marry us either since the Catholic Church was in the middle of changing its rules. Even though we were officially married, having been married by a minister, in the eyes of the church we were not married and living in sin, or was it that we were married but living in sin? Either way, the church said we were living in sin. Now we needed a special dispensation to get married in the church at all.

Can you even begin to imagine how we were feeling now? We were trying so hard to "do the right thing," that is get married in the church, by a priest. There was only one hope left, and that was to return to New Jersey and get married in Mike's church. He was friends with the pastor there, and the Monsignor would do this "favor" for Mike. "Favor!" Indeed.

Oh, no, not again, we had to go back to New Jersey after I swore to myself I wouldn't. The Monsignor would allow us to get married in his church but with conditions. Couldn't everyone just be happy?

Suddenly, I think: Hey, wait a minute, this is my life we are talking about. We are already married. What do I care if the church marries us or not?

"Oh, no," Stephen told me. "This is for the families, Carol. They'll like us better if we're married in the church. The family will accept us back to the fold if we marry in the church. Heck, they'll even come to the wedding." How wrong he was. And what about me? How insecure and anxious to please everyone can a twenty-seven-year-old woman be?

Fearing if I didn't buck up and agree to all this church

business, Stephen would change his mind again, I gave in, fighting and kicking and almost screaming the whole way. With so much turmoil during my pregnancy, it's a wonder to me that Josh was born with the best disposition in the world. He was and is the sweetest, kindest, most beautiful soul you will ever meet.

Back and forth we went to New Jersey to arrange for this church wedding "for the families." Of course, the Monsignor scolded and humiliated us, told us we were bad people and had sinned, and I was not sure, as I listened to him berate us, which was the bigger sin: my being pregnant or the fact we eloped. My God, more sin and more shame.

I had to sit there and be insulted by this pompous priest, who lived in his vacuous world, who didn't know me or Stephen or anything about us and obviously had no interest in knowing. He just wanted to tell us again and again how "bad" we were and what a favor he was doing us by "allowing" us to get married in his church. I kept thinking, "Don't do me any favors, pal, I don't need your blessing or approval. I'd be walking out that door now and not turn back for an instant if only Stephen would walk out with me, if only..."

Instead we sat there like faithful, good penitents, took his abuse, and planned a wedding in New Jersey. It would be small, of course, only immediate family, and Mike and Lee would give us a little party afterwards. Rita was my maid of honor and came from Long Island alone because her husband was either playing golf or taking care of the kids. My parents came with Louis, his fiancée, and Lorrie. So much for my side of the aisle.

Stephen's brother stood up for him as well as his three

kids, Lee, and Stephen's godmother. His parents didn't come to the wedding and his sister didn't come either. I was so glad we got married in New Jersey for the family! My mother told me she didn't tell anyone where she was going, so none of her friends knew I was getting married this weekend. More shame, and no good wishes either. This was the price we "sinners" had to pay for our sins against the families. It was April 10, 1965, more than two months after we'd eloped. I was six months pregnant now and looking it.

This whole ceremony was the biggest farce of our entire married life. Even now neither Stephen nor I celebrate or acknowledge this day in any way. I'd like to have the chance to do it all over again, with loving friends and a ceremony that was meaningful to Stephen and to me and God between us. I can only be angry about this page in our history. I don't think I have ever forgiven his parents or mine for their disgraceful behavior to us at this time. They made us pay a price for being stupid, because that's what we were, not bad or terrible or sinful, really just plain ignorant.

I don't think of it so often, but writing about it now even after all these years, I still feel the anger at the injustice of it all and the smug arrogance of the Holy Church as personified in that most un-Christian-like priest. I don't believe either God or Jesus would be pleased to have this kind of a man represent them. I know kinder people who wear no habit or have no religious affiliation. I had never been a devoted Catholic, but after this experience and after all my dealings with my husband's family, "good" Catholics one and all, I was less inclined to rejoin the "holy and apostolic faith."

Such uncharitable behavior toward me and to their son and

brother, told me the milk of human kindness in the Hrehovcik family had dried up by the time I arrived.

I can't say much better for my own family, except they were not hypocritical about themselves and the church. My mother was never much of a churchgoer, and my father prayed to make up for her, I think. But there was the crucifix above the bed and a rosary in the pocket. After thirty years of marriage to Stephen, my father finally acknowledged our anniversary and told me, "All is forgiven." I wanted to say to him, "Not by me."

Our wedding was simply a preview of the sad and sour relationship we would experience with all of Stephen's family at one time or another. My family was not much better. We were the black sheep, the outsiders. Stephen and I laugh and say when it came to parents we really struck out - 0 for 4. Can you believe there wasn't one parent who was supportive, sympathetic, kind, or even nice to us?

Once in a while we would get a flash of nice from someone, but not anything you could count on, so we tried not to expect anything but disapproval and disappointment toward us. We hoped now that we had each other we could let our families just sit on the sidelines of our lives. After all, Stephen and I were in Washington, D. C., which we loved, and the rest of the family was far away. So why worry?

Prior to the wedding ceremony that didn't solve anything or appease anyone, Stephen and I had more immediate concerns we needed to resolve. One was to find an apartment and the other was for me to get a job so he could continue graduate school. Naturally, I turned to what I knew, teaching. I went to the department of education in the district and walked out that day with a job. This was too curious, too lucky; I was confused but happy.

The next day I knew why I was so "lucky." The job was in the heart of the poor black section of the capitol. When I arrived at the school and my classroom at this so called "integrated" school, I had eighteen black students and two white. I was stunned for a few minutes, but when I got behind the desk and then in front of the class, I had no more thought about color; they were all simply kids, kindergartners for the second time. They were active and spirited, but kids are all the same, and I felt confident I could do some good work there. I also liked the principal, an older, kind woman who had a lot of compassion for her students and the faculty.

There was only one problem for me. When I got the job, I was four months pregnant. Now that I was married this was no problem for me personally. However, in 1965, in the District of Columbia, teachers were forced to leave their position when they were four months pregnant. Ironically, the woman I replaced was also four months pregnant. Once again, I did a dishonorable thing, at least to me, but I felt I must. I had to lie to get the job we needed so desperately. For someone like me who had so much pride in her honesty and loyalty, I felt ashamed that I had taken this job under false pretenses. More shame and more humiliation were to follow.

At the time, nevertheless, I swallowed my pride, put honor on the sidelines and resolved to do a very good job, which I did. I had many approving and complimentary assurances to the effect from both the principal and supervisors. In some way I felt in my heart this made up for my deception. Fortunately, I didn't show my pregnancy until a couple of months later.

My principal and the other teachers guessed my condition in April. When confronted, I broke down and had to bear the disapproval and disappointment of the woman I had come to admire very much. I felt worse than if I had let down my own mother. But of course, I had already done that.

However, because I was pregnant and married and happy to be free, I put the job and its disappointments aside and concentrated on being a healthy and happy pregnant woman. I spent many days at the National Art Gallery and the Smithsonian, riding buses everywhere. I enjoyed walks in Rock Creek Park and visiting the zoo. I made special dinners for Stephen, and while it was still possible, we made love three or four times a day. Our enjoyment of each other sexually had not diminished with my pregnancy.

There was still another difficulty for us to face at this time. I had not yet met Stephen's parents. Originally, when I got to know him, I thought Stephen must come from a wonderful family because he was so nice. Had I met his parents prior to our marriage, I might have changed my mind and become a single mom. I know I wouldn't have made any other choice.

Stephen had a spring break in April, and now, since I was no longer employed, we thought this would be a good time to go to Florida for me to meet his mother and father. Apparently, his father was still especially angry with my husband, and so to mollify him, or so they hoped, his brother and sister-in-law insisted we take their daughter Maryellen with us. She was to be the offering to help reconcile Stephen with his parents. This trip was to be our honeymoon and now we were taking a seven-year-old child with us.

Once again, I agreed even though I wanted to say no.

Maryellen arrived in Washington and the three of us were on our way. I had never driven south of Virginia, so I was excited to be traveling again, determined to enjoy the ride and not think about the destination. Maryellen was a typical seven-year-old girl. She kept brushing my hair the whole drive down and would eat only grilled cheese sandwiches and tomato soup. She was also, it seemed, fascinated with every bathroom between D.C. and Florida. The big problem was at night in the motel room. We had to be quiet whenever we were making love, and for us that was indeed a sacrifice.

When we arrived at the house in Florida, I was pleasantly surprised it was such a nice brick ranch home. In back of the house was another brick building, not quite a motel, but four small apartments that looked clean and new. Maryellen was the first one out of the car and ran ahead. I was by now looking very pregnant and waited for Stephen to take my hand and lead me.

Maryellen's grandfather was delighted to see her and kept swinging her around, ignoring his wife, his son, and, of course, me. Stephen kept trying to introduce me. "Pop, Pop, Pop," he kept saying. "Mike, Mike," his mother said. And I was standing there embarrassed, humiliated, and angry. I was furious that this man could be so rude to me and to his son. I was also waiting for Stephen's mother to say something to her husband. My mother would never have allowed my father to be so rude to a guest. This foolishness went on for what seemed like a very long time, and I thought again I should have listened to my instincts and not brought Maryellen along, and then the man would have had to deal with us directly.

Finally, he stopped the swinging and said hello, it wasn't warm or fuzzy, but very cold and angry, and, I thought, cruel. Right there and then I knew I didn't like this man and probably never would. I also wasn't very fond of Stephen's mother either as I wondered what kind of a woman allows her husband to be mean to his own son and his new wife. I guessed it was more punishment for our "sins." Well, I was pretty sick of this already and I only hoped the days would pass quickly in Florida. All I ever wanted was for Stephen and me to live our own lives, away from his family and mine. I was eager to start our own family and be sure we would be more loving and forgiving parents than our own had been.

I love to go out to eat. To me, it is like theater, entertaining and fun. Naturally I assumed we'd be going out to dinner or lunch sometime during our stay. Breakfast? "Oh, no," Stephen told me. "My parents never go to restaurants." Too bad, especially as I discovered his mother's entire repertoire of culinary ability in those few days. These included the traditional Slovak dishes of rolled cabbage leaves stuffed with rice and hamburg, called halupki, and chicken soup that was not as good or hearty as my mother's. Mrs. Hrehovcik's soup was more of an appetizer than a meal. The rest of her cooking ability was either chicken or steak, all overcooked.

...All right, I thought to myself, there's no contest here, I can out-cook her. Then I discovered her housekeeping method, which was – there wasn't any. After she washed and folded her clothes, she simply put them in whatever drawer was empty. There was no such thing as a drawer for socks, or underwear or towels or linens. Things got put away in a haphazard style, but it was her way and once again I smiled to myself as I thought, There's no contest in the housekeeping department either…

Then how would my mother-in-law and I be competing? It was always a competition, I knew that, especially with sons and mothers and daughters-in-law. Aha! She was holier than I, which didn't take much, as you already know. She prayed a lot, yes, a lot, I mean the rosary was out morning, noon, and night and all the rides in the car in between. "Oh, boy, no contest here, lady. You win as I am not holy at all. I love God, and He loves me, and we have a very nice understanding, thank you very much."

Meanwhile Stephen would help his father with some odd jobs, leaving very little time for us to be alone and explore the area, each other, or to make plans for the future. "All right it's only a week, and then we'll be out of here and we can get on with our lives at last. And hey, they're in Florida after all, how many times are we really going to see them? I can do anything for a week." So, I thought. Surprise again!

First of all, I got the worst sunburn of my entire life. Stephen's parents always talked Slovak, so I never knew what anyone was saying. I felt smothered and thought if I didn't get away from Stephen's father, I would go insane. Finally help arrived in the form of Stephen's cousin and her husband. They took us to the dog races, and I was so happy to be out and around normal people who spoke English. Stephen's father told me now I would have to learn Slovak. "Like hell," I muttered to myself. I don't like anyone telling me what I must do. I did learn one word though, "kapusta," which means cabbage. Somehow cabbage stuck in my mind, maybe because we ate so much of it.

I knew Mr. Hrehovcik and I would be enemies if that was the way he wanted it, and it seemed to be. There was no problem with Stephen's mother, and as I had heard only of mother-in-law problems, I was not prepared to deal with Stephen's father. I got a contest all right, the contest was to be: who did Stephen love more? Me or his father? To whom would he be loyal? Who could hold onto him the tightest, the hardest, the longest? Poor, poor Stephen.

He was in the middle of this tug of war until his father died in 1984. Even then he wouldn't be free. Apparently, Mr. Hrehovcik had no use for the part of the wedding ceremony where you leave your parents and become the man/woman, husband/wife. No, Stephen was a son first and foremost or else, and the "or else" came upon us quickly and often. Oh, if we had only known. How could two such intelligent people continue to be so incredibly innocent?

I knew I wanted his family to like me. I loved their son and thought perhaps that would be enough to make them like me. If I made Stephen happy, they'd like me, right? Oh boy, and did I try to make him happy by doing and saying what he wanted, and not saying what I wanted. I didn't listen to myself or trust my own instincts. I didn't do what I believed was right or honest for myself and again I'd regret it.

Remember I was still afraid Stephen would change his mind and decide just as suddenly he didn't really love me and he'd made a mistake. I had to be sure he would keep on loving me, and the best way I thought was to do everything his way, to swallow my pride, my instincts, my feelings, and yes, eventually, myself. I was losing Carol, little by little, piece by piece after only two months of marriage. Somehow, I didn't think this was the way it was supposed to be.

Graduate school ended sometime in early May and Stephen was looking for a job. By May of course I was quite pregnant and happy we were living our own life at last. We were looking for a bigger apartment so we would have room for the baby who was due in less than two months.

Stephen's father started calling him to come to Florida to watch his house while he looked for property in New Jersey. Of course, I said, "We can't go. I'm having a baby. It's nearly time for the baby to be born. Am I supposed to change doctors and move to Florida now just to please your father? "

But Stephen's father pressed him. "If you don't do this for me, you are no longer my son."

I was concerned for my husband and his struggle to please his father, and I agreed then that we must go. But I was so angry at this point, I didn't know whether I married a man or a good little boy. However, I took a trip to see my parents in Massachusetts before we left. I reasoned that women have babies in Florida too and at least his parents won't be there. Maybe it wouldn't be so bad after all. What an optimist I was turning out to be.

After a week away and with the prospect of leaving D.C. to go to a strange place to have my baby, I arrived at the bus depot in Washington all excited to be back with my husband. I'd written to him every day, feeling then he was with me. My writing made me feel closer to him; I believed he missed me as much as I missed him.

Anticipating that Stephen would be there waiting for me, I was anxious as we got to the station. I looked around eagerly for his smiling face. Alas, there was no Stephen in sight. Oh well, I sighed and thought the bus was early, he'll be here soon. I sit on the bench and wait. After a half hour of sitting and waiting I start to cry. I guess he didn't miss me after all.

Finally, he arrived, very casual, with the top down on the Falcon. He looked at me crying and wondered what was wrong with me. After all he wasn't that late, he said. This was the beginning of my waiting for him at every bus depot, train terminal, and airport. It wasn't long before I discovered Stephen was always late and I would always be left waiting. Many years later, with the knowledge that comes with therapy, we discover what being late really means. Stephen is almost never late now.

I learned too that I do not have to wait for him. After waiting for him all those years I cannot wait for other people more than ten minutes. Perhaps fifteen if I am feeling very good. To me when someone is late and keeps you waiting, they are saying "You don't count. My time is more valuable than yours." I believe tardiness is rude, insulting and all about control. The more important lesson I learned was that I have a choice with my own behavior.

As usual I digress and get ahead of myself, but I believe it is important to share what we learned and hope some of it may help you. Our lives don't have to be a repeat of the same sad behavior patterns which made us martyrs and unhappy in the first place. I've been both a martyr and a fool, and I can tell you honestly you can control your own behavior and your own life. You are not stuck with anything you don't want to be. You are in charge of you. For someone like me, loyal and appeasing, it was a difficult role to change, but I was determined to make it.

Back in D.C., there was good news waiting for me, even if Stephen wasn't. He was happy to tell me his parents had sold their house in Florida so we wouldn't have to leave D.C. after all. I was so excited and happy; we began apartment hunting right away and had good luck. Stephen also found a job with a local construction company.

We found a charming, second floor apartment in Tacoma Park, Maryland. It was conveniently located near a big shopping mall and boasted the best deli in the area. Stephen and I frequently had a meal of fresh hot pumpernickel bread with butter. After all these years we still talk about that bread and our mouths hunger for the taste once again.

Our landlords were very dear and helpful to us, and many of our neighbors were other young couples with small children. Our future looked normal after all. Weren't we lucky to have such good luck! Oh, sure.

Chapter Seven

Oh, Boy

We did our best to furnish the apartment and get ready for the arrival of the baby, but Joshua decided to be born early. I went into the hospital on the Fourth of July, 1965. I thought how grand it would be to have our son born in the nation's capital on Independence Day. Alas, this was not to be, as my labor is very long and very difficult.

I soon learned why it's called "labor." I was not only in pain, but I was also all alone. Where was Stephen? Why couldn't I see him? He was the baby's father; why was I so alone and so afraid? I'm embarrassed to admit I remember screaming, not just crying, but actually screaming. No one told me about labor pains. I was totally unprepared for this birth experience.

Also, dreamer that I was, I pictured Stephen walking up and down the corridor outside the delivery room, pacing like all the soon-to-be fathers in the movies. Other men were waiting out there, but not my Stephen. He dropped me off and went home, to sleep, I think. I did not see him again until after Joshua was born.

This was 1965 and although it doesn't seem that long ago to me, it was nearly forty years ago. As far as I'm concerned, the birthing methods were still archaic. The father wasn't allowed in the labor room in most hospitals, like this one, and definitely not in the delivery room. The husband waved you off and then went about his business. Perhaps there were other husbands and fathers who at least chose to stick around the hospital and ask about their wife's progress. Stephen went home and waited for a phone call.

He did arrive the next morning. shortly after Joshua was born, very excited and very proud. I was just exhausted, and I felt abandoned. I thought something was wrong with this whole idea of giving birth. The father should have been there, holding my hand and comforting me. I shouldn't have been all alone. Perhaps that's why I was screaming; I was so mad to be left alone again.

Joshua had a touch of jaundice so I couldn't hold him for a while. I guess he'd had a hard time too because his face was kind of squished up. I began to wonder if having a baby was worth all this, until the moment I held him in my arms. Then I knew I'd never let him go and this baby, holding him, having him, was the true meaning of my life.

Stephen left soon after he saw the baby, not able to hold Joshua himself. That was another unfortunate rule in 1965. No one could hold the newborns except the mother and the nurses. As soon as I got out of the hospital, I was determined to let this baby know there were two very important people in his life, and two pairs of hands to take care of him.

My other disappointment was I had not seen Joshua being born. In fact, I didn't believe he had been born. I was having such a hard time and had been in hard labor for nearly thirty-six hours. I was finally put to sleep. I woke up saying, "When am I going to have this baby?"

"You already have, a boy." No, I didn't, I thought, where was he? I didn't remember anything. But there he was beside my bed, enclosed in a glass-covered crib, not an incubator, just shielded because of the jaundice.

When Stephen left later that day, the fifth of July, 1965, he went to the unemployment office and passed out cigars. He'd lost his job with the construction company. "Oh, God, now what?" I couldn't worry about that as I was more concerned about how on earth, I was supposed to take care of this baby – this little person who was suddenly, it seemed, all mine. My parents arrived before I was due to leave the hospital, and my father made one of his insightful, witty remarks.

Looking at Joshua through the maternity window, my father said, "Well, at least you can tell it's his kid." This was because Josh definitely had his father's nose, not big or ugly, just Stephen's nose. I'm sure my father wasn't the only one who looked at my son in anticipation. Even Stephen's sister would be appeased that the baby was indeed Stephen's when reports of the nose filtered down to her.

My parents, who were not happy with me most of my life, were at this time very supportive and sweet to both and Stephen and me. They went out and bought a dresser for the baby. I had several hand-me-down baby accessories but no crib. For his first days at home, Joshua Stephen Hrehovcik slept in a dresser drawer we put on the floor. He didn't seem to mind.

I have the fondest memory of my mother the first week I

was home with Joshua. I tell you I was terrified of this baby. Oh, sure, I used to baby sit, but never had I had an experience with a newborn. He seemed so fragile and so delicate. I was afraid I'd break him.

My mother smiled and encouraged me to be brave and just relax with him in my arms, assuring me that he would not break. She gave him his first bath and showed me how to do it so both the baby and I would survive.

I nursed him, and this is the greatest thrill I think a woman can possibly have. It is so natural and fulfilling in no other way I can ever imagine. The nursing of the baby made my bond complete, and I grew more confident by the time my parents had to leave.

I was never close to my parents and couldn't wait to get away from them, but after Joshua was born, I was sorry to see them go. I was sorry the baby wouldn't have grandparents near to love and nurture and cherish him. As much as I felt a sense of loss, I retained the hope that Stephen and I would be better parents than ours. I wanted us to love and care for this baby as we had wanted to be loved and cared for as children ourselves.

After my initial fear wore off, I was confident Stephen and I would be good parents. Because we were young and in love, I felt we were bound to do a better job raising our baby than our parents had done with us. We were educated and curious and I had my copy of Dr. Spock to see me through the doubtful times. Ah, youth!

Let's talk about Dr. Spock. His book was the most respected book about childcare at the time. The philosophy of most pediatricians then was to let the baby cry as long as you knew he was fed and dry. It was advised by all the "experts" not to pick up the baby as soon as he fussed but to let him cry himself out. Otherwise he'd be "spoiled."

There were times when Stephen and I literally held each other back not to pick him up whenever he cried. My natural instincts were to hold him gently in my arms, rock him and kiss him till he fell asleep. I did not listen to myself and have regretted it ever since. Remember, you don't get second chances with your baby.

So, we let him cry, and only Joshua knows what permanent damage this did to his soul. We always apologize to Joshua. "Sorry, honey, you were the first one and we didn't know what we were doing. You were the trial and error baby, I'm afraid." I know parents and experts are smarter these days. Good for you!

Stephen was taking over some family duties, as I insisted he help take care of the baby. He learned to change diapers as well as I did; he gave the baby a bath sometimes, and because I thought it was important for Joshua to know both a mother and a father, Stephen would give him a bottle at least once a day. Even though I was nursing, a supplemental bottle worked out fine for all of us. It is the caretaking of a baby that bonds you to him, mother or father. I'd had the baby, but he was ours now, all the way, all ways.

Although I know Stephen had never considered his role as a father, I know he was pleased to participate actively in the upbringing and caretaking of his son. He was a proud and happy father during this time in our little apartment in Tacoma Park. He'd even bought a rocking chair from the Salvation Army and held it up proudly for me to see. He paid seven dollars for it and was so pleased he'd been able to make such a deal. He had only ten dollars in his pocket at the time. We didn't know where the money was coming from for the next week, month, or the rest of our lives. We were facing another dilemma and tough decisions would soon have to be made.

Stephen was still out of work as July became August. I considered the fact that I would have to go back to work. How would I feel teaching other children while leaving my own behind? Stephen wanted to continue with graduate school, but to what end, I wondered. To become an actor? Would he be happy teaching in a college? There were too many questions and not a lot of answers.

Meanwhile Stephen's brother called us to tell Stephen there was a good job in New Jersey. He and Mike would work together on a special project for a toy company, designing plans for a toy gun. The money was very enticing.

We discussed the pros and cons of such a move. The most obvious disadvantage involved our leaving Washington and giving up our independence. More than that we'd be moving to New Jersey and we'd be surrounded by his family.

However, we had a new baby to consider. Where was the future for an actor? For Stephen and the theater? We decided to go to New Jersey. I felt happy and sad at the same time. Happy because now I wouldn't have to leave Joshua, and sad because we would be living in New Jersey. "Maybe it won't be so bad." (Ha, ha, ha.)

Our landlords were hurt when we told them we were moving. They felt Stephen hadn't tried hard enough to get a job in D.C. I wondered about this myself, as I had always gotten a job if I wanted one. However, I still had faith in my husband, his talents and abilities, so we packed up and moved once more, with dreams and hopes high. I regretted we'd disappointed someone else, again.

Until we found our own apartment we would live with Mike and Lee and their young family of three children. Mike's wife was always coming and going, and her mother, who lived upstairs, watched the kids for her. As I was a guest in this house, I did what I could to help out. Stephen and Mike went off to the Bronx to work every day and I was left to care for Joshua, and make a life somehow while living in someone else's house.

I enjoyed Mike's children very much. They were all sweet and fun in different ways. Maryellen, who accompanied us on the "honeymoon that wasn't," was especially dear to me at this time. She adored my son and loved to take care of him. Joshua was a very contented baby and slept most of the day.

For a new and silly mother like me, this was almost a disappointment as I wanted to play with him. I remember putting him outside in his carriage to sleep and then checking on him periodically hoping he'd be awake. It would be four hours before he'd wake up. Sometimes I think I encouraged him to wake up. Didn't he want to eat or something?

At last Stephen and I found an apartment of our own. There were two bedrooms, a big kitchen, a living room and a beautiful yard. I thought how nice it would be for the baby and us to enjoy the space. I imagined we'd have picnics out under the fruit trees. Only after we moved in, we discovered the yard was not to use in any way. The yard was for looks only. We weren't allowed to walk on the grass or put a blanket down. No, there would be no picnics on Garibaldi Avenue in Lodi, New Jersey.

Our landlords in Lodi were an older Italian couple. I was comfortable with this was I am naturally familiar with the Italian temperament. However, they turned out to be very nosy and interfering. When I finally got a washing machine, Mrs. "Landlord" told me I washed "too much." Good thing she didn't know my mother because my mother's idea of successful housekeeping was to have an empty hamper. Impossible, of course.

A more disturbing aspect of our life in the apartment at Lodi was the constant fighting between our landlords. It seemed as if they were was always hollering at each other. This was too much like home, so Joshua and I went for long, daily walks.

Stephen taught me to drive the stick shift on the Falcon convertible. Since he either took the bus or shared a ride with his brother, I could have the car – more freedom for me and Joshua. This was a challenge for me because I learned to drive on an automatic. I had a lot of fun, but there weren't many lessons before I was set free to drive myself and Joshua around the small towns in northern New Jersey.

Joshua was beside me in his little car seat and off we'd go. I shudder when I think of that car seat. It was attached to the seat by two large hooks and since no one seemed to know any better at the time, I felt satisfied that he was secure and safe.

We went to parks, shopping malls, to not too distant little towns, and wherever else our happy hearts carried us. I stalled that Falcon all over northern New Jersey! Many horns honked at me in anger and frustration . I always believed in the old adage to learn by doing, so undaunted by surrounding drivers, I would continue to learn by doing. It wasn't long before I had the confidence of an A.J. Foyt. Freedom at last!

I was very lonely in those days. Stephen was gone all day and I had no friends. My sister-in-law Lee was working part-time and extremely involved with the church so I couldn't count on her for friendship. Although Joshua and I shared our time and adventures, it was still a lonely time for me. As happy as I was in one way, I was sad in another.

Stephen's parents had moved back to New Jersey and were living in his godmother's house in Linden. It was expected we would visit there at least once a week. I didn't like his father any more than I had when we first met, and I had little use for his mother either. Yet, because of the way I was brought up, I swallowed my pride, held my tongue and tried to get along the best I could. The Slovak language and the traditions were overwhelming to me, and my pride kept me from giving in and learning the language, my pride and my utter dislike of my father-in-law. I thought they should speak English, after all we lived in America.

Stephen's godmother, Kresna, was one of the dearest and kindest people to me at this time. Of all my husband's family, she was the one I liked the most and I think she liked me too. She spoke English for one thing, and treated me as a guest she was happy to see whenever we visited with her. Her husband, Kresni, was also a dear, funny man. He was always smoking a cigar which reminded me of my own uncle Louis. Kresni was both generous and lovable, qualities which seemed rare in this part of New Jersey.

Kresna's mother, Tsetka, reminded me of my grandmother,

dressed in black and often wearing a babushka on her head, a kind of a kerchief. This visit was the way I remembered visiting with my own grandparents. Her husband didn't talk much and was most often in the garden or just visiting with family and neighbors. That part of Linden, known as Tremley Point, consisted mostly of Slovak people and so gave it an old world flavor.

And then there were the weddings.

One tradition I thought was especially fun at weddings in Linden was the dance with the bride. Called the Radovitza, the bride carried a special little purse and anyone who wanted to dance with her had to put money in the purse. I imagine it got pretty full as she danced her way around with both men and women. I did enjoy the Slovak dances, and I must give my father-in-law his due, as he was an extremely good dancer. As I watched and observed these happy rituals, I thought of how Stephen and I got married.

I know our lack of ceremony or support from either family was a grudge I would carry for many years. Not that I blamed anyone but us, I was still sad about the church wedding we never had. Although eloping was in itself very romantic, I would never recommend it. I know how important it is to have the love and support of your family and friends to encourage you and support you from the very beginning. "Regrets, I've had a few," yes, this is one.

Remember as a young girl I would dream about brides and weddings and read the brides' magazines while mother was getting her books at Mitchell's. I loved those magazines and now, alas, I would never be a bride, never, never, never. I'd sigh and try not to feel envy or jealousy, but I wasn't always successful.

Life in New Jersey is not a happy recollection for me. Stephen and I have had some difficult, almost impossible times over the years, but I look back on these three years in New Jersey as the worst in our marriage. I was lonely and angry a lot and not able to share or express my feelings to my husband. Then I discovered the power of the telephone. It became my connection with the "outside" world. At the same time, I knew I was losing touch with myself and who I was.

Because Joshua was such a delightful child and joy to us, Stephen and I talked about having another baby. Sometimes even I can't believe how naive we were. I thought naturally all babies were alike; they were all like Joshua. I got pregnant right away. This was faster than we planned, but there we were, and we were delighted.

I must talk about another example of the clash of cultures. It was our very first Thanksgiving and we had invited Stephen's parents. Since I was a newlywed, I wanted to impress my in-laws with the good choice of a wife Stephen had made. I made a feast. I mean a FEAST. I spent days cooking soup, meatballs and sauce, manicotti, and homemade stuffing for the turkey. I made a banquet like we used to have when I was a kid. I wanted Stephen to be proud of me, and I really wanted his parents to like me, or at least accept me, and the fact that I loved their son and wanted to take good care of him and their grandson.

I had my first disaster when the turkey was too big for the oven. The oven door would not close no matter how hard Stephen pushed or which way we turned the pan. The damn oven door would not shut. Would my turkey cook? His parents would think I was a failure, all the cleaning, cooking, planning would be all for nothing if the turkey wasn't cooked. I had made so much food, I wished I had invited lots of people. I set the table with great fuss and flair and thought, "This is so nice and will be worth all my effort." How could Stephen's parents not be impressed?

Oh, brother!

Just as I was feeling so pleased and proud of myself and Stephen was looking the same, Stephen's parents finally arrived looking unhappy and more out of place. There was very little conversation or talking during dinner, and worse than that, they hardly ate anything. "Oh, God," I thought, "they don't like my cooking; they think my cooking is bad." For a girl from an Italian family, this was a true disaster.

Stephen's parents picked at their food, talked very little, usually in Slovak, of course, which naturally I took personally as an insult to me. My day was ruined, and I thought, so is my life. There was nothing I could do to make these people like me. I was waiting on everyone, running back and forth to the kitchen, hoping they would like something, anything. When they left at last, I just broke down and cried and cried. I felt humiliated, embarrassed, angry and stupid. Stephen did his best to comfort me, and told me how great all the food was. Then he added the crowning touch, "They ate before they came."

"What? They are invited to Thanksgiving dinner and they ate before they got here?" I couldn't believe it. I had never heard of such a thing, such an insult.

Stephen then added, "They always eat before they go to dinner anywhere."

"Why the hell didn't you tell me that before I made all this food?"

Years later we would laugh about our first Thanksgiving. The picture of Stephen pushing the oven door, all the food laid out like a banquet for twenty people and his mother and father sitting there like two orphans not willing to try or enjoy anything I had done. But I assure you it was far from funny on that day.

I learned a lesson. For years I would still keep trying to get them to like me. Was I such a bad person? What was wrong with me? You see, I was perfectly willing to accept the fact that it must be my fault. It was my responsibility, and I was sure I'd find a way to get them to accept me. Never did it occur to me that it might have something to do with them and that it wasn't all my "fault."

However, because of this humiliation, I told my husband we were going to Massachusetts for Christmas. This was not a popular decision with his family, but I was determined to have at least one happy holiday, and we did. We had a wonderful visit with my family, saw a lot of my friends, went to parties, and laughed a lot. My parents gave us nice gifts and I felt like me again. When we returned to New Jersey I was determined to make our life better and more fun and freer from his family. We could live our own life and be happy despite them. Ever the optimist.

Just as life was starting to become routine and we were becoming a family, the three of us, Stephen came home one day that winter and announced he had quit his job at the toy company and was going to work with Equity Theater in Manhattan. For eight weeks. For nothing.

We actually had money in the bank because the pay from the toy company had been so lucrative. But, oh dear, what to do now? I thought if I allowed him (as if I had a choice) to do this job with the theater perhaps he'd get it out of his system once and for all. I would kid myself about this for many years. This was merely the first time.

Since we did have money in the bank, I knew we could get along, and I also felt guilty that he left graduate school and gave up his dream of becoming an actor. I felt lucky, after all, I had what I knew was the most important part of my life; I had Stephen and I had Joshua. What was eight weeks in a lifetime? Where had I heard that before?

There were so many talented, unemployed professionals in this production of "Beau Geste." All were out of work, working there for nothing, hoping some director or producer or someone would see them and give them a job that pays. Stephen wasn't even acting in the play; he was the stage manager and had a small walk on. Where was the future in that? But he was so happy to be around theater people again and involved with what he loved. As the eight weeks passed, I was more concerned and unhappy. I was fairly certain nothing would come from this, but I hoped this would be the end of chasing the theater rainbow. I was wrong.

CHAPTER EIGHT

Oh, Boy and Oh Boy Again

When the show ended, Stephen's commitment was over. With no prospects for a theater job, resolutely he went job hunting. He had a job the next day with Minkus Stamp Co. as the advertising manager and worked out of Gimbals in New York City. The pay was $150 a week, which was very good in 1966. Unfortunately, all our savings were gone, and once more we had to start all over again.

By May I was pregnant for the second time, and because we'd need more room for the new baby, I found another apartment. This one was in Rutherford, which was much nicer than Lodi. We moved there in the fall of 1966. Stephen didn't like the apartment as much as I; he felt I liked it only because the landlords were two cute guys. This was partially true, but it wasn't their good looks that prompted me to move so fast. Mostly, I needed to get away from our situation in Lodi. I was eager to get to a place where the neighbors, that is the landlords, wouldn't interfere with our lives. In Rutherford, the landlords would not be living on the property and there was a nice yard we could actually use.

The other advantage of that location was the bus stop at the corner, within sight of the apartment. We could wave to Stephen as he left for work and when he came home. The town's main street was within walking distance, and as Joshua and I were always taking walks, this was a happy convenience for me. The apartment wasn't closer or farther from his family, so that wasn't an issue. I just liked the neighborhood and the area in general and was happy to be in a prettier town than Lodi.

I enjoyed our time in Rutherford and made some friends at last. In general, I found the people in northern New Jersey rather cold and distant. A friend later told me it was because people were so mobile and transient in the area, they didn't make friends easily. I was happy to have someone to talk with. An older, friendly woman next door gave me much encouragement about child rearing and the joys and sorrows of being a parent.

There was a single mother living upstairs who had two little girls. She was a nurse and helpful to have around. That Christmas Stephen spent several hours putting a doll house together for one of her little girls.

A young couple who lived in the house in back of us taught me once again not to judge people by their appearance. He was a handsome man and his wife looked like a blond southern belle. I thought they were stuck up, but when we finally got to know them, I learned they were very nice, and were working hard to buy a home of their own.

We had our first Christmas tree in the apartment in Rutherford. I remember being so excited! This would be our first Christmas alone together. We got a tree stand, picked out a fresh tree, and looked at each other. "Where are the lights? What about the ornaments?" We laughed. Of course, we never had to think about this before.

Fortunately, the downtown was close by, so we went to the dime store and bought ornaments, lights, tinsel and garland. More than thirty-eight years have passed, and we still have some of these ornaments. They will always be very special to me as they bring back the memory of our first Christmas together. We were young, innocent, trusting in each other and our love, and believed in the goodness of life.

As the ornaments have broken over the years, many of our dreams and hopes shattered as well. I treasure the few decorations that remain. I don't need to hold anything to recapture the memory of that time, but oh, it is so sweet to hold one of those decorations in my hand. When I see the box marked 1966 the pictures of our first Christmas are fresh in my mind and I smile.

Because of this realization, we started a tradition with our kids. Each year all of us would choose a special ornament for the Christmas tree. Now as all the children have left home and are on their own, they decorate their Christmas trees with these special memories and treasures.

It was always fun to unwrap the boxes each Christmas. Who would remember where this special ornament came from? And so, a part of our family history remains with them all. It's funny too, as Stephen and I are alone and miss some of these ornaments when we remember they belonged to one of the kids.

Christmas is fun with a one year old. He was delighted

with the lights and the nicely wrapped packages, happy with one or two toys. This was fun for Stephen and me, not only for the delight we felt with Joshua, but also for the special gifts we had for each other. I gave him a new guitar, and he gave me many pretty clothes. Fortunately, he could get a discount at Gimbels.

Our second baby was not due until the end of February, so Stephen and I made plans to celebrate our anniversary by going into Manhattan to dinner and the theater. The baby had other plans.

This baby was very active all the while I was carrying him. He'd kick me at the most inconvenient times. On more than one occasion I jumped out of my seat having been attacked by one of his more violent outbursts. Joshua had been more sedate, but this guy was active. I had no real instinct about the second born being a boy or girl, although I felt it was most likely a he.

Since this was my second time around, I knew what a contraction felt like, and the contractions began about 3 A.M. on February 7,1967. There'd be no anniversary celebration this year. Stephen's brother came for Joshua and he and his family took care of him while I was in the hospital. I was excited and pleased this baby would be early. I was more than ready to go.

Stephen was eager and enthused about this second baby. He drove me to the hospital in Hackensack. We left in the beginning of a terrible snowstorm and learned later this was more than a snowstorm. It was the worst blizzard New Jersey had experienced in twenty-two years.

We arrived at the hospital safely and while I was wheeled

to the elevator, the nurse told Stephen to go home, and so he did. But as I learn later, he did not go home. He drove through the blizzard to Manhattan and to work. Naturally, under the circumstances he was unable to return to visit or to be with me that day or see his second son.

We said goodbye at the elevator, and I felt abandoned again. I did not have the pain I had with my first delivery, but I had more emotional pain. I couldn't believe I was going to have another baby without my husband nearby. Not only was he not in the hospital, but he was driving to work in a blizzard! The birth of my second child was a worse experience than my first.

However, I was soon very excited when only a short time later I saw Noah being born. This was so thrilling to me. I actually got to see the birth of my son. I was sorry Stephen wasn't there to share the joy with me. I confess there was no pain for me, for whatever the doctor used I was awake but feeling no pain.

Noah was beautiful from the moment he was born. There was no jaundice, no red marks, just a beautiful, blue-eyed, blond little boy. Smaller than Joshua had been, he was looking just fine, and I felt very happy to have two sons. "I wish Stephen were here."

I planned to nurse Noah as I had with Joshua, but because of the blizzard, the hospital was understaffed with no relief nurses available. Consequently, the nurses on duty at the time were not helpful or happy, and they resented the inconvenience of having a nursing mother. Noah and I were not able to bond easily. Whenever I got him, he was asleep and wouldn't take the breast. When I saw him later in the nursery he was crying and screaming, and the nurses wouldn't allow me to take him.

Noah was losing weight at this time and I was afraid the doctor wouldn't let me take him home. I would have done anything to get out of there with my son. I felt imprisoned as if Noah and I were being punished. Stephen was no help to me, and I spent most of those hospital days crying, lonely and afraid.

There was an archaic policy in the maternity ward in Hackensack, NJ in February of 1967. Only the maternal grandmother and the husband were allowed to visit. Since my mother was in Massachusetts, and Stephen was working all day, I spent four days alone with no company, unhappy, scared, and worried about my son.

When the doctor wanted to know how long I'd been there, I said five days. Actually, it had only been four, but the doctor signed me out and I was able to take Noah home as well. His weight loss was a concern, but I was confident once I got him home and could feed him on demand, his condition would improve.

Stephen hardly visited with me while I was in the hospital. Living in his own world as he does, one night he didn't come to the hospital at all. I called him at home wondering where he was and why he wasn't with me. He was writing me a poem. When I had Joshua, he had drawn a sketch of me, which I just loved then he misplaced. Now he was writing me a poem... I wanted him here beside me to hold my hand and he was home writing poetry. What do I care about poetry if he's not with me? Somebody was confused about his role here, and I knew it wasn't me.

The patterns were forming of course, but I was still so

much in love and unaware. I couldn't see anything except what was happening right then. I really could not see a bigger picture. I have always said people live in tenses. I have generally lived in the present tense, now, this minute, this day, not ever having much faith in the future, and to me the past was just that, passed.

Stephen, I knew, lived in the future tense, always thinking ahead to some greater time, making big plans. What time could be greater than now? There were no guarantees, so you'd better enjoy today – that was always my philosophy. Even in the worst of times I would try to find something in the day that gave me pleasure.

My parents were definitely people who lived in the past tense. Everything was always better, sweeter, happier in the "old" days. Later, I would come to believe my parents were never happy and could never be satisfied, past, present, or future.

When at last we brought Noah home from the hospital, I made sure we had a little surprise for Joshua, besides a new baby brother of course. It was one of those little Fisher Price benches that you hammer in the pegs. I gave him this and made a fuss over him while Stephen held the new baby. After what seemed like a good time, I introduced him to his brother and asked if he would like to hold him. Now Joshua wasn't even two years old, so he was curious. However, since Noah wasn't a car or a truck, he soon lost interest in him.

Naming Noah was another interesting game Stephen and I played. We'd had such a difficult time agreeing on a name for Joshua, I thought naming the second would be easier. Since I had always been a big fan of alliteration, I thought Jeremy would be a nice name for our second son, Josh and Jeremy. "Everyone will call him Jerry. I like Noah." Stephen argued. I liked the name Noah too, but I liked Jeremy better. Stephen took a poll in his office, and Noah was voted the favorite there.

Still I wasn't convinced. I finally decided to agree to Noah when my mother announced she told all her friends his name was Noah. That made it final. She didn't seem to hate the name Noah as much as she'd been angry about the name Joshua. "Why don't you call him Thomas? That's a nice name." She would admonish me every chance she got.

Thomas is a nice name and it was my grandfather's name, her father's. Funny too, because she had always talked about her father as a man she did not especially like or admire, yet she wanted one of my sons to be named after him. I am sorry now I didn't use Thomas at all, not even as a middle name for one of the boys, but we used Stephen's names. He's John on official papers, so we have Noah John and Joshua Stephen.

With a name like Hrehovcik it better be good. As we were to discover later, especially when we moved to Maine, the names Joshua and Noah attached to Hrehovcik conjured up stereotypes in the parochial minds of many people there. I love Maine, always have, but in 1970 and to some extent even today, I find many of the people here more than provincial. Narrow-minded comes to mind.

Interesting to note here is the name Joshua or Josh is now one of the most popular names for a boy. Whenever I see something with Josh imprinted, I still get it for my son, not that it makes up for all those years when he endured ridicule of his name, but there is some satisfaction in it nevertheless. I haven't seen a pencil or pen with Noah yet, but I am thinking with the popularity of "E.R" and the actor Noah Wylie, soon I'll be seeing Noah on a balloon or pencil somewhere.

Taking Noah home was a surprise to me, as Joshua had been such a good-natured baby, I assumed Noah would be too. I thought once I had him at home and could feed him on a regular schedule, like when he was hungry, he'd be fine. I was not prepared for Noah's temperament. I was also not aware there was a reason for his crying all the time. As usual I just assumed I was doing something wrong.

Noah did not sleep much at all, but that would have been all right if he were awake and sociable. But Noah screamed and cried almost all day and all night. I didn't know what to do or what could possibly be wrong. I was nursing him, and he would eat, but never very much. I would use the supplementary bottles with him as well. He didn't seem to care if I fed him breast milk or the bottle, neither satisfied him. I could hardly wait until my six-week visit with our new pediatrician.

Aha, I hear you asking, why did I wait six weeks if he was so cranky? I told you I was stupid. Dr. Spock's book was no help, nor were my family or friends. I was lost, scared and more or less on my own. What could Stephen possibly know if I didn't have a clue? I'll tell you honestly and somewhat shamefacedly why I didn't call the doctor: I was embarrassed he'd think I was one of those frantic mothers who calls the doctor every time the baby cries. The "another new mother" syndrome. I had not been so lucky with my pediatricians in the past, so I was a hesitant mother indeed to get off on the wrong foot with this one.

When at last I did get Noah to the doctor, the doctor shook

his head, looked at Noah, felt his abdomen and said, "Colic."

"Colic?" I questioned. Needless to say, I had never heard of colic, much less knew what it was. Yes, yes, I hear you again, saying I was educated, a teacher for goodness sake. But kids in elementary school don't have colic, so how was I to know? But oh boy, did I beat myself up for that one! I tell you to this day I would not wish a colicky baby on my worst enemy.

It was a difficult time for me, for poor Noah, and for our family. The medicine helped relieve some of the symptoms, and there would be some sleep for all of us at last. Mostly time was the healer, but I sure was happy to have a name for the problem and some help for Noah. My mother, naturally, told me if a baby has colic it's usually because the mother is nervous. Thanks, Mom.

Meanwhile, Joshua just wanted to play, with me, with his Dad, with his brother, but here we all were, topsy-turvy with a sick infant. Poor Joshua. All I wanted to do was sleep, but he was an active 18-month-old and the world was his to explore. Joshua was always gregarious and talked and sang at an early age. Stephen's family thought he was the most wonderful and brightest little boy, and he was. At this time of course, Noah was no competition for him.

The apartment had been painted while I was in the hospital, and Stephen's father had reupholstered a sofa for us. I was very pleased with everything when I came home. My husband was very proud of all the work he had done and the fact that his family had pitched in to help with his surprise.

The apartment in Rutherford was small but cozy. The boys had a bedroom in the back of the house, and Stephen and I slept in the front parlor. There was a small kitchen and a large living room adjacent to a long hall. We used the hall for our dining area and fit all the huge oak pieces in that room.

Our living room was just that, the LIVING room. There were always toys all over the place. Prior to this time, I enjoyed having things in a place and a place for everything. When the boys would go for their naps, I'd pick up all the toys. Out the boys and toys would come again after nap time, and I discovered I was spending a lot of time and energy picking up toys. Finally, one day it dawned on me that no one would care whether the toys were picked up after each use or just once at the end of the day. A child's job is to play after all, playing is a child's life. "If I keep this up either I'll have a nervous breakdown, or my sons will." Then I left the toys out and we'd put them away together at the end of the day. This was one of my first lessons in flexibility. I was always very proud of myself for that.

Housekeeping. Another lesson I learned in New Jersey.

I kept my house pretty much as my mother had. I washed the floors every week; I dusted every day, and I vacuumed regularly. Between the cleaning, cooking and keeping up with two little boys, I had a full-time schedule. Soon I was dusting every other day, then that became every third or fourth day, finally once a week. Maybe that floor didn't have to be washed every week; it wasn't that dirty, was it? Then I was dusting whenever the dust bothered me, and frankly, it didn't bother me that much, and it still doesn't.

While I was busy with the boys and revising my housekeeping methods, Stephen was still working with Minkus Stamps in downtown Manhattan. He seemed to be getting along fine, but worked five and a half days a week. On

weekends and several nights, he had to go to Linden to help his
father build a six-apartment brick building. It seemed to me
he was gone "all the time" and the boys and I were left on our
own. Stephen was also busy with church shows, performing
and directing. There didn't seem to be much family time.

His brother and some of his brother's kids were also helping
to build the house in Linden. I was excused, I think because
I had a small baby. Between Stephen's job, the demands of
his father and family, his passion still for performing, I was
feeling less important than ever to him. I felt as if the boys
and I were last on his list of priorities. I couldn't understand
why he could never say no to his father. There were so many
"shoulds" expected of us in those days, always a "should" or
a "have to."

One of the biggest fights we had at this time was the question
of attending his niece's first communion in Pennsylvania. It
was an eight-hour ride and of course the whole family from
New Jersey would be going. "No, I don't want to go. We don't
have to go." Silly me. Guess what his father said? "If you
don't go, you are no longer my son." Where had I heard that
before? If being this man's son, I was concluding, meant that
Stephen had to do everything his father asked or said, perhaps
Stephen was better off not being his son. Naturally we went
to Pennsylvania. We began looking for an apartment outside
of Manhattan; Nyak, Tarrytown, anywhere in the opposite
direction from Linden. "Why do you want to move so far
away?" we were asked. How about so we can breathe and live
our own life and not have to go to Linden every Sunday or be
on call. It really was a case when Stephen's father said jump,
the response was always how high?

This was foreign to me. Say what I will about my parents, and I know in their own way they tried as well to live my life for me, but once I was married, they cut me loose. In fact, my parents were the total opposite of Stephen's. My parents didn't quite ignore us, but as my mother frequently put it to me: "Nobody told you to get married." Or if I happened to call with a complaint about raising children, she'd add, "Well, nobody told you to have kids." With such support as this, how could our marriage be anything but a refuge for us both?

The boys became my life as we had, it seemed, only each other. The time spent with their father was cherished and eagerly looked forward to. We'd sometimes meet him at the bus stop at the corner or just coming up the street. The boys would run into his arms and he'd sweep them up and fuss over them and be a Dad in those moments. Sometimes I was even a little jealous, after all I never went somewhere to come home and be greeted like that. Yet, the memory of those times is precious and fresh still in my mind's eye. How dear, warm, open, loving and eager the boys were to be with their Dad. Daddy.

Gentlemen, do you have any idea of the power you have with your children? They love Mommy and know she will take care of them, but you fathers, oh boy, you are really special. I hope you know that and take it as a trust and a treasure. When people tell you, "Oh, they grow up so fast," believe it, it's true. All you'll have of this childhood time is precious, warm memories or regrets. I wish you a treasure of warm memories. Put them in your heart and keep them there for all those days and years later when no one seems to know who you are or have the time to care.

I ran away with the boys one time while we were living in New Jersey. I just packed them into the car, left a note for Stephen and drove off. "I've gone home to see my mother's new TV." The fact I still called Massachusetts "home," was not lost on my husband... I'd show him, I thought. Let's see how he likes being alone all the time

Halfway to Massachusetts I wanted to turn around and go back. The boys were always good travelers and I had time to think. All I ever wanted from Stephen was his time and attention, for me and our sons. I knew it was a contest between us and his father and also Stephen's own ambitions. I felt I was losing fast and if we stayed in New Jersey our marriage would be over. I couldn't continue this way. No matter what I did, his family just didn't seem to like me, and I didn't know why. Was I really such a bad person? Had my mother been right? Was I selfish and lazy, stupid and spoiled? Was I really that bad?

I thought I was a good wife, and I knew I was a good mother. I loved Stephen and my sons more than I had ever loved myself. What was wrong with me? Who was I and where was I going and what had happened to Carol? I was lost, confused, and sad I had no one to share my feelings with. I was looking inward and thinking it had to be me, my fault. "Mea culpa, mea culpa."

Carol Hrehovcik

CHAPTER NINE

How Ayn Rand Almost Ruined Marriage

I was a good Catholic to a point, but I always questioned many of the practices of the church. Still basically I liked being a Catholic. During this time in New Jersey, Stephen discovered the work of Ayn Rand and became active in the philosophy as taught by Nathaniel Brandon. I had read and enjoyed *The Fountainhead*, and this was as much as I knew about Ayn Rand. Stephen went on to read all her work, including *Atlas Shrugged*, which I had never read, and this book became something like a Bible to him.

We had some very interesting, philosophical discussions. However, suddenly, or so it seemed to me, Stephen decided not only to leave the Catholic Church and denounce all its teachings in favor of his new-found liberalism, but also to renounce his faith and belief in God. I had gone from being married to one of the most devoutly religious men I had ever known, to marriage with an atheist. There was no in between for Stephen; it was either/or, black or white. I expected

135

perhaps an "I'm considering this, or I'm puzzled by that." No, none of that. One day it was, "Christ has risen." And the next day, "There is no God." What now? I wondered. What should I tell the kids and how do I handle this shift myself?

Stephen told me he doesn't want me to talk about God in any way. Soon I was not only confused and bewildered and feeling like I had missed something somewhere, some link, some connection, but God was outlawed in our house. It was years before I was not too embarrassed to admit to Stephen, I still said a prayer (or two) at night and blessed myself whenever I drove, and I sure talked about God with my kids if I chose to do so. I was not so upset about his leaving the Catholic Church since that had been a cause of many arguments. Soon, Mike noticed we were not in church every week and believed it to be his "Christian duty" to tell Stephen's father we were not attending mass every week. Guess who's not somebody's son anymore?

But I was still a silly person who believed if you talked about a problem, you could resolve the problem. When Stephen told me what his brother had done and what his father had (of course) replied, I told my husband to go and talk to his father. "You have to talk to him and tell him how you feel. You cannot allow your brother to talk for you."

Stephen told me it would be a waste of time and nothing would be resolved. I insisted, and finally we both went to Linden to talk with his father and see if we could come to some sort of understanding. Naturally the whole conversation was in Slovak, so I didn't know what was actually being said, but I understood anger in any language. I understood screaming and red faces, and Stephen's mother, the pacifier, waltzing around the two men saying her always effective, "Pop. Pop."

Stephen took my hand and led me outside to the car. He was right and I was wrong. However, this wasn't good enough for Stephen's father. He followed us outside screaming and shouting in very clear, loud English, red-faced and pointing his finger at me, "I blame you. It's all your fault. Before he married you, he was a good man, a good Catholic. The priest in the Army wrote me my son went to church every week. It's all your fault."

Stephen tried in vain to calm his father down, "Pop, Pop," but hey, "Pop goes the weasel," and off we went, another humiliation, another scene, and yet another failure for me.

The funny thing at the time was I truly understood why Stephen's father would blame me. After all, what he said was absolutely true. Stephen was a good Catholic, he would go to mass every week, and he was a good man. What Stephen's father didn't know was the doubt and the questioning had been in Stephen's mind and soul long before he met me. More than that was the fact it was Stephen's own turmoil not only about the Catholic church but about the very existence of God that led him so far away from his religious roots. The irony was not only that I was not the cause or the reason, but I was the one remaining with the faith and belief in God. I didn't need a church doctrine to tell me what to think, feel, or believe or how to live my life, but God was still a part of my life.

Further, I thought if these people, Stephen's family, were an example of "good Catholics" I had made a wise decision long ago to be a free spirit and acknowledge only the part of religion that made sense to me. I didn't think going to mass every week made you a better person. I believed in right and wrong, good and evil, a basic sense of morality and how you lived your life as the most important elements as a measure of any religion.

I did not believe God, or any church gave you permission to be cruel and mean to your own son and his family, or to disown your son anytime he didn't agree with you. No, this was not the kind of God or church I believed in. I often wondered what my father-in-law told the priest when he went to confession. Did he tell the priest he wasn't talking to his son? Did the priest absolve him? Or did my father-in-law think it was all right and not a sin to discuss in the confessional?

And what about Stephen's brother? Was it his "duty" to interfere in this matter between Stephen and his father? What did Mike know about what Stephen believed? The brothers had never talked about it. Not that talking would have helped anyhow. Even I could not say I fully understood all Stephen talked about in his new pursuit for truth. However, I could tell you honestly, given the choice between the devout, guilty Stephen and this new, rational Stephen, I would take the new one any day. Naturally I hoped a balance would eventually take over. I believed this extreme pattern was like a pendulum, first it glides to one extreme and then the other until it finds its natural rhythm. I was soon, no, not soon, to discover Stephen's natural rhythm was not the smooth balance of the pendulum, but always to be at extremes. Balance was not a word in my husband's vocabulary, any more than it was in his behavior.

Yet I was hoping, and praying in my own way, for a

resolution to this problem with his family. Sides were taken as they often are in any family dispute, and once again and as always, Stephen and I were cast in the role of black sheep, the outsiders. I knew more than ever if our marriage and our immediate family were to survive, we had to get out of this environment. We could not grow or flourish here.

The opportunity for a move arose soon after this time. Stephen had already expressed impatience and unrest with his job at Minkus and had been looking for a job once more, yes, in the theater. I didn't care where he worked or what he did as long as it was far away from New Jersey. In fact, I believe distance became a prerequisite.

He interviewed at theaters in Springfield, Mass. in Hartford and New Haven, Conn. I especially hoped he would get the job in New Haven as it was very neatly in between the two families. I liked the city very much. The Long Wharf theater was doing many interesting and challenging projects, as well as being a very respected regional theater. I could be happy here I thought, and so could the boys. The boys and I traveled with Stephen to all his interviews, so each job audition was an excuse to get away and became an adventure for me and the boys. What fun it was to be able to just pick up and go. Sadly, there didn't seem to be any theater job out there for Stephen.

Not only was this time of personal unrest, but major social upheaval as well. Martin Luther King Jr. was assassinated in April, 1968, and two months later Robert Kennedy was gunned down in California. The Vietnam conflict was still going on with no end in sight, and people at home were fighting one another. Tanks moved into the nation's capital, and rioting was widespread. I learned to lock my doors and be afraid during this time in New Jersey. I'd never had a lot of faith in the future, but events were so overwhelming the possibility of my fears for the future becoming a reality was too frightening to contemplate. Now with Joshua and Noah, the future was very important to me and my one prayer at this time was for my sons to never have to carry a gun.

At the same time our landlords sold the house and told us we had sixty days to move out. This was one of those "good news, bad news" declarations. I saw this as the opportunity to get away from the area, job or no job. Stephen was unhappy with his work, and I was just plain unhappy. I wanted to "go home." At least it would be a place to start. We discussed it, and even though Stephen was hesitant, the prospect of moving away was not totally unacceptable to him.

On August 1, 1968, Stephen and I packed up whatever furniture and goods we owned, loaded a U-Haul truck and the Falcon, and prepared to leave New Jersey behind. Joshua drove in the truck with his father, excited about the adventure before us, only caring for the fact he was riding in a truck. Noah drove with me in the Falcon, in that little over the seat, car seat, and off we went. No jobs, no prospects, uncertain of the future and what lay ahead for us, knowing only we had to leave to survive as individuals, as a couple and as a nuclear family.

Years later I thought if my kids ever did something like that I would probably go crazy. I'm sure I would argue and protest. Yet, Stephen and I were young and healthy and had the belief in ourselves and our future that fear never entered the picture. We had only high hopes and good air we could breathe without feeling smothered. We were at least and at last in charge of our own destiny. Or so I thought.

I remember it was a beautiful day, the sky and the road ahead and the future were all bright with possibilities. We were going to stay at my brother Louis' for a while until we found an apartment. What a frightening sight we must have been when we arrived in my brother's driveway. What to do with us? We managed there for three weeks until it became clear we had better make other arrangements. We did.

We moved into the third-floor apartment of my parents' house. I was not happy about this but hoped it would only be temporary until we got on our financial feet. Stephen was looking for a job during the day and working at a gas station at night. As soon as school started, I got on the substitute list and started teaching again. I didn't mind this time since I knew the kids were safe with my mother watching them. They even had playmates next door the same ages. It was the first time we were in a neighborhood with other children. I thought this arrangement might work out all right after all.

I was hoping for a permanent teaching job but was busy everyday substituting. Stephen finally got a job in Cambridge as the advertising manager for a bank in Harvard Square. It was a commute, but nothing like he'd had in New Jersey. Still, it made a long day for him. We began to look for an apartment closer to his work and away from my parents.

I can only imagine how cruel this must have seemed to Stephen's family. We didn't move away to hurt them, we wanted only to live our own life, our way, right or wrong, Catholic or non. Years and years would pass, and even to this day, Stephen's family blames me of "dragging" him away, making him leave his family and his home. My mother's litany of "No one told you to get married, have kids, etc." was followed by Stephen's family's chant: "No one told you to move away."

Sometimes, I must confess, my husband's family continues to confound and amuse me. Don't they have any knowledge about Stephen at all? Do they know him in any way? The answer is and always has been no, of course. Stephen never told them, and they never asked. I used to feel perhaps I had "dragged" him away, maybe without me Stephen would have stayed close by his family. But where had he been all those years before we met and married? Had he been living in the bosom of family and "home"? No. If his family ever stopped to think about it, which would be a miracle in itself, they would realize Stephen was always running away somewhere. He could no more bear to live near his family than I could, or than I could be too long around my own.

This fact became evident once more to me when my mother called me at school one day. She hollered at me to tell me how bad my sons were, especially Joshua. She couldn't do a thing with him. Joshua, a bad boy? I don't think so. Perhaps he misbehaved, or didn't listen, or worse in my mother's eyes, had a mind of his own and just went about his business. She screamed and carried on over the phone so much so I decided right at that moment she would never take care of my children again. She had screwed me up and there was no way she was going to do that to my sons. If anybody was going to do the messing up it was going to be me, but of course I didn't plan on doing that. I would love them and cherish them, and Joshua and Noah would not be afraid or scared they were unlovable, as I had grown up to believe about myself. After all, if your own mother doesn't love you, who will?

I quit teaching that day and made child-rearing my full-time job. The family could manage now that Stephen had a good position. Oh, did I love that bank! We bought a new car. Stephen sold the Falcon and bought a blue Opel station wagon. I remember when he drove it home the first time.

He had chosen the car all by himself; I had no idea what it looked like. Joshua and Noah and I were so filled with anticipation. When he drove into the driveway with much beeping of the foreign sounding horn and grinning like a conquering hero, we all clapped with delight. It was a perfect car and the boys and I just loved it. We took all the neighborhood kids for a ride that night.

The back of the wagon became the "way back" and was always the favorite place for the boys to ride. Of all the cars we've owned over the years, this blue Opel station wagon is still my very favorite. Is it because I have so many good memories of the car and this precious time in our life? Or is it the fact Stephen chose it all by himself and drove home so proudly? Or perhaps it seemed life was looking good and promising and we finally felt like a family.

I know now giving up the convertible for the station wagon was more significant than I realized. In some way I knew this or at least sensed it, and believed Stephen was now ready to be a husband and a father and our life would only get better. It was after all the job at the bank that enabled us to get the new car and also allowed me to be a full-time mother, a job I so ardently wanted.

Joshua began nursery school in the fall, which he didn't care for at all. Noah was reading and learning to read faster than I could ever teach him. He was devouring words like one of his favorite dinosaurs.

I hadn't realized Noah could read. I thought, at first, he simply had an excellent memory as we both read to the boys all the time. He was barely two years old, how could he possibly be reading? Before he could walk, he'd always sit on my mother's floor with the World Almanac on his lap and look at the printed pages. Since there were no pictures, only print, he'd turn the pages and be very content.

At the same time, Joshua was very active, sitting still was not something he did willingly, except to be read to. No, Joshua loved his cars and trucks and announced he was going to be a race car driver "when I grow up." He was captivated by the cartoon "Speed Racer," mesmerized by any kind of car race. Joshua's love affair with cars and racing continues to this day, not fixing them, just driving them and wanting to race. Naturally, as a mother, all I could think of was the terrible risks involved, but he was a little boy and why should I worry now?

Noah, on the other hand, was quieter and more intellectual. While Joshua just wanted to play, Noah wanted to be left alone to read and learn things. He loved learning and he loved words. My sister-in-law, Carol, was the one who discovered Noah could actually read. She made some word cards and placed them in sequence and changed them around and sat Noah on her knee. Noah read them all. He wasn't even two years old! He thought this was a grand game. My God, I wondered, what do I do with this child?

How smart must he be and how could I help him? I started to work with him at the blackboard while Joshua was in nursery school. Later Joshua would sometimes join us, but mostly he didn't have the patience nor inclination to read at this time. This was perfectly normal and all right with me. I knew how smart Joshua was, but he wanted to do more important things, like building with his blocks, racing his cars, and playing games. Kids' stuff, of course.

My mother was very taken with this newfound knowledge of Noah's ability to read. She bragged about him often, sadly in front of Joshua, to a point where Joshua would introduce himself and his brother like this: "Hi, I'm Josh and this is my brother Noah, he can read, and I can't." This was both cute and sad at the same time. Funny thing was Noah could read more words than he ever talked. Joshua was the talker and did almost all the talking for Noah, sometimes I think it is still that way.

I felt this blatant favoritism from my mother particularly would be a problem for Joshua's future self-esteem and it was time for us to move out and on. We had never intended to stay in the apartment for very long anyhow. I was too well aware of the damage my parents, unwittingly to be sure, had caused my own spirit, I didn't want to see that happen to my sons. We were looking to get away once more when Stephen came home in February of 1970 and announced he had quit his job at the bank and taken a position with a fledgling theater company in Cape Elizabeth, Maine. Goodbye security and trust for a long, long time.

Stephen would be in Maine selling the new theater group to the businesses in and around the Portland area. Part of the plan with the owner of the company was for our family to be housed on the family compound in Cape Elizabeth. Stephen had the use of the owner's Jeep and would come home on Wednesdays and Friday nights for the weekend. Neither the boys nor I liked it very much, but with the promise of the summer in Maine, we all held on and enjoyed each homecoming as a special treat. At least this time I was not alone. I had my family who spoke English, some friends and the boys had their playmates.

Again, this was not my idea of a marriage, but I thought if Stephen had finally found a job with a theater and he'd be happy, then I'd be happy, too. I tell you I was sorry to see that job at the bank go. Man had landed on the moon that summer, but Stephen who always seemed to land on his feet, may as well have been on the moon as far as I was concerned.

When Stephen took me to visit the "compound" in Maine, I was overwhelmed by the obvious wealth of the family. I thought as we drove around the many acres, complete with a main house and several cottages scattered about the area, this must be something like the Kennedy compound in Massachusetts. There were the swimming pools, a farm, a barn that housed a bowling alley and upstairs a stage where the theater would be. I thought to myself, "all right, I can live around here or the nearby beach" Now the owner wasn't quite sure where the Hrehovcik family would be housed. Higgins Beach was nearby, and the family owned several properties there. I was beginning to feel perhaps this wouldn't be so bad after all, a summer in Maine.

Once again, however, plans did not work out as expected. In the spring of 1970, only four months after Stephen had left his job at the bank, and after all his work getting support for the theater, he was fired. He was fired!

Carol Hrehovcik

The boys and I were waiting for him at a bus stop in Newburyport. It was not unusual for him to take the bus home some weekends as the owner would use the Jeep herself. The bus, as always happened with my husband, was late. I am not a patient person, and am less so since being married to Stephen, but this beautiful spring night, with two lively little boys running around and having been the sole caretaker for months, I was especially tired, restless and cranky. As soon as he got off the bus, I knew there was a problem. I was not prepared for this particular problem. I don't believe there was any preamble. Stephen has never had much of a sense of timing, never mind time. "I was fired today." What? "Fired, let go. I'm not going back." Why? "I think her best friend didn't like me, so Millie gave Ronnie my job."

Now, I have said a lot of things about my husband, but one of them has never been that people don't like him. In fact, one of Stephen's main goals in life is to be a nice guy. That is very important to him. He was always the nice guy, so it was hard for me to imagine someone not liking him. Although there were times when I didn't like him a whole lot myself, this was different. I had to live with him; he was my husband and the father of my children. I could see where he might come on too strong for some people, and some women didn't always appreciate his sense of humor. But, fired? Oh, God, now what? Here we go again.

CHAPTER TEN

A Summer Playhouse and the Move to Maine

I didn't understand why this man couldn't hold a job. We'd been married for five years and he had at least as many jobs in that time. He'd been fired once before, just before Joshua was born. Usually, he'd just quit while he looked for a job in the theater. Since I'd been fired from my job in New Hampshire I didn't feel there was any shame to it, sometimes there's just a personality conflict or the chemistry is wrong, I can understand that. But I thought, this man is thirty-two years old, it's time for him to grow up. How do you say "grow up" to a grown man?

I know I wasn't very nice, and it was hard for me to be supportive of an idea which a) I hadn't been consulted about, and b) I never believed in the plan anyhow. Perhaps now (silly me) I hoped he'd get a regular job and forget the theater and we could be a family again.

It seems odd to me now that Stephen and I never really

sat down and talked about our values and priorities. I thought because we loved each other, somehow, they were naturally the same. I really believed it; otherwise how could we love each other? How could I love someone who didn't think, feel, and believe the way I did, at least about the important issues?

Yet we never, never talked about what we wanted from our life together, from our marriage. We didn't discuss our hopes and dreams for our children or for each other as individuals or as a couple. We simply never stopped to ask any of these questions. Stephen could overwhelm me with his enthusiasm and faith in our "future."

Where was this future? What magic would occur to make this future he kept talking about really happen? I didn't need or want a lot of material things. I didn't need the best of everything or diamonds or Lenox china or sterling silver. All I wanted was what I had, my family, and a husband to share life and living with me and my sons, to be healthy and strong. I wanted Stephen to be a husband and a father. I wanted him there with me and with us. I wanted our family. That was what I wanted, but I never knew until years later what it was Stephen wanted.

In my heart I knew family was the most important part of life. I believe raising children is the most valuable job anyone can ever have. Taking care of your children is taking care of the future. I thought Stephen felt the same way. But if actions speak louder than words, and I believe they do, and if behavior is indeed everything, then Stephen was talking to me loud and clear in a language I either chose not to understand or I simply could not accept.

It was obvious to everyone but me this belief in marriage

and the family was not one shared by my husband. That sharing of any kind meant to him controlling, and yes, he was doing what was important to him, and that was to keep going back to the theater in any way, shape or form he could be involved.

I began to doubt myself, my abilities, my instincts. Perhaps I had made a mistake and should have worked while he finished graduate school. Then maybe he would have been happy teaching drama in a college or university somewhere. I doubted myself and started to feel guilty for not encouraging him to finish graduate school. I began to blame myself for his problems. Why not? I'd had a lot of practice.

The concept of someone being responsible for his own actions was not one with which I was familiar. I felt responsible for everyone's happiness, but at the same time I thought Stephen was responsible for mine. I couldn't be happy if he were unhappy. I couldn't be happy if my children were unhappy. I was beginning to think perhaps we were not meant to be happy here on earth at all. Maybe Mrs. Dylan Thomas was right, "Hell is right here on this bloody earth," or as Stephen's mother used to say: "Life is to suffer." Still in my own heart I didn't believe it or accept it. I didn't think that was what God had in mind for us. Yet happiness, except for brief, fleeting moments scattered about like tiny stars, eluded me and eluded us.

I questioned myself over and over. "What is it going to take to make you happy, Carol? Can you ever be happy or is it impossible for you? Is it in the genes, this unrest, this misery? Is the most you can hope for a moment here and there of happiness? What about joy? What about delight?

And wonder? And love? What is happening to love?"

I didn't have any answers, but I certainly had a lot of questions and I knew something was very wrong. As usual I thought it was with me, my fault. After all, Stephen was working hard, no one worked harder than Stephen, so why were things going from bad to worse? Some bad luck? Some bad breaks? "Hey, we're young, we'll be fine. We'll be all right." I believed it.

Stephen was not feeling sorry for himself for very long. He was on the phone making calls and appointments the next day, all revolving around the theater. Soon he was back in Maine at a summer theater in Kennebunkport. I knew the Kennebunkport Playhouse from my single days when friends and I would drive to Ogunquit. We'd check out the playhouse in Ogunquit and later wander over to Kennebunkport to see what was playing there. In those days both playhouses featured big name stars in popular Broadway productions.

At the time Stephen interviewed for the job in Kennebunkport, the theater had been purchased by two men from Massachusetts. They were producing plays with a repertory company, an assortment of professional actors and actresses. Stephen's job would be public relations and publicity. It wasn't what he wanted, but it was a chance again to be involved in theater, and since he had no other prospects at the time, he accepted. So, we'd have our summer in Maine after all. I was not unhappy to be leaving my parents' house, but the boys, especially Joshua, missed their playmates. Only many years later did we discover how deeply this last move affected him.

One hears all the time how resilient kids are, how they are so capable of adjusting to new situations and that was what

I thought too. I could never foresee anything but our family together once again, independent and living our own lives away from the influence and dependence of our families. I guess I was so excited to about going to Maine, I couldn't think beyond the summer. I felt sad the boys would be leaving their friends, but happy again to get away from my family. Kennebunkport wasn't so far away after all, but far enough for us to live our life the way we chose. I can see now I was out of touch with reality, bedazzled and still so much in love, I would go anywhere with Stephen if I thought he would be happy at last.

Stephen used to play the guitar when the boys were little and we'd all sing, yes, "Sylvie." Another one of our favorite songs was "500 Miles." It's a sad, but lovely song. In the summer of 1970 as the four of us sat in our little rented cottage at Goose Rocks Beach, Maine and sang that song, Joshua began to cry and asked us not to sing that song. To this day, he cannot bear to listen to that song, "away from home, away from home," too much sorrow still.

Aside from not anticipating Joshua's sadness at the loss of friends and playmates, I also did not foresee my life at Goose Rocks Beach without a car all day and many nights as well. We had no phone in the cottage, no car, and as we had moved into the cottage on Memorial Day, there weren't a lot of people around either.

Fortunately, the boys and I liked to explore, so we walked all over Goose Rocks Beach, and I dug more holes in the sand than I care to remember. The lights seemed to go off at least once a night as there were many storms that summer, this added to the charm of it all in a way. We played a lot of games by candlelight.

As the summer season began, more families with children arrived and the boys finally had some playmates to enjoy. The one problem was just as the boys would get friendly with the kids, the families would pack up and leave as their one- or two-week vacation ended. This must have been the summer from hell for poor Joshua. No friends, or new friends soon gone away, and more than that I made him take swimming lessons in the cold Maine Atlantic.

Fog, fog, fog. Joshua hated the water and soon so did Noah. But being the good protective parent I thought I was and thinking once again kids adjust, I made them continue with swimming lessons. After all they were going to be living by the water. I was sure in time Joshua would get over his fear of the water and his near hatred of it, but not Joshua. I can't apologize enough to Joshua and can only hope he has forgiven me.

So now we had two unhappy little boys, a lonely and sad mother, and a father who worked and was gone all the time. Such is life in the theater. I thought the hours might not be so bad as he wasn't an actor, but the theater was trying to reestablish itself this season and it was Stephen's job to promote it. That summer was difficult for Stephen, and the only time we did get to see him was on Sunday. We'd be driving up and down the southern coast of Maine and New Hampshire dropping off the current posters in all the motels and restaurants along the way. It was fun for the boys and they felt useful and happy to be with their Dad, and I was happy for us all to be together.

As unhappy as the three of us were at the beach that

summer, Stephen was struggling to do a good job to promote the playhouse and the current show. It was soon obvious this Kennebunkport Playhouse was not going to be as successful as the old playhouse had been. First there was Ogunquit to consider, a grand and well-respected summer theater. It had some of the top names in show business and was a major draw for vacationers and people living within the North Shore.

Meanwhile here in Kennebunkport, the director of the new theater was going to "educate" the public with "good theater," whatever that meant to him. Beware of any director or manager who wants to "educate" the public. Most people on vacation, particularly in the summer, do not want to be educated; they want to be entertained. That's what vacation is all about. But no, not this fellow. I wonder why the season was such a bust with such well-rounded fare as "Juno and the Paycock," "Crawling Arnold," and others in that same vein.

Soon Stephen realized he was in a thankless position. If a show managed to make money, it was because the show was wonderful, the actors and technicians and the director were all talented and grand. On the other hand, if a show fell on its face, the fault was always Stephen's lack of getting the publicity out or they said his work wasn't good enough. Never did it seem to occur to any of them the good shows were the comedies, the light summer fare that people enjoyed, like Neil Simon's "Star Spangled Girl." But Sean O'Casey? Really!

I am sure many of you have been in a similar position where the boss takes all the credit for the good work, but somehow never seems to take any of the blame for what goes wrong. Well, imagine twenty bosses blaming you for everything that goes wrong, but the same twenty bosses not once giving you credit for the things that do go right.

More than that, it was evident to Stephen and later to me that he was considered an "outsider", not an artist. We'd go to opening night parties and no one would sit with us or talk to us. Someone did talk to us one night, he wanted to borrow our chair. It didn't take too many of these parties for me to say no more for me, thank you. Who did they think they were? I have had a strong dislike for actors ever since, especially amateurs, and these people in my mind were amateurs.

Perhaps it is necessary for an actor to have an ego in order to survive, but I cannot understand nor forgive rudeness and arrogance. Of this summer group, we've seen only one performer in films or on television. I often wonder how long the rest of the troupe pursued their dreams of the stage and movies or TV. Where are they now?

One good thing about that summer, I had a great tan. I was thinner than I'd been in a while and I was making some friends along the beach. I decided I liked living there in spite of the inconveniences and later the fact that some people thought we were Jewish. This was very interesting to me. The boys' names are of course from the Bible, but these are old New England names as well. There was Joshua Chamberlain from Maine and Noah Webster from New Hampshire.

I was washing the dishes in our cottage when I happened to hear one of our next-door neighbors talking with another neighbor. I could not believe what she said. "I won't let my children play with them because they're Jewish you know."

What? I couldn't believe what I was hearing. First of all, the woman who said this was the "good Irish Catholic" neighbor next door. Oh, that Catholic thing again. I was stunned, I didn't know whether to run outside and cry we are not Jewish, we are Catholic just like you, or to confront her with what I had overheard.

I had never encountered this kind of prejudice before. I was as I told you, brought up to treat people as individuals and I never thought about someone's religion or nationality, all I ever cared about was whether they were nice or not. The next day on the beach I called my sons "Josh and Noah O'Riley." I know it didn't fool anyone, but it made me laugh, and I am ashamed to admit I did not confront this woman. After all, what would I say to her and why would I give her the satisfaction of thinking I even cared what she thought?

Yet it was a harsh lesson for me, and I think for my sons as well. As they grew older this belief would occur many times because of their names and our strange last name, strange to the people in this part of Maine at least. Even one of the school principals thought we were Jewish and wanted Noah to study Hebrew. I said sure, thinking nothing of it one way or the other. I didn't mind if Noah studied Chinese or Japanese or Spanish or Hebrew, it was all enriching to learn another language and culture. After several lessons it was revealed to Noah only the Jewish students were studying Hebrew. Noah said, "I'm not Jewish. I'm Catholic." The principal called me feeling very embarrassed, which he should have, and apologized for assuming the family was Jewish because of our name.

I had witnessed prejudice in Washington, and I could understand the color issue, and I surely learned some humility and greater understanding as the only white passenger on a bus. I knew prejudice existed and we all had some to one degree or the other, but I was puzzled by this prejudice against Jewish people. I felt such sympathy for them as I learned firsthand the prejudice against them has nothing to do with them as individuals. What the problem is, I simply do not understand and I don't think I want to because I don't believe it will ever make any sense to me. I don't care to have something explained when there can be no explanation why a person would not allow her children to play with someone else's children because of some ethnic difference. Children are all children after all. It didn't matter to this mother that my sons were polite, funny and smart. What was she teaching her children? How could she go to church and pray and be so guilty of this great sin against innocent children? I don't understand cruelty of any kind, but I have always wished this woman ill; I am Sicilian after all.

The summer was coming to an end, and somehow the boys and I managed to recover from our sense of abandonment and disappointment. The "future" was here again and now what do we do? It was time for Joshua to go to kindergarten as he turned five this summer in Maine. Although there was no public kindergarten in Massachusetts at this time, I had enrolled him in a school in Haverhill. Yet the prospect of returning to the apartment in my parents' house was not one Stephen or I welcomed.

During the summer Stephen had gotten friendly with the advertising manager of the small, local paper. When the manager decided to leave his job to return to school, he offered the job to Stephen, and recommended him to the editor. The paper was the York County Coast Star and Stephen took the job for $150 a week. This was much less money than he'd been making in Cambridge, but the benefits of living in a small town in Maine were more valuable to us. This time we did talk about his decision and together chose to stay in Maine. We thought what a wonderful place for our children to grow up, where they might learn more basic values and together we could enjoy a good and simple life as a family. This theater experience left Stephen with bad feelings and it seemed he was ready at last to leave the glory of theater behind.

Having been married now for a little more than five years, I had not lost the glow of faith and love for this man and was ready to settle in Maine. I didn't need a lot of money and was willing to go back to work for a better life and to pay back all the money we owed.

Up to this point, I have not talked about money (or sex, but more about this later). In case you think all these moves were cost efficient, I assure you they were not. With every move, with every change from job to job, from place to place, we were digging ourselves into a bigger and bigger financial hole. We owed so much money I doubted we'd ever be debt free. At least now we were starting fresh, we'd both be working, and perhaps with a simpler life in Maine, we'd get on our financial feet at last.

What mattered the most to me was we had agreed on where we were going and what we wanted to do at this point in our marriage. Stephen started his job at the *Star*, and I made the rounds of realtors looking for a place to live. I was of course looking for a year-round rental and was laughed at almost everywhere I went. "Year-round rental." Unheard of in 1970 in Kennebunk or Kennebunkport. It surely was different here from where we had lived previously, but since it was basically a vacation area, there were winter rentals available. We went around town looking at some winter rentals and decided we'd worry about summer when the time came. One realtor asked what we were looking for and I replied a house with two floors. "What else do you want?" he asked. "The moon?" I was not happy with him.

I had never lived in a house before, not in my whole life. I had lived in apartments and finally the little cottage at the beach, which was actually smaller than some of the apartments I'd lived in. So, when I thought of a house, my vision had always been upstairs and downstairs, and this person was telling me I wanted the moon. All right, so I'd be moving again, summer and winter, but by God, I'd get what I wanted.

Because Stephen worked for the paper and was in charge of the advertising, he had access to the local realtors. One day he came home to the beach cottage all excited. "I've found the perfect house." Sure, I thought. He took us for a ride and drove to this charming red, two-story house, set back on a small incline, only a short distance from the town beach and not so far out of town from his work. I fell in love with it immediately. As we drove up the driveway, I knew this was indeed the house of my dreams. I didn't even need to go inside, I loved it; I loved it and oh, I wanted so much to live there!

"I think I can get it for $125 a month, but you can't come in with me. One look at you and the price will go up." Stephen went into the realtor's office alone while Joshua and Noah and I sat anxiously in the car. Soon he came out with a big smile on his face, the keys in his hand. "I got it for $125 a month and we can move in anytime." Yes, there was a God, and He loved me, and so did Stephen; he'd made a dream come true for me. I was so happy, I vowed I would never complain about anything ever again as long as I could live here.

To me the inside of the red house was even more perfect. There was nice furniture, a TV set in a built-in cabinet, a dining room with lots of dishes and flatware, a huge kitchen with a dishwasher and a washer and dryer. Three bedrooms, a den and two bathrooms. For the first time ever, we would have two bathrooms! And a dishwasher!

The yard was very spacious with a big old apple tree in the back, a circular driveway, and a big sprawling lawn out front. I thought this was the most wonderful house I could ever have imagined. To me it was like living in a fairy tale. I was thirty-three years old and I was living in a house just as I had always dreamed. I was in love. I never minded working if I knew what I was working for, and now I'd be working to live here in this lovely house, and maybe, just maybe, one day we'd have a house just like this of our very own.

When I look back at all the years we've been married, I believe this time at the "red house" was the happiest time in our marriage. We still had our problems, of course, but we lived in this wonderful house with so many amenities; it seemed like we were going to have a regular life after all. Our goals and plans were the same, I thought. I treasure still the years in the red house as the most special. The boys were growing and happy. Stephen had a steady job and I was back to work and the future looked promising.

In spite of the overwhelming debt we incurred, I was optimistic we could pay it back at last. Yet I was afraid to go to the mailbox or even answer the phone. I took all the nasty calls and threatening letters very personally and felt like such a bad person because we couldn't pay our bills. That was the only bad part, well, all right, there was another.

Stephen continued to work long hours, but he was home most weekends and we usually had dinner together during the week. I hadn't remembered that happening for years. The boys seemed to do well here although they didn't have friends close by. When Joshua started kindergarten, his teacher said to me, "Joshua is a very smart little boy, but I have the feeling he'd rather be anywhere else than here." She was so right.

Noah was attending a nursery school and day care center where Joshua could walk to when he finished kindergarten class. The director of Noah's school told me one day, with a "heavy heart," she believed Noah was "brain damaged." Since both of my sons hated it there anyhow, this remark convinced me to pull them out of there immediately. "Brain damaged" indeed. Her problem was, I thought, that at three years old, Noah was already more intelligent than she dared to dream. We would find this attitude in one way or another with other teachers at different times in Noah's school career. His obvious high intelligence and creativity could be intimidating to some teachers whose self-confidence was already low. Other teachers welcomed the challenge of a child like Noah.

I have found that the mentally challenged get more care, attention, funding and programs than the gifted children in our public schools. I have no idea what private schools do with their gifted youngsters. At any rate, in 1970, in the state of Maine, which to be sure was behind Massachusetts in its educational progress, there were no programs for the gifted child I was aware of.

Fortunately (or not), Noah had a mother who was aware and took great pains to see he got treated with respect for his intelligence. Not that I expected teachers to make a fuss over him, but I had hoped he'd have the experience with many who would rise to the challenge and be excited by the possibilities he'd offer to their teaching. Some were indeed just that way.

The price Noah seemed to have to pay at the time was a very weak physical nature. Since his birth Noah had been a sickly child, first with colic, then with his hip displacement and the brace across his feet, and then with one virus after another. Because he had walked much later than most children his age, and because his hip was still out of alignment, Noah was a year behind his peers in physical ability.

Yet he was able to do anything any other child could do, except he got tired a lot quicker. When I finally took him to an orthopedic surgeon, he assured me Noah did not need an operation on his hip. As long as he could run and jump and ride a bicycle, he was all right. What would it matter if he weren't ever to be a marathon runner? We should just let him be unless at some later time the hip gave him problems. Because of this weakness, Noah began dancing lessons to build his strength and stamina.

I was very fortunate in the fall of 1970; I found the most wonderful babysitter for my two sons. She not only took good care of them but nurtured them and played with them and taught them and I think loved them. She was the original natural food disciple and with her husband owned one of the first natural food stores in the area. Sometimes her husband and she, Cindy, would take the boys to the store or to the beach. The boys called Cindy's husband "Big Bird" and still talk about how he taught them to skip rocks. He was a gentle giant of a man, complete with long hair and a beard. The boys adored him.

Every day I left the house to go to work I was sad; I hated leaving them. Knowing they were in such kind, good and loving hands helped ease my sorrow as I drove off each day. I still can see them waving goodbye to me each morning, with their little boy faces pressed against the window. It is one of those pictures time doesn't erase, yet I know how much luckier I was than so many other working moms.

Fortunately for me things were going well on the home front with the boys flourishing under Cindy's care and guidance. Stephen was doing well at the paper and the advertising dollars were growing every week. There seemed always to be a celebration at the office whenever the inches grew. I, on the other hand, was neither flourishing nor doing well. The first grade class I had taken on as a full time job with such high hopes and promise turned out to be more difficult than even my first grade Army class.

The principal and I had totally opposite views on teaching children. Since I had become a mother, I understood so much better who a child was. I often thought this principal would have liked me better when I first started teaching, before I knew what a child was really like. I had enjoyed being more of a disciplinarian in those days, and even though my standards still remained high, I had a different vision of how to attain them.

Especially having two young sons, I understood better that school was not conceived with young boys in mind. Yes, primary grades were generally where the girls excelled, but the boys were the challenge and often the delight. I knew now that children had to be physical, that to be still or quiet was not their true nature. Although I still demanded and expected attention and no talking when I was teaching, there were acceptable times to wander and even whisper, to play together, to explore and to create. I cannot tell you how many times that principal came into my room "shushing" me and all the kids. It got to a point where I could predict when she'd arrive and time her entrance.

The word soon spread in this little school about that rabble rouser in grade one who would not conform to the rules. The rules at that time being: no talking, no running, no playing, no having fun in the schoolroom or schoolyard. Now there were several teachers who thrived in that kind of atmosphere, but I had never been one. I believed children needed to run, not in the schoolroom, but outside for sure. These kids were not allowed to run outside until they had walked, in file, out and around the entire building. I thought this was ridiculous and almost cruel.

I had never been wise enough to follow the old fellow's advice from my first year of teaching: "Don't make waves." I neither understood nor accepted this advice. These were our charges; their lives were our responsibility for more than six hours a day, five days a week; they were our future. Were we to raise them to be like sheep? To be timid and to follow? From where would we get the leaders of tomorrow if we couldn't allow some individuality now? Since I didn't like to be a follower myself, how could I expect it from these children? Needless to say, the principal and I were at odds all the rest of the year. She kept coming into my room shushing,

To Love and To Cherish

and I kept rebelling. I had one kindred spirit teaching next to me that year. She was always in trouble too, and we knew neither of our contracts was going to be renewed.

Just as I began to fear what the future was to hold for me professionally, and where in this small town I would ever get another teaching job, the superintendent of schools and his assistant visited me in class one day. Since as you may recall I wasn't too keen on administrators, I was a little concerned, expecting the worst. I was then genuinely surprised and delighted when I was offered a job for the next year teaching the fifth grade where they both felt my "talents and abilities" would be better appreciated. Wow! "Talents and abilities." Appreciated! Wouldn't that be something completely different?

I always knew, no matter what this principal or any other said to me, I was a good teacher. I knew from teachers who had my students after me. They would often tell me how my kids were the best prepared, especially in math and reading. I admit I wasn't very good with art or science, but with the basics, "reading, writing, and arithmetic" I was good and proud of it. Let someone else who was good at it teach them all the science and geography and nature. I knew what I was good at and I enjoyed that part of my teaching career.

I loved the teaching of teaching. When you see someone really grasp an idea and understand, then teaching is the most fulfilling job a person can have. There are days of course you wonder if what you are doing makes any difference at all. There were the days for me when everything clicked, and I used to wish I had an audience to see how good I was. Classes in creative writing or great arithmetic lessons, or reading, or

166

teaching time. Then of course there were other days I was glad no one could see me, or they'd wonder why they were paying me, and anything must be too much. I suppose in any job you have your good days and the other kind.

One quality I know I brought to all my classes was a genuine respect for each child. I think in all the years I taught school, no, I know in all those years there was only one child I did not like, and I was aware of it although not aware at all of the reason for it. Fortunately for both of us, he left soon after the new year started. I respected each child as an individual, you see Lowell was not completely lost on me, and these children taught me respect for each life here on earth. I treasured them as people, not simply as children, and I know I learned from them as I hoped they had learned from me.

The one wonderful aspect about education and teaching to me is it is perhaps one of the few jobs where there is a beginning, a middle and an end. If this school year went badly, or this year's job wasn't as successful as I had hoped, I got another chance to start all over again in September. To this day I still regard September as the start of the new year. Although I must confess, I am happy to be out of it all now.

How times have changed. When I started teaching in 1960 and even again in 1970, women were not allowed to wear pants to school. We dressed "professionally." In 1970 pant suits for women were just coming into fashion, and many of us thought this made a lot of sense. I bought one, a red plaid, I remember, and wore it to school, taking a big chance. I mean what did I have to lose at that point, and it was an awfully cold winter that year in Maine. Naturally, it was the cause for gossip and staring and whispered remarks, some rude and some merely inquisitive. Soon after I wore my suit to school, several of the other teachers wore one as well. I guess the principal couldn't fire all of us. I had to laugh to myself; you see what I mean about sheep.

I also recall talking in the teachers' room and having not one, but two of my peers brag about the fact they had never, ever been out of the state of Maine. They were as proud of this fact as I was appalled. This was something a teacher should be proud of? What was I doing here? Where had we moved to and why? I'd been in some odd circumstances, but this was scarier to me than working in the ghetto in Washington. These people were teaching our children, my children, and they had never been out of the state of Maine. No wonder the schools were behind. A little voice inside me kept crying, "Run, Carol, run."

I was happy to see that school year end and I was excited about being "promoted" to an upper grade at a larger school. There were several men on the faculty there, so perhaps there would be more of an interchange on a higher intellectual level. I welcomed the challenge and looked forward to being appreciated, and yes, maybe, heavens, good lord, could it possibly be? –

Understood!

Chapter Eleven

The Most Beautiful Girl in the World

Meanwhile Stephen and I made plans to rent the same cottage at Goose Rocks beach the summer of 1971. This summer would be different. We had more security together as a family, I knew the area and what to expect, from the Irish Catholic neighbors for example. Also, I had a car of my own. Living in a rural area in Maine with two jobs demanded it. I drove the blue Opel which I loved, and Stephen drove a little red Ghaman Khia convertible, which he loved. Except in the winter of course, when he didn't love it all that much.

We were paying off our bills, slowly, steadily, making friends, loving the red house where we lived and the beach house in summer. At this time, we started to think of buying our own home. Naturally I wanted to buy the red house, but when we asked our landlord he firmly and kindly said, "Oh, no, we'll never sell this house. It's been in the family for years and we'll probably retire here." I was devastated. I loved that house, still do, more than I thought one could ever be attached to a house. At least we knew where we were going for a change and had the security of going back to the house in the fall.

Stephen was on a regular schedule at the paper, and I insisted we have a phone in the cottage this summer. Yes, once again life was full of promise and hope. Joshua would be starting the first grade and Noah would be in kindergarten. I would be working full time and Stephen had a steady job which he seemed to enjoy.

We moved back to Goose Rocks beach, enjoyed the "bloat" and Mr. Butts' store and the return of many of the summer families we'd come to know. We had lots of company that summer too, and because Stephen was home more often, the boys were much happier than they'd been the summer before. Cindy would continue to baby sit for me in the fall. Yes, I was still young, in love, hopeful and even happy. I decided I could live in Maine after all, away from both of our families.

Hope, promise, and, yes, even love soon would be lost. In the summer of 1971, I got pregnant and I didn't know how or when. Oh, sure I did, but I didn't. By this time, I had tried every form of contraception and had now returned to the good old rhythm method. Oops, guess what? It didn't work!

Yet, I say God knew what He was doing. Good thing too, because I sure didn't. I cursed and blessed the day I discovered I might be pregnant. I felt almost like I felt the first time, unmarried and afraid. Again, I made excuses, denying what I feared was the reality. "Perhaps with all this moving, the stress of teaching this year, all the uncertainty there could be another explanation for my not getting my period. Couldn't there?" I hoped.

I would never learn. "Yep, you've got a touch of pregnancy." Dr. Buell laughed. As for me, I didn't know whether to laugh or cry. Yet somehow, somewhere inside me, I was happy, excited and proud.

We could always get a house later, I mused. Here was a new life, another child to enrich and enlarge our family. I think I cried later when I told my husband, but he was happy and excited and hoped it would be a girl. I was too now, but sad when I had to resign my teaching job. I would have enjoyed that fifth grade position, but now I had a new job to look forward to, once again with fear, excitement and hope.

How would we get along without the second paycheck? Perhaps it would only be for a short time and then I could go back to work. At the same time, I was scared and anxious at the thought of being the one now to wave at the window. No longer would I see the sad faces of my sons at the glass every morning. I loved my children more than anything and I treasured all my time with them. Not that I never got angry or cranky or disillusioned, but mostly I knew Joshua and Noah were the treasures of my life. Each day with them was a gift I valued and cherished with all my heart.

During this summer of 1971, my pregnancy confirmed, we got on with the business of enjoying this season at the beach. With Stephen there to participate and being busy with friends and family visits, I was happy, secure and optimistic.

The boys were taking swimming lessons again and hating every minute of it. But, hey, I was a conscientious mother, and I thought I was doing it for their own good. When I look back, I see how much I thought I knew, and how little I really did know, especially it seems about my own children. Me, "Miss each child is an individual" couldn't seem to get it through her (do I have to say thick?) head, these boys of mine were different and it was okay.

So, what if they didn't swim at five or six? Couldn't they learn to swim later? Who wouldn't be miserable learning to swim in the very cold, Maine coastal waters? But oh no, not me. I was listening to my head and not my heart, and just as I had let Joshua cry when he was a baby so not to spoil him, I let my babies, no I didn't let them, I made them go to those swimming lessons every day. After all, I thought, not only was it for their own good, but if those other kids could do it, by God, so could mine.

Such arrogance out of such righteousness. Perhaps people shouldn't be parents until they are fifty or something. Does wisdom necessarily come with older age? No, I don't think so. It is only looking back, hindsight, that teaches lessons, at least that is how it works for me. If ever I am a grandparent, I hope I will be wise and gentle and patient and kind and loving. I like to think this is the kind of mother I was, but honestly, I know I wasn't. Perhaps I was like that some of the time, and I believe I was a good mother. I knew my job as a parent was the most important work I would ever have and have ever wanted. Yet I know there were times when I would have liked to run away.

My kids grew up knowing that as well, and yet I hope they remember I was the one who was always there for them. I always hoped they would grow up knowing they were loved, above all else they were loved, yes, and cherished by me. I may have failed in other ways, but I really hope I did not fail in this. I wonder why God entrusts these poor mortal little innocent children to fools like us. No course can ever prepare you, no experience except the experience of doing it, and for me it took three times to finally get it, if not all right, at least pretty good.

Parenting is the most difficult, complex, confusing and frustrating job you will ever have. At the same time, it is one of the most rewarding and fulfilling. The trick, no it isn't a trick, the treasures come in little ways, at odd, unexpected moments, little nuggets of joy and satisfaction that allow you to think perhaps you aren't doing such a bad job after all.

I thought I had an edge because I had been a teacher, and the lessons my own children taught me made me a better teacher. The teaching in many ways made me a better parent. For example, I knew about boundaries, long before that became a mainstream word. I knew about discipline and following through on your threats and keeping your promises.

I also knew about bribes, and I say here I believe in bribes, all right, some of you may call them "incentives." This may sound silly, but I use the term bribes in place of promise or incentive. Who doesn't like the idea of a reward for doing something? A job, a lesson, or something unpleasant is more pleasant with the promise of something delightful or nice at the end of it. I would advise you, however, to use threats and bribes very sparingly. I know how important it is, especially to a child, that promises once made must absolutely be kept.

I will say here in this one area of promises Stephen and I had a major difference of opinion. Actually, we had major differences on the entire matter of child rearing. I was the disciplinarian, the bad guy. My husband, on the other hand, used the laissez-faire method of childcare. He would make promises with abandon, not understanding that a promise to a child, to most people, is a sacred bond of trust. Stephen would make the promises, break them, often not keep his word and then expect the children to "understand." He had no idea what it was like to be a child, as apparently, he had never been allowed to be a child himself.

I believe I hated this above all, not keeping promises, but then I didn't drop my promises around like jellybeans at Easter. Of course, who do you think was left to explain, pick up the pieces, comfort two sad boys who had believed what their father said? This was not a legacy I chose to leave and yet here I was with what seemed to me at the time no choice. Co-dependency was not something people talked about in the early 70s. Nor was I aware of addictions and addicted behavior. I had a lot to learn.

In those days I felt like a single parent most of the time. To go to work and come home to a place where you could just forget everything else, dinner was either planned or on the table, I always felt this must be the easy way. Many men at the time could come home, put their feet up, not worry about dinner or schedules or a clean house or dishes or paying the bills or even the socialization for yourself and your family. Nope, a friend once said to me every woman needs a good wife. I have always felt there is much truth in that remark.

I believed my husband surely had a good wife. He was definitely king in the castle. The boys still fussed over him when he came home. Daddy's homecoming was still a big deal at the time, and now he was home more often than ever. At least his body was there. Ah, but his mind, that could be anywhere and usually was. Without knowing or understanding, I knew Stephen was not "all there" or here.

During my pregnancy that winter, Stephen and I directed another production for the PTA of Kennebunkport. We'd done a show each winter we'd lived there, and this would be our third. Stephen's experience in the theater made him a natural choice to direct the local PTA plays. There were always people who wanted to act and find fulfillment in amateur theater productions. It was nice for both of us because it was a way for us to get involved in the community and to meet people and feel part of a town at last. The first year we did "You Can't Take It With You." The winter of '71 we decided to do a more ambitious theatrical undertaking with a production of the musical "Bells Are Ringing."

I would suggest if you really want to get to know a community, get involved with the local theater group. The first year we did the PTA show we were astounded to discover how many people in the cast were cheating on their spouses. I continued to be so naive I thought a small town like Kennebunkport was like "Our Town," innocent and honest and simple. I couldn't have been more wrong. People were cheating on one another at what to me was an alarming and disarming rate. Once again, I wondered where we were and what we had gotten ourselves into.

Cheating seemed to be a way of life up there, like drinking. Now, I know winters are longer in Maine, but still... I don't get around so much anymore, so I don't have the knowledge of whether or not there are statistics available in the regard of affairs per capita, but in the early 70s it really did seem to be a way of life in this area of rural Maine.

Anyhow it made for some mighty tense moments on the set several nights. Stephen got involved when he discovered a couple backstage and the husband threatening the other man. Ironically, the cuckolded husband was having his own fling at the time.

During the second show, things among the cast were not as chaotic. "Bells Are Ringing" was a labor of love for almost all of us who were involved in the production. We had a great music director and so many wonderful voices. Our leads were strong with experience in both music and theater. We believed this would be our last and best show. As I was pregnant now, the late nights got to be more difficult for me. Some nights we'd take the boys with us to rehearsal, and other nights we were lucky to have a babysitter the boys liked and who in turn enjoyed them. By now, Joshua and Noah were very comfortable with all their babysitters, and I felt lucky to have such reliable girls.

When the boys did come with us to rehearsals they used to love to get on stage and perform. Their big number was Ernie and Bert. Both boys were avid TV fans and Sesame Street was their most favorite of all. They knew Ernie and Bert's routines and would switch roles at will. We had two performers on our hands, after all, how could they not be?

It was nice for me to be out doing the show with Stephen as I was home all day with the boys, chauffeuring and cooking and cleaning and doing all the household chores. Doing the show was a nice change of pace and necessary for me to share something with Stephen that he loved. Not being left out or left behind was very important to me. I also liked the people and enjoyed the challenge of making a show come together. Stephen was an excellent director and I was his assistant. Even then I had ideas of my own and would frequently make suggestions, some of which he would accept, but mostly everything went his way.

I love the music in "Bells" and that old, buried part of me that had wanted to be a musical star would rise up from my heart to my throat and stay there. Why wasn't I performing? Fear. I was quite simply afraid, afraid to be bad, afraid I was no good after all. No, I thought better for me to sit on the sidelines, in the background. And the sidelines, the background is where I would spend most of my married years.

I never fully realized how much I resented the role. Yes, all those years of being the "supportive" wife, the good mother, doing what I had to do, should do, felt compelled to do out of necessity, made me one angry lady inside. I didn't even know how angry I really was. After all, if I didn't do it, who would? And then, what would happen? I carried co-dependency to an art form, except I didn't know what I was doing. I was doing what I'd been taught to do, and that was to do what everyone expected of me. What exactly was expected of me, and by whom? I was expected to be perfect, by everyone including myself. I simply did not know any other way to be.

I had spent my life for the most part being a good girl, doing the right thing. The few times I had rebelled, and I could count them, what had happened? Something tragic, or so it seemed to me. Then I would go back to being responsible, to putting my own dreams on hold. "On hold," I'd been on hold and would continue to be for another twenty years.

But in the winter of 1971 and in the early months of 1972, I did not question my life or my husband or my future. I was pregnant, busy, and I thought fulfilled. I had two beautiful sons; Noah would soon be five and going to school half days; Josh would be seven and in the second grade. This new baby would be special and precious, and even though the timetable was to set back our future, I was content.

My concern at the time was for the baby to be healthy and strong. I was thirty-four years old and scared I was too old to have a healthy baby. I think I read too much. But Dr. Buell quoted me statistics that cheered me, and another friend who had five healthy children said, "Look at them. Your baby will be fine, too."

There was a terrible blizzard the night of the first show, naturally this affected our audience. We kept some people from the cast overnight at our house. That was our best show ever with no audience to see and appreciate it. Even though we were snowed in, the show went on as scheduled. By now I was so big and so tired I just wanted the whole thing over with, the show and the baby. I felt so badly for all of us involved, especially the actors and singers who had worked so hard.

What could be worse than to give a show and not have anyone come to see it and applaud? It was like planning the biggest party only to have no one show up. I decided this would indeed be our final show, and to my surprise, Stephen agreed. It was disheartening to work so long and so hard for so little reward, and I don't mean money. Joshua and Noah were complaining about having babysitters "all the time" and our being gone so much, nights and weekends. I think the boys and I longed for a "normal" life, a routine that would include some fun and play and relaxation, not just work.

I was restless, very big, and, I thought, ugly. The last month of pregnancy, especially a third pregnancy, is not beautiful, or at least it wasn't for me. This baby was not like the boys had been. I was used to being early; this baby was not early. She wasn't even on time. "Late? What you expect me to carry you around for more than nine months? We'll see about that!"

I needed the baby to be born. All those remarks: "What? You still haven't had that baby?" or "When are you finally going to have that baby? It seems like you've been pregnant forever." Tell me about it! Did people think I was keeping it in for fun?

Stephen was hoping for a girl. I was afraid of having a girl because I was worried we wouldn't get along, that it would be like my mother and me. Yet I was just as concerned if we had another boy. I could not imagine what it would be like for a boy to have to compete with his two older brothers. And compete I was sure he'd have to. My sons always seemed to have some sort of sibling rivalry going on. I must say I never understood it, wasn't happy about it, but accepted the fact that it was.

I remember before Noah was born, I was concerned I wouldn't be able to love him enough, not love him like I loved Joshua. Isn't it funny the things that go through your mind during those nine months? "Let's see, what can we worry about today?" As if worrying was really going to help. Yet for some of us, when we worry, we actually believe we are accomplishing something. Hey, I'm only human and more so when I was pregnant apparently.

As soon as I saw Noah, there was no doubt in my mind

I had plenty of love to go around. Finally, I understood the concept of the heart expanding, and the heart expands the more people you love and have to love. Any doubt, any fear vanished even before the moment I saw him. As I watched him being delivered, I felt so blessed and so lucky to have another someone to love.

If there are parents out there who are afraid to have another child because they think they may not be able to love him or her, trust me on this one, the heart grows and so do you. I think perhaps because of my own childhood of feeling unloved and unlovable, I thought love was like a big pie, and there wasn't always enough to go around. I have discovered over the years this may not be such an unusual belief. Why that is, I can't say, but it surely must be rooted from a lack of something in childhood, and I don't mean a lack of toys or clothes or material goods.

That was my anxiety with Noah. Now I was afraid of having either a boy or a girl as I could foresee problems either way. Mostly my concern was for a healthy baby, and as for the rest, I'd cope the best way I could. I knew I'd love this baby as much as I loved Joshua and Noah. At least I knew that much.

St. Patrick's Day, 1972. I had an appointment with Dr. Buell. Already two weeks late, I was sure he'd send me across the street to the hospital that day. I was so eager to have my baby. "Nope, not yet," he said. "I'll see you next week."

"What?" I shrieked inside myself. "Oh, no, not another week." I was so distraught and upset I went to Dunkin' Donuts and had coffee and a big sweet roll. "I'm fat enough already, what's the difference?" And besides, as some of you women may recall, after getting weighed at the doctor's office, sometimes you had a small binge after. After all, you had sacrificed all week to get on that scale.

I went home and cried and cried. That night I was so mad. I walked around the house in a rage, up and down the stairs, over and over and over. All the while saying to this baby inside of me, "There is no way I am going to carry you around for another week. You will be born now. I'll make you come out if I have to walk around all night." Around and around the house I went, and up and down. I would not sit still.

Now this may have no scientific basis at all, remember I'm the girl who flunked several of her science courses (all right, I did pass a couple), but I swear all that anger and walking around must have helped. My beautiful baby girl was born the very next day!

On March 18, 1972 I was awakened by sharp contractions. Hey, I'd had two children, so I knew a contraction when I felt it. Believe me, ladies, there must be very few women as ignorant of the natural childbirth routine as I was. However, with this third one, I was finally smart. I got out of bed, walked around a little, went downstairs and started to time the contractions. Oh, good, they were steady but far enough apart, so I didn't have to wake anyone yet.

I sat in my rocking chair and smiled and felt very smart and wise and happy. I had made this baby pay attention to me. Finally, about 7:30 A.M. I woke Stephen who then got the boys dressed and ready to go to our friends' house. My, my, I felt so civilized. It was a Saturday, which was convenient. Stephen was home. Our friends and their children were all home, so we went to their house and all of us sat around and timed my contractions together. How pleasant it all was. Even my contractions weren't as painful as I remembered them.

About noontime the contractions were close enough to call the doctor and Stephen drove me to the hospital. This time he was going to stay with me. He had no excuses, no work to go to, the boys were taken care of and now he'd have to stay with me. Wow!

I asked the nurse if Stephen could come into the labor room with me. "Oh, yes," she said. "Just as soon as we have you all prepped." I was in heaven, well not exactly heaven, but at least I knew I wasn't going to be alone this time. Maybe that is why everything went so well. Just as soon as Stephen got into the labor room with me, my water broke and I could feel the baby wanting to come out, and oh boy, did I want this baby now. Stephen was scooted out, the doctor was called and the nurse kept telling me, "Don't push." Easy for her to say.

I was wheeled into the delivery room, saw Dr. Buell's smiling face, the lights and all the activity, and suddenly for me, lights out. "Hey, wait a minute, we didn't talk about this." It wasn't long though because I saw them cleaning the baby and everyone in the room was laughing and giggling. Did I miss something? Dr. Buell was laughing so I knew everything was all right. My fears, as usual, had been unfounded. "You have a beautiful baby girl," he announced.

"Have you told Stephen?"

"No. I thought you'd want to do that."

"Oh, no, you tell him, Dr. Buell. He'll like that. This is the first time he's even been in the hospital."

When I was wheeled out, Stephen greeted me as if I had given him the best gift of all, a little girl. We were both excited and happy. He called the boys to tell them they had a sister. Both Joshua and Noah expressed some disappointment at first because they wanted a brother. Later they assured me it was "okay that she's a girl."

This girl was born with a smile; I have always said that. I swear she smiled at me as soon as she was in my arms. I held her and I knew she and I would get along just fine; we wouldn't be like my mother and me. My heart grew once more, and I blessed God for giving us this beautiful baby girl.

I had decided on a girl's name many years ago. A book I'd read by Evan Hunter was the first time I had seen the name Gillian. I loved the name and the character and kept the name in the back of my mind for many years. I pronounced it with the hard G and told Stephen this was the name I chose. He wasn't sure he liked it all that much, but I would not change my mind. After all, I reminded him, I'd given in on Noah. He could choose the middle name. He thought about Amy, and then as he looked at Gillian he said, "Joy. Because she's made me so happy." So, Gillian Joy Hrehovcik it was.

Now, do you think my mother liked this name? Even though I told her it came from a book by one of her favorite authors, she gave me grief. "Where did you get a name like that?" I told her again. When she visited me later in the week at the hospital, she was so disagreeable about the baby's name, I was ready to punch her and throw her out of my room if she continued. When she finally told her friends and they said they liked it, she decided the name was all right.

Once again, I made a mental note to myself: when my children have children, no matter what name they choose, I will say I love it, how wonderful. More than that I will love all children's names when told by their parents.

Gillian took to the breast as naturally as she seemed to take to life. She fed, she slept, she smiled and was a delight to me and all the nurses. For a couple of days, she was the only girl in the nursery so she was always preened and pretty. They loved her and so did I.

Meanwhile, an acquaintance of ours who had come to the hospital right after us, had a baby boy. Sadly, he was born with Down Syndrome. I was so sad for her as she was about my age and this was also her third baby. She had two other boys about the same ages as Joshua and Noah. When I went to visit with her, she cried, "I never thought anything would go wrong; I never even thought about it." I couldn't help thinking how I had fretted about such a possibility and now I had the perfect baby and this poor woman had the sick one.

During my stay at the hospital the boys would send me notes. I could also see them in the hallway outside the maternity ward. They were so precious and so dear to me and so excited, but mostly they wanted Mommy to come home. I would send them little treats and notes in return.

My niece, Lorrie, who was only fifteen at the time, came up to Maine to stay with the boys and take care of them while I was in the hospital. It wouldn't have mattered if they'd had maternity leaves for fathers at the time, because it simply would not have occurred to Stephen to stay home and take care of his sons.

I have always thought how nice it was of Lorrie to do that with her cousins, and I know it was a good experience for her. Stephen told me he'd take a week off from work as soon as I got home. He assured me he'd take care of the children and help me adjust to the idea of having three children now.

I believed him and trusted him to be good to his word. I still had a lot to learn, but there were things I would have preferred not to learn at all.

Another sad event happened that year. My brother and his wife were expecting their first baby. Lorrie was of course Louis' by his first marriage. When my sister-in-law held Gillian, I could see how happy she was to be having a child of her own at last. After being married for seven years their first child was due in September. Carol was thirty-five and this was her first pregnancy.

She carried to term, but the last week before her due date, the doctor knew something was wrong. There was no heartbeat, and she delivered a still born baby boy. She never got pregnant again and there would be no children. Before his wife came home from the hospital, Louis and his friends cleared out all the signs that a baby had been expected there. Since Carol had a shower prior to the due date, there were a lot of presents and baby furniture and clothes, and Louis and his friends just took them all away.

In a rare moment of confidence, my sister-in-law told me how badly she felt they had done that. She said she would have liked to do it herself because it would have helped her grieve.

Here I was once more, Miss Worrywart, and I had three beautiful children, and people I knew were having unfortunate and terribly painful experiences. I don't know whether or not I felt guilty because I was so lucky. I don't know what I felt. I was sorry it had to happen to anyone, but perhaps like any survivor I was, at the same time, glad it wasn't me. Why it has to happen at all, only God knows, and do you think one day we'll know the reason? Is there a reason do you think? I used to believe there was a reason for everything, but as the years go on, I am less inclined to believe that.

CHAPTER 12

Marriage Ain't No Picnic

During my pregnancy Stephen and I had been hoping to buy or build a house. I wasn't sure how we could afford this without the added income of my salary. Stephen, as usual, had enough confidence for us both. I assumed he knew what he was doing, and I wanted to believe in him. Also, I knew I wanted a home of our own very much and thought if I just went along, everything would work out.

Somehow my husband convinced one of our local banks to grant us a mortgage to build a house, using what was then called "sweat equity." In other words, his work on the project would qualify as the down payment. We found a nice piece of property in Kennebunkport that was reasonably priced in a neighborhood with only four other houses. Building a house seemed more economical at the time than buying a house for the same money. This way we'd have a house the way we wanted it, no tearing apart and building up again.

The year 1972 was a big year for the Hrehovcik family. We had a new baby and made the decision to build a house. Stephen was going to work with the builders and subcontracting the work, at the same time he'd be working full time at the paper. Both boys would be attending the Consolidated School, Noah in kindergarten and Joshua in the second grade. This little school was as close as you could get to a country school, at least in 1972. I liked the school, the administrators, and the teachers. Since I had substituted in all the schools in the district, I had selected this school for our children, and so the decision was made to build in Kennebunkport.

And build we did, in spite of every obstacle and all the events that followed. Building a house together is very exciting and emotionally tumultuous. We heard stories of couples getting divorced while building a house together. I believe it. Things went wrong from the very beginning.

We'd seen other houses the builder had completed, and although the designs were not exactly prefabricated in the old-fashioned sense, these homes were pre-built in a factory and then assembled on the site. We'd had a tour of the factory and been very impressed with the quality of the workmanship and the efficiency of the entire operation.

Stephen was to contract for the plumbing, electric, the land preparation, the interior and the finish work, most of which he planned to do himself. It sounds good, doesn't it? Reasonable. Except nothing fell into place as planned.

We had worked together on the design of the house and had fun and shared ideas and even managed to compromise. He wanted a gambrel roof, well, I didn't know a gambrel roof from any other roof until he drew it for me. Aha. He then went on to explain this particular roof line had no lost space, so it was more efficient.

All right, although I personally always liked a Cape style house. I agreed none the less and we worked on the interior design together. We made compromises as you always do for the sake of money, but generally we had a wonderful time planning our dream home. And I, who often had no faith in the future, believed things would get better as time went on. Later we could add to the house as our situation improved.

After Gillian was born in March, the spring of '72 slowly arrived. Stephen and I and the children, baby included, would drive to the property and begin to clear the land. Stephen would cut the trees with his newly acquired chain saw, and the boys and I would clear away the brush. We had fun, some of us. Often Noah would stay by the car or in it with the baby. He was afraid of most bugs, and there were plenty there. We worked hard clearing and cutting, but we didn't mind because we were working together for a dream we shared.

Gillian was a good baby and a happy girl, but she didn't like to sleep very much. I always said she was sociable and didn't want to miss anything. She especially loved being up late into the night, which actually was all right since she would sleep later in the morning. I was used to sleeping babies and nap-takers. The boys still took naps or at least I'd send them to their rooms for quiet time. I confess this was more for me than for them, but I needed that time to myself. They would play quietly and more often than not fall asleep anyhow.

Although Gillian was a reluctant napper, I enjoyed her later mornings. I was tired all the time in those days – three small children, building and planning a house and now getting ready to move out of the red house for the summer. Stephen who had "promised" me he'd take a week off after the baby was born, somehow never managed to take off even a day. I came home from the hospital, my niece left the same day, and Stephen was gone all afternoon. I never saw him again until six o'clock. Something he "had to do at work," he told me.

Meanwhile there were two hungry boys to feed, a baby to nurse, and no one around to help. I was still suffering from hemorrhoids after childbirth. Even though Gillian was my easiest birth, she was also my biggest baby. Having hemorrhoids is not a glamorous affliction, and yet I tell you, it is so painful. I spent most of my hospital stay in the sitz bath. Whew, saved my ass, literally.

Back at home I was still hurting, but managed, martyr that I was then, to make supper that night. By the time Stephen finally came home, supper was on the table. The boys and I were eating, and I was in a fury. I'm sure I cried, even though I know I was supposed to be calm for the sake of the children. I just couldn't believe he would let me down like this again. I still believed the man when he made me promises.

The next day and the rest of the week he went off to work as usual, and I'd lay on the couch when I wasn't feeding someone and cry or try not to cry. When would I ever be able to count on Stephen? Would he ever be there for me and the children? Could I ever believe anything he said to me again? I was sad and I was angry. I felt cheated and abandoned. Again.

At the same time, my husband was trying to do it all outside the family. He was finalizing the plans for our house, working full time at the paper, and going to the land to get it ready for the building. Since he was subcontracting, he was constantly calling plumbers and electricians and the town for this permit or that test. Do you think we were both young and foolish? Yes.

We were young and healthy and believed we could accomplish anything with hard work and determination. I believed everything would get better. After all I was brought up to believe that hard work leads to an easier, better life. Everyone struggled in the first years of marriage, I thought, but hard work brought results and rewards. I'd never heard of work for work's sake. I still had a lot to learn about my husband and his family and the way he was raised. What he had learned as a child and what I had learned as a child, well, we may as well have come from two different planets, and this was long before Dr. Gray's Venus and Mars theory!

I didn't mind working to make the dream of our own house come true. After all the moving we had done and now with three children, my need to nest was very strong, even overwhelming. I wanted a home of our own. I was willing to do whatever needed to be done to attain this goal. We still needed a place to live in the meantime. The house at the beach was not available that summer; I suppose we waited too long to call the landlord.

Secretly we both hoped we could stay in the red house, but that too was rented for the summer. We asked again about buying it, but once more the landlord told us he'd never sell. A year after we moved into our house in Kennebunkport, the red house was sold with the furniture and all for $42,000. My heart sank. That had been the house of my dreams; if only we had waited, if only, if only...

We did a lot of waiting that spring and summer and fall of 1972. I've said everything went wrong and it did. It began with the land. We discovered two horrible facts: one was the ledge that needed to be blasted away, and second was a natural spring which ran underneath the edge of our property. Ledge and water. We had not budgeted for these problems.

The two fellows responsible for the land preparation and excavating were new in the business and just getting started. They were nice guys all right, but they weren't very dependable. Truthfully, they were not reliable at all. Sometimes a week or more would go by and there wouldn't be any work done. Nothing. Then they discovered the ledge problem and there was much chin holding over that. Next was the spring, and there was more nodding and looking and pondering. Two hostile elements rooted in our dream land.

Then came the perc tests, endless perc tests, and our land kept failing to a point where there was a question whether or not this land was buildable. What the heck is a perc test? And who knew about it anyhow? After all these years I don't believe I could explain it to you. Only a word of caution: before you buy any property, be sure the perc test has already been done and passed!

So much money we had not accounted for was going not quite down the drain (remember we hadn't passed that darn perc test yet). Yes, our money was dwindling away on land fill and dynamite and still we had not even a road or hole big enough for a foundation. When a hole was finally dug, we'd drive by each day expecting to see a foundation. No, nothing but a hole, a big hole, and I thought about how all our money was going into it.

At last we managed to get a summer rental at Hills Beach in Biddeford. The cottage was right on the water, and normally I would have been thrilled to be there, but this was a letdown for me. The house itself was dirty and old, and I couldn't get the smell out, the mustiness clung to everything. Still we were lucky, and I knew it, and the price was fair.

There was a lot of commuting and running back and forth that summer. The boys were happy. They didn't have to take swimming lessons that year, and we had a lot of company. Sometimes we would dig for clams right in front of the house. There was an island where the gulls nested, and we could walk there at low tide. There were many friendly people at Hills Beach, and most of the time the boys and I and Gillian were busy and happy.

All of a sudden, out of the blue it seemed to me, as I felt all our hard work was coming together, Stephen made an announcement. He wanted to quit his job and start a theater of his own. Was he joking? Where had this come from? Was he serious? What about the house? What about the baby and the boys? What about all our plans and what we'd been working so hard to accomplish?

"We can still finish the house," said Stephen, the dreamer.

"How can we do that if you have no job?" asked Carol, the realist. We'd argue and argue, and I was baffled, puzzled, and confused. What happened? Had I missed something? What should I do? What did I want to do?

Believe me, it wasn't often I would ask myself that question. "What do *I* want to do?" No, more often it was "what do I *need* to do?" Most of my actions were reactions. I would respond to whatever crisis arose at the time and there was always a crisis. This was another one of those times I didn't see it coming, whatever "it" was. There was no way I could have foreseen this turn of events. I was paddling my canoe as fast as I could while he was out on the open sea in a motor launch.

Finally, I said, "I can go back to work. I'm sure I can get a job teaching again. But I won't go back to work so you can start a theater. If you want to start a theater, you'll have to do it without me." This made Stephen furious, I mean furious. We spent the next days and nights in constant battle.

I was definite this time. The new baby made me strong and I knew what I had to do to take care of my kids. "I want no part of it this time, what you do is up to you. I feel I've been more than supportive to you and the theater. We've just had a new baby and we're in the middle of building a house. I'm not willing to sacrifice myself or the kids anymore so you can chase some rainbow. You do what you have to and so will I." I meant it and he knew I did.

He railed against me as he never had before. This was the first time in our seven years of marriage I had said no to him, and he didn't like it. It was a dreadful time and I wasn't sure what he was going to do. I did know I would survive and take care of my three children with or without him. In my heart I felt I had given him enough chances to try the theater and I wasn't willing to do it anymore. I had too many responsibilities.

So did he, but he didn't think about anyone but himself, it seemed to me. Years later we were in therapy together and the doctor asked each of us what was the worst time in our marriage. No contest for me. "New Jersey" was my instant reply. Stephen's answer surprised and stunned me. He reported this time when he'd wanted to start his own theater and I said no, he'd been "emasculated," he told the doctor. I remember staring at him in disbelief. Of all the times, and there were worse to come, this was the worst to him.

He decided at last that summer perhaps this wasn't the best time for him to start a theater, but in my heart I knew he would never forgive me; I'd pay for this. Of course, he could have done it on his own, as I was perfectly capable at the time of taking care of myself and the kids. I could have worked, gotten my sitter back and managed to get along. The kids and I were used to being alone so much of the time, what would it matter after all?

I felt guilty about this decision for years and it would reflect many other decisions I would make later or more to the point, not make. Out of guilt of being firm this one time, and even though I know what I did was right, I felt so badly for having hurt Stephen that I went along with all of his other schemes and dreams. There were more to follow.

It was always his dreams and almost never, ever mine. My dreams for myself or for the family didn't matter, only his dreams mattered. I think sometimes I am a very simple person. I had my priorities in line. I was a mother with two little boys and a new baby girl. My primary goal was to take care of them, love them, and hopefully provide them with some security, emotionally and financially. This didn't appear to be a goal shared by my husband. Truthfully, I believed he didn't even think about it. Sadly, I would fail to provide the security I hoped to give my children. I did try awfully hard though, and I think they will acknowledge that now.

We had more bad news that summer of 1972. We had no phone at the cottage that year. I'd walk to the store a few blocks away to the pay phone, when it was working. One day I had to call Stephen about something, luckily the phone was in operation that day. He told me about Bob Hilliard, in an almost off hand sort of way. "Lynne called me this morning. Bob died of a heart attack last night."

"What?" I shrieked into the phone. "Bob died and you didn't come home to tell me about it? I should be calling her; she'll wonder where I am. How could you not have told me right away? He was our friend."

To this day I don't believe Lynne has ever forgiven Stephen for not telling me or being there for her. After all, Bob was the reason Stephen had finally decided to marry me. He was the closest to a best friend Stephen would ever have. Yet he couldn't take time out from his work to come home and tell me Bob was dead. Stephen wouldn't allow me to be with my best friend in her time of need. He was taking away all my independence. I was not my own person anymore; my life was out of my control and I was scared.

At last I was able to reach Lynne, and she was surprised to learn I had only just now heard the news. I made arrangements to spend some time with her after the funeral. I wondered how Lynne could endure so much loss. Her two little girls and her first husband and now Bob, her second husband. At least she still had her son Michael.

It turned out their marriage had been in jeopardy from his gambling and an inconsequential affair Lynne had with one of her colleagues. Stephen and I had gone there a few months earlier to calm Bob, he was explosive to the point of being dangerous. Now he was dead, and she discovered the extent of his gambling. It wasn't just horses and cards, he'd turned to bigger stakes in real estate, at huge losses. Also, she learned her diamond ring was really zircon.

What right, I thought, do I have to complain when this poor woman has lost so much? Next to Lynne, I felt like the luckiest person alive. I'd better start counting my blessings and stop complaining. And so, I counted my blessings: 1) Joshua, 2) Noah, and 3) Gillian. Was Stephen a blessing or a curse? Had I made a very big mistake? I began to consider the possibility of leaving him. Where would I go and what would I do? My resolve of a short time ago vanished as I fought with my feelings for him. I still loved him dearly, but I had so many doubts at the same time. Was love enough to hold two people together?

I had many questions, plenty of doubts and no answers. To whom could I turn? Who could help me? Not my parents, not Stephen's family, not even my friends, friends that I seemed to be losing one by one. I felt so alone, worse than alone.

Marriage was not working out for me, at least not the way I had hoped and dreamed and planned. I was married and happy to be so. I loved my children more than life itself. At the same time, I knew something was missing, and what was missing was a man dedicated to me and to his children.

There were signs from both boys that the strain between Stephen and me was taking a toll on them. But I didn't know how to read the signs. I was so busy just trying to get through each day, each week, working to get our new house finished. I thought once we moved into our own house and didn't have to move so often, the boys would feel more secure. Gillian fortunately was still a baby.

At this time, I noticed Joshua speaking in different voices. I didn't pay much attention to it at first, but I thought it was odd. Sometimes I'd kid him about not knowing which voice was the real Joshua. That summer he wrote a letter to the Jackson Five, his favorite music group at the time, and invited them to our house at Hills Beach. He didn't expect they would come, but he invited them anyhow.

Noah, on the other hand, had what he called a "magic lightning finger." Each time we passed the water tank in Biddeford he'd proclaim, "There's my space rocket. I am going to space to get away from all of these people." Stephen made him a lightning bolt to put on his finger. Noah would wear that, suck his thumb, and still hold onto his blue blanket.

Gillian Joy, aptly named since she was such a joy for all of us at the time, would sit in her swing at the beach for hours watching the ocean. She was very content there. I have often wondered if this contributed to her love of the water. She is the only water baby I have, always has loved the water and is one of the few people I know who dives into the cold Maine ocean, jumps up and invites you. "It's not that bad." Brrrrr to me, but not so for Gillian.

Our house was moving along slowly, slowly. We were at the site all our free time. Sometimes the boys would rebel and beg for time to play or go out for some fun. Fun was fast becoming the "f" word in our house. We still joke about that, fun being the "f" word. But it was the summer of 1972, Joshua was seven years old and Noah was five, naturally they wanted to play, but Stephen and I were so focused on the new house, we had little time to play.

Bob Hilliard had died, and I was trying to be a good friend to Lynne, as good as I could be living two states away. She was making me look at Stephen in a new way, a way I didn't want to look, but I couldn't explain his behavior to her any more than I could understand it myself. I knew something was wrong, something was missing, but Stephen was such a good man overall, I thought it had to be something in me. There must be something in me that expected too much or asked for more than I should. As usual I was confused but relieved we had averted the theater crisis for now.

With the arrival of the fall of '72, Joshua was entering the second grade and Noah was in kindergarten. Since we could no longer stay at the Hills Beach cottage, we were once again looking for a place to live, temporarily, until our house was finished. At the rate the men worked, or as more often was the case, didn't work, this "temporarily" could be months.

We needed to be in Kennebunkport near the bus route and hopefully close to the new house so I could check on the progress, or lack of. This time we were fortunate indeed to find an apartment literally around the corner from the new house. It was large enough for the family, the bus would stop for Joshua and Noah right in front, and I could walk to the house with the baby.

By now the shell was up, and I eagerly walked down the street to see it. "My God, the house is orange!" It was the color of a pumpkin. I was horrified and even embarrassed. I mean, how would you feel if one of your neighbors erected an enormous pumpkin house? This was not the color we had chosen.

As I walked closer to the house, not only was the color horrible, yes, it was horrible indeed, but there was another glaring problem to me. Contrary to our plans and my expressed instructions, the front door was in the middle. I wanted the door on the side of the house to prepare for the addition I had planned in my mind. Now there would be no balance.

More disappointment followed when I went inside the house. The living room was so small because the builders had neglected to follow the plan. Was anything ever going to be right with this house? Our dream had become closer to a nightmare. Nothing we planned or envisioned came close to this pumpkin patch.

There was however one part of the house which was mine and went ahead as planned. The kitchen. The carpenter and I worked together every day discussing possibilities and choices. I had collected pictures from magazines and had many ideas. He had built many kitchens, and together we made the kitchen of the house the one room that was perfect.

I say this kitchen was perfect because of the efficient workspace, the many cabinets, the window and shelf above the sink overlooking the woods outside, my range top, built-in oven, and the best piece of all, a roll out butcher block and cabinet. I have dreams about this kitchen even now. I loved it that much.

I have a new house now as we were brave enough, (or foolish enough) to build another house. Only this time we knew what we were doing, and the house turned out exactly as we had planned. I say it takes two houses to do it right. In fact, we had such a great experience this time we are considering building a third house. No, I think we will quit while we are ahead.

It is difficult for me to look back on this time of our lives. The old house as we now call it, came to represent everything that was wrong with our marriage and in our lives together at this time. There was no end to the work we had before us, and soon Stephen's "sweat" equity became not only sweat but tears, grief, misery, depression and unhappiness.

Because we were doing all the inside work ourselves, every spare moment was spent working on the house. I didn't mind at first because I knew this was the only way we could ever have a house of our own. At the same time, I felt there must be an easier way. I was thirty-four years old, and although I was still young, the toll of having three young children, including a new baby, moving three times in the past three months with one more move yet to come, exhausted me.

I wish I had been happier with the house itself. It was ours and I felt lucky to have it, no matter how much work was involved. I continued to do it all because I had to. It was simple. I painted and stained all of the kitchen cabinets. I had no idea the detail work involved, "inside, outside, all around the cabinets." I didn't think the job would ever end. I didn't hate doing it, it just seemed endless. There certainly was satisfaction when I finished at last. I vowed I would never paint another thing after that kitchen.

Here was how it went: I started to paint and the baby cried, I put the brush down, comforted the baby, started again and Noah was home from kindergarten, brush down again and I made lunch and talked about his morning, hoping the baby would nap along with Noah. I would start again and then it was time for Joshua to get off the bus. Now it was snack time and play time and I would start again but soon it was time to get supper ready and still I tried to accomplish something more.

This went on and on and on. I tried so hard to be all things to all my family, not to ignore anyone or any duties I needed doing. We moved into the house on Columbus Day, 1972. The water company hooked up our pipes that morning and we moved out of the apartment that afternoon. Now I could work at the house all day and all night. How convenient.

Our decor was very avant-garde, one of a kind. Stephen's table saw was the central theme in our living room in combination with plastic that draped the side wall where the fireplace would be one day. There were no doors anywhere inside as my husband intended to build them all. Of course, we had no rugs or linoleum but the natural unfinished look of particle board. Sheet rock cried out from all the walls "paint me, paint me."

Mattresses placed for the efficient use of space in the den and kitchen supplied our resting places. Gillian's crib was the only piece of furniture we owned at the time. Everywhere you looked there was work to be done, and no one to do it but Stephen and me.

Those were the days when I believed I could do anything. Those were also the days when I discovered I could not. One thing I couldn't do was use the power saw. I would grab that saw and the vibration would make my hand shake so hard I couldn't hang on. I wasn't much better with a hammer either. Oh, sure, I could hammer all right, but sometimes (all right, often) I would miss the nail completely. More often than not I'd have to pull the damn nail out and start all over again. So, I was left with all the painting and staining. I could do that, as long as I didn't have to hurry, speed was not my long suit.

I was also in charge of childcare, grocery shopping, cooking, cleaning up work areas before and after, laundry, and the general gofer – "go fer this, go fer that." Time for myself? Forget it. I couldn't even go to the bathroom alone. Since there was only a sheet on the door, one of the kids would always be coming in to "keep me company." I admit it was awfully cute. Stephen would get home from work, change clothes, eat and work on the house. Such was life in the fast lane at Maplewood Drive in the fall of 1972.

CHAPTER 13

A Mixed Bag of Bedlam and Blessings

While we were in the process of building our house, new neighbors moved up the street. They were a couple about our age with three little girls, almost the same ages as our boys. The kids and I went up the street to meet them. Her name was Nancy and her husband, Art, was the new superintendent of schools in the district. They'd moved into the big house at the top of the hill. What a lovely home it was. There were rugs and curtains and floors and wallpaper and doors and everything! Even the basement was finished. "So, this is the way my house is going to look some day?" Sure. Still Nancy had plans to decorate the house to suit her style and taste.

I would talk about my plans and visions for my house and sigh. Nancy would talk about her ideas and go out and buy. I couldn't imagine what it was like to talk about something and then actually do it. Didn't she have to talk about it forever and maybe one day she'd make the dream a reality?

Not at all. Nancy could do it all; she'd buy it and then do all the work herself. She painted, she papered, she planted, she entertained, she really did do it all. I was amazed and a little envious. I was jealous of her aptitude and enthusiasm for getting things done. She didn't wait for Art; she just did everything. I admired her a lot.

At this point, as I was beginning to feel less and less adequate, not knowing what to do next, thinking all this work was too overwhelming for me, I decided I didn't want to take any chances of getting pregnant again. One particularly bad day Gillian was so fussy and wouldn't stop crying, I called my husband at work and demanded he get a vasectomy. "Now?" he asked.

I was not laughing. "I'm not having any more children. I've tried all kinds of birth control and now it's up to you." He was able to calm me down, probably just by agreeing with me, whether he meant it or not. Just the thought that I wouldn't have any more children was a comfort to me.

I was scheduled for my appointment with Dr. Buell soon and Stephen agreed to come with me. Together we'd talk about the vasectomy and get the name of a good doctor. Understand Stephen agreed to this just for me, not because he wanted to do it. He always said he'd like to have five children. I thought he could have five when he stays home and takes care of them. No way, so vasectomy, hooray!

Aha. Once again, a plan B. As it turned out, my uterus had dropped, a prolapsed uterus it's called. Which means my uterus had fallen to a point where it was practically falling out of my vagina. "Didn't you feel it?" asked the good doctor.

I adored Dr. Buell, but I believe he was under the delusion I was as enchanted with the mechanisms of my body as he seemed to be. No. "Well, have you been tired a lot?" You bet.

He called Stephen into the office and as we were discussing my options, whether to lift the uterus or to get rid of it, I could see Stephen was so relieved he wouldn't have to have his vasectomy that he had missed everything the doctor said. I was sure all he heard was oh, good, not me, her. Whew. He swears this is not true. I still don't believe him.

I asked about each operation and what exactly was involved – time, cost, advantages, disadvantages, recuperation. Dr. Buell told me there was no significant difference in time or cost or danger whether we lifted or removed the uterus, except, then he added, "You won't have any more periods or be able to conceive again." Bingo! He said the magic words.

"Let's take it out." No more periods, no more danger of pregnancy. "Out, out damned uterus."

I was thirty-five at this time, I'd had my three children, and I knew, absolutely knew I did not want any more, so a hysterectomy was my choice. I do not recommend this of course as a method of birth control, but I can tell you very honestly, I have never regretted my decision, not even for a moment, not before, after or since.

I was lucky my operation was not complicated. I made sure I followed Dr. Buell's advice. He told me, "If you do what I tell you, you'll be fine for the rest of your life. If you don't follow my advice, you'll regret it for the rest of your life." His advice was to take six weeks to recover, this included no lifting, no vacuuming (break my heart), no heavy work, or driving.

Since I had my little girl who wasn't even a year old at the time, I would have to have someone come in to take care of her and the boys and the house, such as it was. In other words, we would have to pay somebody to do my work. On the other hand, I consoled myself with the knowledge that six weeks was such a short time in a lifetime. I know it was difficult for me to give up caring for everyone and everything, but being healthy was most important to me.

I am glad I did heed the doctor's advice and took the time and cared for myself. I have no idea what the instructions would be today after such an operation, but I am relieved I was fortunate. Dr. Buell later asked me if I could tell when I would be having a period, when I was ovulating. There he went again thinking I had some clinical interest in my body. I merely laughed and said, "No, I never think about it. Only when I walk down that aisle in the store and I smile because I don't need any of that stuff anymore." I can't even begin to tell you what a delight it was for me not to have a period anymore, not to worry about getting pregnant again, free to have sex anytime we wanted, without fear or anxiety. God, it certainly was a different time.

Just think of the paraphernalia we women had to endure during our periods at that time. Those thick napkins, the belts that dug into your skin and you swore everyone could see through your clothes. I often wondered what the women wore in the older days. How did they manage their periods? How about the Greeks and the Romans under those togas? How did they endure that time of the month? Did they use rags? Take to their beds? I wonder who even knew what this whole bleeding process was about?

Well, at least those days were over for me and I could wonder about all the women in history and in the future all I wanted.

Once again Stephen was not there for me. He was home with a cold, flat on his back in bed the entire week I was in the hospital. When he did manage to get out of bed to visit me, he ran out of gas on the highway, or he forgot the time and got there when visiting hours were over. The nurses must have felt badly either for him or for me, and they let him in that night.

I was crying, of course, and then he started to cry too. Instead of comforting me, I ended up comforting him. The important part of this to me was it was the first time I had ever seen my husband cry and it touched me very deeply. I was naturally softened by his tears. We'd been married eight years, and this was the first time Stephen had cried in front of me. I hoped it wouldn't be the last, but many years would pass before I'd see him cry again.

I never agreed with "men aren't supposed to cry." After all, what made them so special or so different they couldn't cry? Crying is a natural release the body established to help us deal with grief and pain. I thought it was strange Stephen never cried, but then I thought it was odd that he never got angry either. I remembered his mother and her "I never cry" badge of honor and thought perhaps this had something to do with it. Stephen was a funny person and could make people laugh, but I was discovering something else about my husband.

This man was funny, but he wasn't a lot of fun. You may think this a small and silly distinction but think again. Someone who is funny, makes you laugh, you automatically believe he is therefore fun. I was discovering Stephen didn't know how to have fun, how to relax, or how to play. Next to him, for whom work was the most important aspect of living, I felt like the laziest person in the world.

I would try to work as hard as he did, but I was of the school which believed first you worked and then you played. I was still waiting to play with Stephen. The only playing I did in those days was with the kids. For my husband, play was like having surgery, he'd put it off as much as he could, for as long as he could. When he did find some time to play, there was always a timer.

Work was his God, his Bible, his reason for living. I wondered further, if a man works so much, shouldn't there be some reward at the end of it? Shouldn't our lives be getting better financially? Wouldn't there be some progress in our lives we could see, like getting caught up or ahead to a place where we didn't have to work so hard all the time?

I was beginning to wonder when our lives would get better, easier, and concerned it might never be any different at all. The house was nowhere near finished, not one room completed at all. The big project this fall was for Stephen to build the fireplace. His father was a mason and Stephen had worked with him many summers; the fireplace was something he wanted to do himself.

The boys and I dug up rocks from the road in front of our house. Since the contractors had laid the wrong kind of road, huge rocks instead of the smaller pebble like stones, we got a beautiful field stone fireplace from it.

I will never forget the day Stephen sawed the big hole in the living room wall. He stood outside in the footing he had poured previously and was reading the book *How to Build Your Own Fireplace.*

"I thought you knew how," I shouted.

"I do," he replied, "just checking."

Talk about faith. Do you know what? He built that fireplace, almost single handedly. It took months and months of part-time work and a week here and there. Every weekend he worked and so the kids and I worked with him. We hauled all the rocks, mixed the cement, operated a pulley system Stephen had rigged to get the rocks to the top. Every time I walked down the road, I'd be looking down for more rocks, or the "perfect" rock. I have to catch myself today not to pick up rocks anymore. Stephen since then says, "I built a fireplace once, and I'll never do it again." He's right: he'll never do it again.

When he was finished at last, the fireplace looked wonderful, a great big fieldstone, friendly fireplace with a mantel made from wood my husband had picked up from the dump. Stephen had lovingly sanded and varnished and stained the wood, and now it hung in this place of honor. One thing I have always said about my husband is he is resourceful and yes, clever. He was always amazing me with his skills and abilities.

Stephen lit some papers to check the flow of the damper as the whole family stood around waiting to light our first fire. Suddenly I was afraid. "What if it's just beautiful but it doesn't work?"

My husband whose normal response to such a query would be "don't worry," looked at me and doubted himself for a moment, lit the paper and the wood and the smoke rose up the chimney, just like it was supposed to. We all clapped for relief and joy and out of pride for what our young, small family had done.

The date and the children's names were etched into the sides of the hearth beside ours. I assume they are there still, at least I like to think so. Just in case, Stephen confessed later, he put all the names at the top of the chimney as well. Perhaps one day in the far away future someone will see all our names and the date, 1973, and wonder what happened to the family who lived here? Were they a happy family? Where have they gone and what became of them? It's funny to think about the future because I really believed at the time, we were a happy family. With all the doubts, and pain and loneliness I still thought we were a happy family.

In spite of all the work there was yet to do on the house at Maplewood Drive, there were some good times too. All our neighbors were very friendly, and the kids had playmates on the street. The road was safe enough for them to be out sliding in the winter or building forts in the summer. There was even a small pond across the way to ice skate safely, and the woods were always available for exploring.

There was little league in the summer for the boys. Their team won the championship one year and they got to go to their first ever Red Sox game. One of the ironies of life happened many years later when Joshua went to work for one of the local firms. His former little league coach was the warehouse manager and Joshua worked with him there for a time. It really was a small community after all.

We became even friendlier and closer with the Hedberg family up the street as we began the most sociable period in our marriage. A tennis and swim club opened in Kennebunk and we sent the boys there for more swimming lessons; you can imagine their delight. Stephen and I played tennis every Sunday with three other couples. Life was good and bad at the same time.

I took a part-time job at the club, the Meadows, to help out with the bills and the escalating cost of working on the house. The idea was for me to work the hours when Stephen would be home to take care of the children, so we would save money on babysitters. That was the idea. The reality turned out to be something quite different.

The nights I worked when he was supposed to be home so I could get to work on time, there was always a phone call saying he'd be late. I'd take the kids with me and he'd come by the club later to pick them up and hopefully feed them and get them into bed. I was lucky they were all such good kids. For them the most fun was when Stephen would take them into the pool and play with them. He'd toss them around and they all loved it, even Joshua and Noah, but most especially Gillian.

The weekends were a little easier for me to get to work on time. I had only to get myself ready. I never liked it very much, leaving everyone at home, I always felt as if I were missing something. Still, I liked my job; I didn't have to think about anything when I got home, not like teaching, and the little money I made helped out.

Stephen would work on the house while I was gone and hopefully there'd be some surprise for me when I got home, like a completed door, or windowsill or molding. I remember he was making a door for the den and I looked forward to that door with great excitement. His vision was a door with an arc, and he spent one Saturday desperately trying to get the wood to bend.

All he accomplished this day was to break one piece of wood after another. He was very discouraged and so was I. "Let's just buy a door." No, no, he insisted he would make all the doors, but perhaps there'd be no arcs. At last there was a door on the upstairs bathroom, and this was soon followed by another door for the downstairs bath. Some privacy at last, somewhere, and even some progress. Sigh.

Perhaps Stephen and I were too hard on ourselves and each other. All we saw was the work that needed to be done, all that wasn't finished. We never took or gave credit for all the work we had accomplished. Two perfectionists, how could it be otherwise? I yearned for one room to be completely finished. I wanted to go there and say "Ah, peace at last." We lived in that house for eleven years and we never finished one room, not one.

Mr. Hrehovcik built us beautiful, wide brick steps outside with a planter on the side. Stephen and his father worked together for a week on the steps. I loved the steps and cherished the planter. Even though I still disliked his father, I thought it was very nice to have some of his work as part of our home and legacy.

I spent a little time with my mother-in-law, hoping to get to know her a little better. However, she spent most of her time outside working with "the men," mixing cement, pouring dirt, digging plants from the woods, and pouring scotch later in the day. "The men need a drink now," she would always say. I think she frequently enjoyed a drink along with them. Scotch was a "man's drink" according to my father-in-law. He announced this to my father one day when my father asked for a whiskey. This did not endear either man to the other.

I was involved with the kids and school and my part-time job and working as I could on the house. Nancy and I became good friends. I think we were best friends; that is until my husband decided to get involved in the district's education policies. He was going against Art and I was afraid Stephen's interference would damage my relationship with Nancy. Stephen assured me, "Don't worry." With those words I knew there was cause for immediate alarm, but I knew also there was nothing I could do to stop him.

My relationship with Nancy became awkward and strained for us both, and eventually Art forbid any of the Hrehovciks to come to the Hedberg house. Nancy had to be loyal to her husband, but I couldn't understand why she didn't tell him he was an ass and her friendships were her business and not his. I, on the other hand, had no trouble telling Stephen what I thought of his behavior.

I started at this time to do jigsaw puzzles to keep my hurt and unhappiness out of my mind. I blamed my husband for being so bullheaded and causing me to lose another friend. I was losing friendships at an alarming rate. Most of my old friends were no longer part of my life, and I wasn't sure whether it was me or them. I see now it was a combination of both. After all, I'd been single and available to come and go for so many years, but after I got married my life was really not my own, or at least so I thought. I had no knowledge at this time of a co-dependency issue.

After losing my friendship with Nancy and remembering all the other friends I'd lost along the way, I decided I would never again entrust my love or loyalty to another woman. I would not trust myself to have another best friend. I would always hold something back, just to protect myself. I'd been too open, too honest, too loyal, too trusting, and too vulnerable. Expecting my friends to be the same, I was wide open for disappointment.

I believe friendship is an absolute necessity for a woman. We talk the same language of course, but more than that, women have issues we just can't discuss with men, even husbands. There is a part of a woman only another woman can understand or share. I know I have always needed and even depended on the friendships I've shared with other women. I am sure in large part because of my family, where I never truly felt loved, I sought love and acceptance with girlfriends. They became my family, my support and my validation as a decent human being.

I have often said losing a friendship hurts more than breaking up with a man. After all, when you break up with your boyfriend you can always talk to your best friend and she'll share your pain and grief and then bolster your spirit. To whom do you turn when you break up with your best friend? Not to my husband surely. He shook his head and went on about his business. He had ruined my relationship with Nancy. I didn't care about Art one way or another, but I felt my friendship with Nancy should have been separate from Stephen and Art. She should have stood up to Art. I had a hard time with that, yet we all do what we have to do to survive. I learned later she had a lot of surviving to do with him.

It wasn't long before the Hedbergs moved from their house on the hill to one of the big houses on Summer Street in Kennebunk. This was a more prestigious address. I think if Art had been a woman, we would have called him a social climber. Fortunately for him he received instant status as the superintendent of schools. The Hedbergs and the Hrehovciks patched the friendship together later, but that's all it was, a patch. Never again would there be any trust or respect, only a tentativeness.

With Nancy's move to Summer Street, I felt the break between us was more than complete. She had recently finished redecorating her house, every room, every wall, every space had been decorated just as she chose, and now she was moving out to start all over again. I gave her a lot of credit, but she simply sighed. It was what Art wanted.

CHAPTER 14

Fear of Success vs. Fear of Failure

In 1977 Stephen had been at the paper for seven years, the longest he'd ever held a job either before or since we were married. I was starting to feel secure at last. (Oh, oh.) Gillian would start kindergarten in the fall, which meant all my children would be in school. We'd made some new friends and life was moving on. I wanted to write, and this seemed like my time at last.

My idea for a musical about the golden age of movies and Hollywood had me reading books and biographies of the most famous people of that era. This research led me to the theme of the story. Loosely based on the lives of Bette Davis, Joan Blondell and Hedy Lamarr, the story is about three women coming to Hollywood. They become friends, live together, all rise to stardom and take different paths, yet through it all they remain friends. Naturally one of them meets a tragic end, as our central heroine ponders the question: "Is it possible for a woman to have it all?"

I had more fun reading and writing about the movies. I couldn't write the actual music, but I wrote most of the lyrics and had music in my head for some of the songs. I could see it all in my head, the scenery, the set, the costumes, I could hear all the music, and visualize the dances. My musical would be wonderful. I was excited, eager, and not very confident naturally as I always doubted my ability, but I forged ahead, nonetheless. Broadway, I had decided needed a blockbuster musical.

Just as I was feeling secure and gaining confidence in my idea and my work, Stephen decided to quit his job at the *Star*. He came home one afternoon and announced his intentions to start his own advertising agency and work out of the house. At the time we had eleven dollars in the bank.

Panic does not begin to describe how I felt. Here we go again. Will I ever have any security with this man? Will we ever live a normal life? Will I ever get to follow my own dream? Feeling totally out of control, I did what I always had to do. I found a job and went to work. My dreams were on hold once more.

My concerns and anxieties were for my three children and how to take care of them. I worried about the practical things, like eating and paying the bills. Just as life looked as if it might be on an even keel, Stephen took me down that huge roller coaster dip and I never knew if we were going to come up or not. But I knew about survival, and those skills came forward then. I didn't like it, but I'd do "what I had to do." I was good at that after all.

"You do what you have to do." How many times has someone

told you that? I was brought up on it, to do the right thing, to be a good little girl, do what had to be done, and not to feel anger or resentment or whatever else I was feeling. "You shouldn't feel that way." How many times had I heard that one? I was still fighting my demons from childhood where I believed I was stupid, lazy and selfish. Naturally I did what I had to in order to survive, for my children to survive. Yet in my heart I knew life was more than survival.

And what did Carol do, what was the one thing she knew how to do? Teach. I was lucky. I got a job in a nearby high school working in the library, and I would be team teaching one English class. I thought this was going to be terrific. Except I wasn't really team teaching, I was a backup for this teacher, and I was usually on the bench.

I liked the high school kids. They were often funny and smart. You could have intelligent conversations or discussions with them. At the same time, I was hesitant about disciplining kids who were usually bigger than me, but I could bluff my way around most of them. I liked my boss in the library who taught me well, and the English class was interesting.

I came from an elementary background where lesson plans were handed in every Friday. I mean you passed them to the principal, and he checked them over, and woe to you if you were sick and a substitute arrived in your classroom with no plan book. This particular teacher's style was very different from what I knew. Most days she'd say, "Let's wing it." Now "winging it" may have suited her style, but I confess I was sometimes appalled at her lack of planning. Nevertheless, she almost always managed to pull it off. After all, she was highly esteemed by everyone in the school, so who was I to say anything different?

Life in the library was not going smoothly either. There was one group of kids who acted as if they had it in for the library and the librarians. This group started a fire in the library wastebasket, and one of the boys actually tripped me, put his foot out and tripped me. Was I in the blackboard jungle in Wells, Maine? Soon I was afraid every day, never sure what was before me when I came in or went out. When you've taught in a ghetto in Washington, D. C., you feel pretty confident that that is the highlight of your teaching career, but I didn't expect to be afraid in rural Maine. This was still the seventies, remember, before kids were actually bringing their guns to school.

The job at the time was a temporary position and although I desperately needed the money, every day I was sick to go to work. My mother had her first heart attack that fall, and later, just before Christmas, I lost my job. I wasn't fired, the school board decided not to continue the funding for that particular position and so the job just ended.

Since I had an appointment with Dr. Buell that afternoon, he was the first one I told of all my woes. I cried and he smiled in his usual unruffled, off-hand manner way and said, "I think you are in what's called a situational depression, and as soon as your situation changes, you'll be fine."

Hell, I could have told him that, it was exactly because of my situation I was depressed. Was this situation of mine ever going to change? I was so confused. We worked so hard and yet everything was always getting worse and worse. What was wrong with this picture? Knowing something was very wrong, but not knowing what it was, naturally I decided it must be me. Me, being lazy, selfish and stupid, as I was taught to believe I was.

Stephen was working very hard and trying so hard; yet he never made any money. To me this did not compute. My equation was simple: work equals money equals the more you work, the more money you make. Stephen didn't seem to be operating under the same laws of arithmetic as I. His way was to work hard. Period. Money will find its way to you, I'm not sure how it was supposed to do that, but you must remember this was the "lily of the field" guy. Did Stephen have something against making money? Or was his problem the money itself? Was he one of those "money is the root of all evil" followers?

Here was another difference we discovered. I believed money was freedom, money was fun, and let's not forget, money was a necessity. Sure, it was only paper, but that was the way of the world. How could you explain to three kids all the time there wasn't enough money for this or that? How could you always say no? How could you keep making and breaking promises? What were they learning from us? Who could they believe?

Now there were more arguments, more fights. At least I was fighting, but not Stephen, he wouldn't fight back. All my kids were afraid of me. Me? I thought I was the reasonable one, the fair one. Why me? Many years (and therapy sessions) later I understood why my kids were afraid of me. Even though I have forgiven Stephen for this, I can't forget he was the reason all my kids were afraid of me. "If Dad won't fight with Mommy, then she must really be scary."

I loved my children so much I would have done anything

for them, given them all I had, but I was tired, weary, and I felt like such a failure. I'd get up to be knocked down again. Surely, they would all survive without me. I had nowhere to go and no one to turn to. There was no support from my family, and I felt as if I didn't have a friend in the world. Everyone had deserted me. "You're on your own, Carol, you're on your own." I just didn't know what to do next. I was lost, feeling helpless and hopeless.

What had happened to the Carol I knew so long ago? The girl who went to Germany for a year all by herself? The girl who left security to return to school in Washington, D. C.? Surely that girl wasn't a coward, she wasn't afraid. Where did she go? How could I get her back?

"Maybe my brother could help me. After all I had helped him when he needed it. He should understand; he could help me," I reasoned. "Maybe I'll leave my husband and go back to Massachusetts and get a job and start all over again with my children. I bet I could figure something out if someone would just help me, guide me, support me."

I hope if you ever feel this lonely and abandoned you get professional help. People can help you. I learned you don't have to suffer. Please don't suffer.

I got neither love nor support from Louis, nothing but a shaking of the head and a quick exit. My poor sister-in-law was left alone with miserable me. What could she say and what could she do? I'm sure she was still in a lot of pain after her loss.

I never went to my brother again. Louis is a nice guy; everyone will tell you that. In fact, I'm sure everyone likes Louis a lot, at least that's what I'd been led to believe from my mother. "Why aren't you more like your brother? Your brother can talk to anybody. When we lived in Pennsylvania, he used to talk to all the truck drivers." Personally, I never knew what was so darn special about that, but it seemed important to my mother. "Louis and I would go to the movies all the time. We'd walk everywhere."

"Yes, mother, so what's your point?"

Then she'd go on, "I was in the hospital for more than two weeks when you were born. I was really sick." I still am not sure if she almost died giving birth to me, but whatever it was, she seemed to be saying it was My Fault.

Years later she told me because of me she couldn't have any more children. At the time I thought that was probably a blessing, since I surely would not have given my mother a mother of the year award. No, my mother was a cold woman. Except for those awful adolescent years, I have always been an affectionate, warm person. Hey, I even thought I was lovable. Apparently, my mother felt otherwise. I sometimes think she was always mad at me because she couldn't control me, or perhaps because I was the reason she couldn't have any more children. What difference does it make really? I knew only she didn't like me very much, and for most of my life I doubted she even loved me.

All I ever wanted to do from the time I was a little girl was to have a good time. I wanted to have fun; I was truly one of those girls you know, "Girls just want to have fun." I didn't want to hurt anyone, including myself, and I surely didn't consider the issue of control. Yet there must be something about me that made people want to control me. I would often look at my husband and listen to what he'd say either to me or the kids, and I'd think, "My God, I married my mother," or sometimes, "My God, I married my father."

Later I would advance this theory to "My God, I married both of my parents." Stephen fell into the pattern my parents had established with me all my life. He discounted my feelings, my needs, my dreams and my desires. Once again, I was made to feel lazy, stupid, and selfish. I didn't know what to do about it. Was I really that bad?

Trust, respect, and love were disappearing from my marriage, little by little. All the ingredients for a good marriage were fading, not fast, but surely and slowly. Love was dying a slow, painful death and I was the only one at the funeral.

Still I didn't trust myself either. I lost all my self-respect, and I no longer believed I was lovable. Naturally then I couldn't love myself. What did I know about self-esteem? I wasn't aware of high or low self-esteem, all I knew was I didn't like or love myself very much, all right, not at all. I knew the words, but to me esteem was not a word I would have applied to myself or anyone else I knew. To hold in high regard, I think, is to esteem someone, and I certainly didn't hold either Stephen or myself in much regard at all.

Just as I was considering, perhaps, I was too tired to go on and wondering how many aspirin it would take to kill myself – it was after all the only form of a pill we had in the house – I knew it was silly. Even so, I thought about it. Just the thought of how to do it is one step closer to an action. Again, I kept thinking how silly I was. It reminded me of the day in Washington, D.C. when I contemplated ever so briefly the thought of stepping in front of this very large, Mack truck.

I thought one step is all it would take, just one step off this curb. Then my imagination got hold of me and I considered how painful and messy that would be. What if I were like Ethan Frome? What if the truck became my sled and I only maimed myself and didn't die?

I suppose after all I am not the suicidal type. My mother always called me "the actress." I knew I was like a character in the old cowboy movies I saw as a kid. I basically wanted to ride over the hill to see what was on the other side. Life was so often such a darn good mystery; I wanted to find out what was going to happen on the next page. "Who dunnit? What did they do and can they (or I) make it better or get out of it?"

Yet on this day at Maplewood Drive, in Kennebunkport, Maine, I looked into the medicine cabinet and counted aspirin, thinking, "Okay, I can probably get some real pills. I wonder if anyone ever managed to kill themselves with aspirin?"

I thought about my children, Joshua and Noah, the boys. The boys I thought would be sad, but they were young, and they could get along. But what about Gillian? She was just a baby after all, and she needed me.

I remember soon after that moment in the bathroom, Gillian woke from her nap (it was one of those rare days she actually napped) and when I went in to pick her up, she smiled at me. She just smiled at me like she always did, just as she had the day she was born. She smiled at me, believing in the goodness of the world, that it was an okay and safe place to be. Somehow in her smile I felt as if I couldn't possibly leave this little girl whose smile always meant the whole world to me.

Please don't think I didn't love or care for my sons. They

were so dear and precious to me, but at this time they were getting older and more complicated. I adored them and cherished them. I knew how wrong it would be to leave them. Noah was finally regaining his health and his strength. Joshua was more difficult for me to understand, and yet he was so good and so dear. I may have even thought my sons would get closer to their Dad if I weren't around.

Boys especially need a father, a strong father. Stephen would fool around with them when he was home, but mostly Stephen was involved with Stephen. I think he believed the family would be there for him when he had done whatever it was he felt he had to do. Whenever he proved whatever he needed to prove to himself and naturally to his father. Father and son, oh my, what a complicated relationship!

I desperately wanted Stephen to pay attention to me, to love and cherish me. Not only me, but all of us. The children were wonderful people, loving and precious and so needy of their father. Just when he should have been nurturing and cherishing all of us, Stephen was off fighting windmills and chasing rainbows. He was always working, but never making any money. He didn't seem to equate money with work or was it work with money? His was a dizzying pace, and, like the mouse on the treadmill, it was getting him nowhere. I was left out of the maze altogether.

After I lost my job at Wells High School, and knowing I was in a "situational depression," I decided my abilities might best be used to help Stephen with his advertising business. He taught me about copywriting; I also managed the accounting and some of the typing. Often, we would brainstorm about his accounts and I discovered what fun advertising was. Now all we needed to do was figure out how to make money. I was sure I would help in this way too.

The hard part of owning your own service-oriented business is pricing yourself. When you must put a price not only on your time but your creativity, the question becomes even more difficult. You don't want to price yourself too high and out of the market, but at the same time you don't want to be so low that you work for nothing. Guess what we did?

No matter if the money was a fair amount for the project, Stephen always underestimated how long the job would take to complete. Because of his perfectionist-driven personality, no job ever made him any money. More than that he was never satisfied with the results. He'd change, modify, move layout and copy over and over, rewrite, redraw, rethink, striving for the impossible achievement of perfection. Who's to measure what is perfect anyhow? A word here or there often is merely a matter of personal preference. A layout is something you could move all ways, always.

Before there were PCs and desk printers, Stephen frequently had problems with the people who were printers, the men who printed his brochures and layouts. The most minuscule blur or edge I knew a normal reader would not notice, Stephen would fuss over and do it again and again. I was never entirely sure whether the printers we dealt with were all that bad or if it was just impossible to please my husband.

At last he found a printing company he trusted and whose work he respected. Whew, at last. Yet at the same time I could understand his reluctance to accept less than quality work. After all it was his work, his name and his reputation.

We took on even the smallest of jobs, met a lot of nice people and felt compassion for small businesses who were starting out on a shoestring just as we were. Although I think more appropriately for us with our $11 in the bank, a "shoestring" was too generous a term. Thread, perhaps, either that or a very long rope with which we were slowly tying into a noose. It turned out to be the noose.

The two of us were working at the business together. I liked the variety and the challenge of what we were doing. Of course, I was certain with the two of us working together we would succeed on a grand scale, or a modest one, but succeed we would. I enjoyed the flexibility working at home allowed me. I could take care of the kids and do what I had to do for them. As most mothers out there know, much of what you do with young children in the early elementary and middle grades is a lot of chauffeuring around. Three kids, three different ages and interests, I was always coming and going, dropping off or picking up. Still I was optimistic this time (again) Stephen and I together would make a better future for ourselves and for our children.

As business picked up, Stephen decided we needed some help and so he hired our former babysitter. She would learn layout and design and help him with the visual aspects of the job. I would continue to do the billing and accounting, some copywriting and whatever else needed to be done. I believed this was a beneficial arrangement for all of us. Debbie needed a job and we needed some help.

Aha! I hear you saying. "Here it comes, the good part, the juicy part, the real problem. I bet Stephen has an affair with Debbie." No. For two people who have been married almost forty years, (somehow miraculously) I believe Stephen and I are an unusual couple. Not to keep you in suspense any longer, but neither Stephen nor I have ever been unfaithful. I've never had an affair and neither has he.

I am not saying I never thought about it, but I never did anything. For me, an affair would be to go out to dinner. Even in my mind I never get any further than dinner and conversation. To me this would be the most intimate of evenings.

Sex was almost always good between Stephen and me, unless of course there was something else going on. Overall, we continued to satisfy each other sexually, so I would never have needed an affair for sex. No, I wanted only dinner and discussion, and so far, I haven't found anyone to fulfill that fantasy.

About having an affair, Stephen would say, "You don't have to worry about me, Carol. You know I could never organize my time that well." And we'd both laugh because this is true. Although I am sure if he were motivated, he could manage.

Later when we were in counseling, the first question I was always asked was "Are you sure he's working?" Usually I would laugh until later I thought about it. After all you read and hear of the stories about men supposedly working late, maybe he was just using the old "I'm working late" ploy? Because I was so used to his working all the time, how would I ever know if he had a girlfriend or not? Easier for him to have an affair than for me. Oh no, he would counter, it would be easier for me because I was home alone most of the day. Ha, with Joshua around, I don't think so. Joshua would have known and of course talked.

I'll tell you now something I had never thought of before. I laughed and made jokes about having an affair. I even fantasized, contemplated and wondered, but I am so happy I never did anything for a reason I would not have imagined.

Gillian has always had an inquiring mind, and during her teenage years she was acutely aware of kids in her class either coming from broken homes or the parents that were in the midst of divorcing. One day she asked me straight out, "Did you ever have an affair?" From me a big gulp and thanking God I was able to look her in the eye and honestly reply I never had. "Did Daddy?" No.

I don't know about you, but honesty with my children has always been very important to me. How could I expect them to be honest and respect me, if I didn't honor and respect them? The fact I could look her in the eye with no shame, guilt or secrets, made the decision of never having an affair very worthwhile to me. I don't say this in any way to be judgmental, only that for me this was most significant.

Perhaps if you are considering straying, you may want to think how you will face the day when one of your children asks you the very same question. How much does the respect of your children mean to you? You must answer for yourself.

CHAPTER 15

Abandoned

Affairs aside, I had more important issues to deal with at the time. The agency was beginning to get more business and we believed soon we'd no longer be working out of the studio/bedroom. The opportunity for this occurred during the summer of 1979. A man from Kennebunkport whom we had seen but never met, approached Stephen with a proposition. This man, Hank, heard many good things about Stephen and knew his reputation around town was solid, golden even. Hank was starting an agency of his own and wanted Stephen to join him as his partner.

My husband was naturally flattered that Hank would come to him. I, on the other hand, good-natured skeptic that I am, wondered why this man wanted Stephen for a partner? Stephen had no money to contribute to such an agreement. What then would be his role? What could he possibly contribute to a partnership with Hank? We learned later what Stephen had that Hank did not, and that was Stephen's good reputation and his creative talents

When I finally met Hank, I decided immediately I didn't like him at all. Moreover, I didn't trust him. "Don't do it," I advised my husband. "I don't like it. Something is fishy. After all we have no money, so how can you be his partner?"

Oh, no, Stephen wouldn't listen to me, he "could make it work," he assured me. "He came after me and I think this is a great opportunity." Oh, I didn't like the situation or Hank at all. Once more my opinions and instincts were quickly cast aside by Stephen, thus making me doubt once more whether I was indeed without value. What did I know after all? How could I possibly have any self-esteem when my opinions, judgments, instincts and feelings were always rejected and not even considered? Because my husband gave them no value, I thought I had no value myself. More dirt on the pile and all over me.

I did nonetheless get my way about one condition. Stephen agreed he and Hank would not be partners, only associates. There was no way we were going into a partnership with this man. Stephen's association with Hank was the beginning of a downward spiral that would engulf and envelop us like a rapid ocean current. Down, down, and down we went.

The truth is together Stephen and Hank could have been a brilliant combination. Stephen was the creative genius. Hank knew how to make money. That was all he knew, but he was darn good at it. I really admired his ability to turn a dime to a dollar. He could make all money matters come out to his benefit. Yes, indeed, Hank was a money maker.

After an initial interview with Hank, Debbie was hired as the office manager and secretary. Hank brought along his wonderful graphic artist, Cecile. Cecile and Stephen thought alike and were on the same wavelength almost all the time. It was fun to see the two of them work together and listen to them talk with such excitement about whatever project they were developing. I was doing Stephen's books and billings and helping out anywhere I could be useful.

At the same time, I got another job for the summer, selling shoes in Kennebunkport. This was the year of the gasoline shortage and gas lines, so it was not a successful season, still I didn't mind the job so much. I'd work at the store, go to the office, take care of the kids and do all the running around. It was a hectic and unfulfilling schedule. Work was all there was, and life continued to be like one bad job after another. Unable to find happiness anywhere outside of myself, I wrote a lot of poetry to ease my need for self-fulfillment, but more to express the growing despair inside me.

Yet I enjoyed the challenge of the business world. Stephen and I continued to work together at the office when I was there, but I got to do all the detail, dirty work. Stephen did all the creative, showy projects. When occasionally I did get to write some copy, he'd change it all. One time however, an account liked my original copy better than Stephen's and so he had to let me change it back. At the same time, Debbie and Cecile often complained to me about Stephen and his constantly changing their layouts. Not to be out of the loop, Hank complained to Stephen regarding our billings and demanding more money to run the office.

The only solace I found in these days was our accountant. He was understanding and extremely helpful to me. It was a constant but losing battle with Stephen to pay attention to details, to get receipts for everything, to keep track of his mileage and his time. Details were not anything Stephen found important and so we were fighting all the time. He continued to be the good guy while I got to play the heavy once again. I didn't like this role, but I sure had it, at work and also at home.

Whenever you try to be all things to all people, you can't win. Why did I keep trying? Why was I keeping all the balls in the air and then running frantically to catch them only to toss them up in the air again? It was a circus act on a high wire and all I could do was fall and fail.

Prior to this I never thought of failing. I didn't venture into this agency with Stephen or Hank to fail. I maintained still my belief if you worked hard enough, you would succeed at whatever you did. So, I continued to work hard, we all did, and I thought once more "Aha, this is it. We are going to make it at last."

"Carol, Carol, Carol, silly Carol, wrong again." How could I have possibly known anything about other people's agendas? Didn't we want this agency to be productive and successful? Weren't we working toward the same goal? No.

With the work both Hank and Stephen were bringing in, the agency was looking as if success were possible. We paid Hank whenever we used Cecile's time. Again, I admit to admiration for Hank's ability, no it was more than ability, I believe it was genius. Yes, Hank was a genius at making money. He had not one creative bone in his body, but this didn't stop him from using other people's creative talents to further line his pockets.

Taking money from Stephen, he later admitted, was like taking the proverbial candy from a baby. Stephen was innocent and pure; how could Hank stop himself? Years later I would understand and forgive him for what I judged his trespasses.

My husband believed no one would ever cheat him or treat him unfairly, after all he was a "nice guy." This was one of Stephen's fatal flaws. Hank's was his inability to resist the impulse to take money from whomever and wherever the opportunity presented itself, and Stephen was first in line.

Our visions of the agency were from two vastly different perspectives. Stephen and I wanted the agency to grow and flourish, and I think both Cecile and Debbie wanted this too. Both men had natural talents that would only complement each other. Since neither man communicated with the other, Stephen too busy being a whirlwind and Hank too occupied with the bottom line, the agency was indeed doomed to fail.

As for me, I was neither here nor there, but trying desperately to be everywhere for everyone.

CHAPTER 16

"What, Me Worry?"

While Stephen and I were struggling to make the agency productive and successful, Noah skipped the eighth grade and advanced to high school. At the time this move seemed logical for a boy with Noah's talents and abilities. Only years later would I question our decision.

Because Noah was now a freshman, and Joshua a sophomore, I was afraid of the effect this move would have on Josh. It turned out to be a problem for him as well. Meanwhile, happily, Gillian was busy being a little girl and that was refreshing for me.

Now I was worried all the time. I worried about the children; I worried about the agency; I worried about money. In fact, I was very worried about money. My life at this time was full of worry, doubt, and anxiety. Remember I came from a family of worriers; I had learned from the masters, or as I called them the "hypothetical twins." What if this or that happened? I don't know why it is, but we feel that we are doing something when we worry something, as if in some way we are being productive, when of course it is just the opposite.

I wondered about everyone and everything and forged ahead. I believed if I just loved my children enough, they would be all right. I thought if I worked hard enough, I could make the agency a success. I loved the thrill of the business, discovered I was good at it, and enjoyed both the economics and the creative aspects of it all. I never doubted when we began that we would be anything but successful. Stephen was a creative genius and Hank was clever at turning a profit. This should have been a winning combination. Too bad.

In 1980, Hank and Stephen decided to incorporate H&H. I wasn't exactly sure what this meant, but I knew I didn't like it. From the beginning I hadn't trusted Hank, and I was concerned about giving him too much control. After all, he had so much money and we had very little. We were working harder than ever and yet we still had no money. In truth, we were eligible for food stamps, and the kids could have had hot lunches at a reduced rate. What was wrong with this picture?

Josh was always making plans to go to work, to make money and support the family. He was fifteen years old and felt the family was his responsibility. He knew we should have more to show for all our time, effort, and hard work.

Kennebunkport in the 70s and early 80s was a diverse community. Affluence started to infiltrate the town and affect the children and their possessions. It was apparent to both my sons they had fewer advantages than most of their friends. When they visited others' homes there was always plenty of food in the refrigerator and "lots of treats." Plus, all the houses had real floors, painted walls, and regular doors that actually closed!

We were, it seemed, the perpetual "have-nots." Mostly what we had not was Stephen's attention or devotion. I know we all would have endured almost anything if we had that. More than a nice house or toys or games, we wanted to be a regular family. The kids wanted to be just kids, not have to be concerned about money all the time. They wanted to play and learn and have fun, have their friends over and not be ashamed. Josh believed our family was "different" from his friends' families, and he didn't like it at all.

At last events at the agency looked promising. We'd lived in our house for eight years and yet no room was finished or complete. Still every room was unfinished and incomplete. Not one room was entirely done. So, Stephen and I decided to take a second mortgage to finish the house. This turned out to be the biggest mistake of our marriage.

We got carried away, both of us, with grandiose dreams for our house. Instead of taking the money and finishing the house we had, we decided to build a bigger house! We added a huge addition. I thought we were looking ahead and planning for the future, the time when the children would need their own space.

I always wanted a big house, and I got a big, unfinished house. My father took one look at it and proclaimed, "My God, it's a mausoleum!" I guess he didn't like it. There was no encouragement or support, just the usual, painful criticism.

Yet, I am almost embarrassed to tell you when I drive down the road and see the house now, my father was right. What on earth were we thinking? I know exactly what I was thinking. I wanted everyone to be happy. Josh was sleeping in a room that used to be our den. Noah had the upstairs bedroom to himself, and Gillian had her room. But no one's room was finished. We added a studio apartment over the garage which the kids could use now as a room to play with their friends. There was a pool table there, and for a time there was fun for us all to share. I could also see when they were older and needed to come home this would be a refuge for them, their own space. I certainly had the right idea about kids coming home and needing their own space.

Stephen used this area as a studio for himself, a place away from the traffic of the family and wonderful light for drawing or painting. We had the right ideas all right; what we didn't have was the money. Although we hired a contractor to do the actual building, Stephen still planned to do much of the work himself. Because of such careful planning and close cooperation with our builder, I thought this time there would be no surprises or disappointments. Wrong again.

Because the bank believed in our ability to finance this project, I believed it too. We even had plans to rent the little apartment in the summer as extra income and not a lot of inconvenience. We were in "Vacation land" after all You see I had figured the potential and all the possibilities except... Except...

Stephen's parents came to visit and to help with our big, new project. Right away we had a problem. Stephen's father hated our plans. He wanted us to fire our builder, and proceed with his ideas, whatever they were. Naturally, Stephen and I argued, fought, disagreed and quarreled about this. Both sets of parents were critical, judgmental, and insulting. With such support how could we fail? How could we do anything but fail? And fail we did. Big time.

The very next day Stephen's father had a heart attack. Now he didn't tell us he was having chest pains or was in physical duress in any way. No, he was sleeping, almost all day. When both Stephen and I remarked about this unusual behavior, my mother-in-law replied simply, "He's taking a nap." Because the man had suffered at least two previous heart attacks, he knew what was happening to him, but for whatever reason decided that day to keep it a "secret."

When I think about it now, even after all these years, I am still shocked by the stupidity of my in-laws' behavior. That night when his father didn't eat dinner or have his Scotch, both Stephen and I knew something was wrong with him.

Finally, Stephen asked his mother again what was going on; she replied, "Pop's sick." Still we were in doubt what to do. Then my husband took charge and called an ambulance. Later the driver told Stephen if he hadn't called the ambulance his father would be dead by now. Mr. Hrehovcik was then rushed to the hospital in Biddeford, but when the extent of the damage to the heart was discovered he was transferred that same night to Maine Medical Center.

Early the next morning we received a call from the doctor requesting the family come in. The doctor said, "You know what this means." (Oh, brother, I'm thinking, Steve's father comes to Maine and he dies, that will really do it for us.) His family blames us for everything as it is, this is beyond even my imagination.

Yet, for some reason I didn't believe the old man was going to die, not now. At this point of course I hate the man so much I think nothing will kill this guy. But off we go to the hospital, each with our own private thoughts. As if it happened yesterday, the scene at the hospital is clear in my mind. When we arrived and were ushered into the room, I encouraged Stephen to go alone with his mother; this should be a private time for him and his mother. As usual Stephen insisted I accompany them and pulled me into the room, beside his father's bed.

There were at least eight medical people assembled around my father-in-law's bed. I wondered why so many people were here. For a death scene? Perhaps it was a teaching seminar. Whatever the reason, I found it very odd.

Then Mr. Hrehovcik began to tell his wife where all the bank books were hidden, that he still had an account in Florida, and other secrets about his assets. My ears perked up at this point as all the money secrets unfolded. Just as the information was getting really interesting, Mrs. Hrehovcik interrupted him and said something to him in Slovak to the effect of "Be quiet; you're not going to die." (I think: "Of course he isn't, damn it.")

This call to rally around the dying spirit was a big show; I'm not sure for whose benefit, perhaps for all those spectators. If they were here for the big death scene, they were surely disappointed. ("This old guy ain't going anywhere, gang. No, he's going to haunt me here on earth awhile longer. Thanks.") Meanwhile he told his wife to pray for him; he couldn't pray for himself he told her. After all, he wondered, "How could God do this to me?" How indeed?

As much as this episode may make me sound like a spoiled sport, I honestly do not wish anyone ill and most especially to die. However, this man made and continued to make my life so miserable and since he was always spouting about heaven being "home," I thought perhaps he'd be happier there. That is if I believed there was an actual heaven and if I believed he'd actually get in. But that is another book.

Alas, Stephen's father was not ready to go anywhere. Yet I did find his proclamation of being mad at God hypocritical. After all, this was the same man who wouldn't speak to his son for months because Stephen stopped going to church.

How could a man who professed to be such a devout Catholic, which is Christian, right, be so cold and unforgiving to his own son, and, yes, to his son's family? If this was an example of a good Catholic, then I was right years ago to question, to doubt, and finally to reject the Catholic Church. So, yes, there was a part of me that wished Stephen had not called the ambulance that night, and that the doctors had been right about the old man's imminent death. Once again that would have been another story and not this one.

As you can imagine, the call to arms in the Hrehovcik family rang out. Soon Stephen's brother and his wife arrived to check out what was being done for Mr. Hrehovcik here in "the Maine woods." Were there competent doctors here? Did they have any experience with heart patients? Should he go home to New Jersey where he'd be "safe?"

The decision made by the doctors was that my father-in-law should not be moved back to New Jersey or anywhere else. He needed bypass surgery if he were to survive and live a "normal" (ha ha) life. And, so, Mr. And Mrs. Hrehovcik would live with us until it was safe for him to travel again, sometime after his surgery.

Now I was instructed by my in-laws how to celebrate the

upcoming holidays, Thanksgiving and Christmas. At this point I left the room and retreated to the bedroom upstairs. No one was going to tell me how to have Thanksgiving or Christmas. ("Oh, sure, Carol, fat chance.")

Meanwhile Stephen's business was ignored. Hank was angrier and more impatient with our lack of producing revenue. I was scared and angry myself and confused about my life. Nothing made sense to me. I could not understand how two people worked so hard and yet their lives never got better. The hole we were digging got bigger and deeper. Failure was never a consideration in my family, and so I never conceived we would fail.

Then of course there was still the question of our addition. Again Mr. Hrehovcik insisted we fire the builder. Stephen, his father and the boys, ages eleven and twelve, would build the addition alone. My father-in-law after all had declared Josh and Noah as "men" and "old enough to work like men." I think he would have let them drink Scotch if he were allowed to drink anymore.

At this time, I was working part time at the Meadows, a recreational facility in town. I was also going to work at the office every day and trying still to maintain some semblance of a "normal" family life at home.

Stephen, poor guy, was trying to appease his father, take care of his mother, run our advertising business, work on the addition with our builder (who we did not fire), and keep peace between our family and his parents. I knew he was trying, but he couldn't manage any of it.

This was not only one of the most unhappy periods in our marriage, but by now I began to feel as if our life together would never be any different. Perhaps our marriage would be filled with nothing but pain, arguments, disagreements, sacrifices and suffering. Maybe his mother was right when she said, "Life is to suffer." She taught her son well. But that wasn't how I saw life at all. I later made a joke out of it: "Our life is full of the three s's: struggle, sacrifice, suffer."

We were deeper in debt and I was more in doubt about my marriage, my husband, and our future. I was feeling beaten and depressed. I lost respect for Stephen as I watched his father and his brother push him around, at least that's how it looked to me. Just once I wanted to see him stand up to them, to stand up for himself, for me, for the children and for us. I was lost, lonely and confused. Even though I didn't know the word for it, I felt abandoned.

Stephen and I were on opposite poles on every issue, including politics. One more thing we didn't need to add to our already unhealthy mix. Stephen had abandoned his religious roots and became a devout follower of Ayn Rand. Then he was zealous about the Libertarian Party. Plus, he decided to sell Amway products. There was not enough time in the day for all these activities and a family; sadly, most of the time the family was last on his agenda.

While I have talked more about my father-in-law, I can't say I was any fonder of Mrs. Hrehovcik. Remember the first time I met her, and she did not step forward to stop her husband from being so rude? This behavior was foreign to me, in more ways than one. While I admired her religious convictions, I'd never met anyone so afraid of everything. I wondered if you have such faith in God and believe He is the answer to all life here and beyond, how could you be so afraid all the time? She would not go anywhere alone except in our woods where she'd uproot and transplant trees and generally play with the dirt.

More than that she insisted always that Stephen take her to the hospital. Whatever her feelings were about me, there was little doubt she didn't trust me. Looking back now I imagine I was as foreign to her as she was to me. Nevertheless, Stephen had little time for business, and so our part of the agency was ignored.

One day I drove her to H&H. Our business was on the second floor, so I parked directly in front of the door where I could watch Mrs. Hrehovcik go up the stairway. The stairway was well lit and straight up, so I said I'd wait for her to go in. She shook her head. "No, you take me." I shook my own head in disbelief as I escorted her up the stairs to where Stephen was waiting. Even my husband was surprised by his mother's odd behavior. This dependence was more significant in her later years, especially when we learned the phrase "passive-aggressive."

I didn't know much about my mother-in-law's background, so it was difficult for me to understand her, and I like to understand people. I know my mother-in-law was not taken seriously in the family. Stephen's family was patriarchal; there was no doubt who ruled the roost.

Only after my father-in-law's death did any of us discover how Mrs. Hrehovcik in her quiet, submissive way manipulated not only my father-in-law but the family as well. Her little homilies about life and marriage: "Life is to suffer." "Marriage ain't no picnic." "We can't be rich." did more damage to us than all her husband's bullying.

During her stay with us she told me she didn't want to know about any of her children's marriages. Her daughter, my mother-in-law confided to me in one of her rare moments of English conversation, was not happy in her marriage. "But," she said, "John has a good job; he doesn't beat her, and he makes good money." Then of course she added, "Marriage ain't no picnic." (I wanted to add "especially if you are married to a Hrehovcik.") Curious remarks, don't you think?

I was not prepared for this experience with Eastern European culture. I knew I could deal with loud, bossy Europeans, after all my family heritage was much the same. However, I was used to a more open display of emotions such as anger, pleasure, even grief. The behavior of my in-laws was unfamiliar to me and so difficult for me to cope with. I was lost in more ways than one.

My immediate family, my children and my husband were and still are my number one priorities. I resented any interference and resisted when others told me how to run my life, my home, or my children. I had always wanted us to be free to live our lives together as we chose, not with his family or mine. This attitude caused great conflict between Stephen's family and me.

I think Stephen didn't know which way to turn. He wanted to be a good son, but the definition of that in his family was to do as you were told and not think for yourself. Other rules included to live within the accepted radius of his parents, attend the Byzantine Church every week, and pay daily homage to his father.

Stephen was failing on all counts, and I, naturally, was the "bad woman" who had taken him away. His family seemed to forget rather consistently, that Stephen had left home and his family long before he ever met me. He told me that was one of the reasons when asked if he'd mind going to Korea while he was in the Army, he'd simply replied, "All right."

He knew instinctively, not on a conscious level, he had to get away from his family or they would smother him. But it was easier for the family to blame someone else, me, for any problem he had with the family. As I was used to taking blame for almost everything and anything, I felt as if it were my fault. Perhaps if it hadn't been for me, Stephen and his family would get along better. I was soon to learn better.

CHAPTER 17

Do the Right Thing

I continued to feel as if I were in the way until Stephen's sister Anne arrived. She came to stay with us for two weeks prior to her father's operation. I didn't know Anne very well except for her remark, "Are you sure the baby is yours?" So, I wasn't very hopeful she would be any different from anybody else in the family. That is to say I expected her to be bossy and annoying. I was pleasantly surprised to see she was helpful and respectful of the fact this was our house.

With Anne's arrival a noticeable change occurred in Stephen's mother. She laughed. She actually laughed out loud! Stephen and I had been married fourteen years and had seen his parents a lot more than I cared to, and I never, ever had seen Mrs. Hrehovcik laugh. I thought perhaps since the woman never cried, she probably never laughed either.

Yet at the mere sight of her daughter, my mother-in-law's face literally lit up with joy and happiness. It seemed Anne's very presence made this old woman grin and smile and laugh. Just as Mr. Hrehovcik was all happiness whenever he was with Mike, as if they were one and the same person, Mrs. Hrehovcik was that way with Anne.

These observations stunned me into discovery. The problem with Stephen's family wasn't me after all as obviously there never was any place in the family for Stephen. His parents were taken before he came along and there was no room for a third child. Dad had Mike, Mom had Anne, and Stephen? Lost.

I believe Mike was the only person Mr. Hrehovcik truly cared for, and why not? Mike and his father were the two proverbial "peas in a pod." Mrs. Hrehovcik's attachment to her daughter made the old woman complete and even joyous. I know my mouth was wide open at the very sight of this behavior. I believed somehow this was not a normal situation, or even very healthy. All right, I confess I thought it was sick. Does the word dysfunctional come to mind? Please remember this was long before any of that kind of knowledge was available.

When Stephen's mother insisted Anne share the bed with her, I was truly appalled. I had arranged for Anne to have a bed of her own, but my mother-in-law was insistent, and to keep the peace Anne slept with her mother. I admit I felt a little prudish about my reaction. After all, I reasoned, perhaps this was just another Eastern European habit. I know there was a time when it was not possible for everyone to have her own bed, but I still couldn't help feeling uncomfortable about the whole thing.

Anne stayed with us for two weeks and was a manic force in our home. She took care of my mother-in-law, seemed able to pacify my father-in-law, helped with the cooking, sewed drapes for my dining room, made a fresh balsam wreath for the door for Christmas, and in general was a pleasure to have around. For two glorious weeks I was able to take care of myself and my family, and I was free to come and go without being concerned about my in-laws. All this, plus, Anne was the one who got the lice out of Gillian's hair.

Ah, lice I say. How could I have possibly forgotten to talk about another Thanksgiving from hell. Lee and Mike arrived at our house for Thanksgiving to be with the family. As Lee was combing Gillian's hair, she noticed something odd, and to my utter horror it was lice. How could my daughter have lice? I felt ashamed as if I were a bad mother. And of course, it had to happen when my in-laws were there.

Everything, you see, in those days was a reflection on me. Joshua still laughs about that, "reflection on me." I had no idea what to do and it was Thanksgiving morning after all. We found a drugstore that was open that morning and Steve and his brother rushed to get there before it closed. The druggist told Stephen what to do to get rid of the lice and it sounded so complicated and like a painstaking endeavor.

Meanwhile I washed all the linens and boiled the combs and brushes. I literally boiled them, like a lobster, and the combs and brushes disintegrated. Everyone laughed at me for being so foolish, yes, and "stupid." At the same time as I was washing and boiling, I had a turkey in the oven and was preparing the rest of the Thanksgiving meal to serve to a very large and hungry group of people.

No one volunteered to help me in the kitchen, so I was running back and forth between sheets, turkey, combs and brushes, and Gillian. All I wanted to do was sit and cry and take care of my little girl. But Stephen and Mike were washing her hair and combing through the lice remover. Whatever it was it didn't work.

When we sent her to school the next week, she was sent home because there were still lice in her hair. We tried other products and remedies, but those damned elusive lice evaded us. I was afraid I'd have to cut her hair to get rid of the lice, then Anne arrived. She patiently and skillfully sat with Gillian one afternoon and combed through her hair strand by strand and removed the lice. Gillian happily was accepted back to school the next day.

It's funny what you grow up believing. I remember as a kid having the school nurses go through everyone's hair looking for lice. I never worried I'd have lice, after all I had this cleanliness fanatic for a mother; I am sure she would have died of humiliation had I ever come home in such a condition. Lice was something also I was uninformed about, or misinformed. I thought only the kids who lived in a dirty house got lice and didn't know it could transport so easily by using someone else's comb or brush or hat. It was astonishing to me how one person's lice could afflict an entire grade and even a school.

I admired Anne from this day forward. I admired her energy and her skill with her hands. She had a talent that was beyond manual dexterity, for Anne was also clever and imaginative. She could sew and craft and copy a dress or suit she had seen in a magazine or in a shop. I believe she could have been a designer of some importance. Say what I will about my in-laws, their kids are all exceptionally bright and talented, each in a different and unique way. If Anne had stayed with us longer, I am sure we could have helped raise her self-confidence and self-esteem,

It was sad to me to see so much of Anne's talent and ability wasted, and to see how little she believed in herself as well. But after all, who was I to talk about wasted talent and ability? And who had high self-esteem that I knew? We each make our own choices after all, and live our lives the best we can. I am sure Anne was as happy as she could be with the choices she made. Was I any different?

I have always been interested in people and their behavior. I like to understand why people are the way they are and do what they do. I can't always understand, but I like to try. I have built stories around complete strangers just by watching them. Perhaps this curiosity of mine is why strangers feel free to talk with me. I have had people confide in me on trains and buses and planes, in transportation stations and even in stores where I worked. Somehow strangers feel safe talking with me and I am generally always interested in what they have to say. Even when life was sad or unhappy for me, I enjoyed listening to people talk, and I still do. I think it must have something to do with the mystery of life.

The situation with Mr. and Mrs. Hrehovcik was not going to last forever, it just seemed like forever to me. Maybe if Stephen and I had been getting along better, this time wouldn't have been so unhappy for me.

At last Christmas arrived and my father-in-law had successfully come through the operation. The New Year, 1980 began for me as it always did, with hope and a promise of better times ahead. Accustomed to being called a pessimist by Stephen, still I was optimistic about our future.

Soon after the new year Mr. Hrehovcik was free to return

to New Jersey. He was well enough now to travel, and thank you God, he didn't die in our house. When the kids and I heard the good news, we began to jump on my bed, up and down holding hands and all but shouting "hurrah." Freedom at last, our lives to live, getting back on course with our business and our family. My in-laws had been with us for more than three months, and while I wouldn't say they were exactly the months from hell, oh, perhaps more like a purgatory, if you believe in that kind of thing, they were not fun either. As hard as it had been to have Stephen's parents with us, we discovered it had been more difficult for Mike to have his father here and not at home with him. "Mike, believe me, if there had been any way, we would have sent him home with you."

My marriage was way down on my list of priorities now. The marriage was stagnant at this point and neither Stephen nor I had a clue about what to do to get it moving again. My love for my husband had eroded like a garden after an earthquake. Over time I had lost love, trust, respect and all of the adoration I once felt for Stephen. I begged him to help me get some of it back. My garden of love needed nurturing and care and a lot of attention.

I spoke plainly to him. "We're having some problems. What should we do? I think our marriage is in trouble."

He replied he was fine, thank you very much, and he was sorry I was having a problem, but it had "nothing" to do with him. Further, he told me, "It's your problem."

Having always been a glutton for punishment, I pursued the subject. "If there is a problem in a marriage, don't you think it has to do with both people? If I have a problem, don't you have a problem too?"

Nope. "Your problem," he told me, "is that you are such a pessimist. I always see the glass as half-full and you always see it as half-empty. That's your problem." That damn glass! That was the end of discussion and the end of problem solving between us. I remember when I had mentioned to him I was thinking about suicide, he said, "Really? Why? I don't see that." and turned over and went to sleep. Stephen had more important matters on his mind than me and our marriage or our family. He had to save the world after all.

Perhaps most men respond to this kind of predicament in a similar way, but I knew our problems had to do with the two of us. For once I wasn't going to take the blame. As I have already told you, I took the blame for almost everything in my life, but with this problem in my marriage, at last I realized I was only partly to blame. I knew it couldn't be just me, it had to be both of us who had a problem.

I also knew and sadly went on to discover absolutely, a problem with a child is a family problem. It would be many years before I forgave myself and stopped feeling guilty about my children and the mistakes I made. It would also be many years later before I started to give myself some credit as well. I was so immersed in the debit column that I never gave myself any marks on the other side of the balance sheet.

The miracle of my forgiving myself and ceasing to feel guilty was then I could forgive Stephen. But this was a long time away at this point.

Meanwhile in the new year of 1980 I believed that since Stephen's parents had returned to New Jersey we'd get on with our lives, make our business grow and flourish and even finish our house at last. We'd been in the house for eight years at that point and it still looked as if we were living there temporarily. Sadly, things went from bad to worse. More heartaches and heartbreak followed as Stephen and I drifted on the sea of disappointment, disillusion, yearning and despair. Would there ever be any happiness for the Hrehovciks in Maine? Were we doomed to fall and splatter? To fail and never finish anything we started and to never succeed? There was still not a place to turn for a "piece of peace" or as Noah would say, "When am I going to have a piece of quiet?"

CHAPTER 18

He's Not Heavy;
He's My Husband

The beginning of the new year was not a beginning of anything new for Stephen and me. Here we were with our priorities out of order again. Stephen and I were on two different, and separate paths. Even the children could not provide the glue to keep us together. Why did we never talk about our values? Our priorities? Our hopes and dreams? Where were we going? Could we ever look back and take the time to ask ourselves what we had learned and where we were going from there?

I know I tried to get Stephen to talk with me, to share with me, but the most I could ever get from him was, "Yes, the family is important to me." Then he would carry on with his life as if we would wait for him forever, as if the kids would be young always and just be there whenever he was finished with the rest of the world, with "issues that really mattered."

An important issue for Stephen in 1980 was politics and

the Libertarian party. He believed the only way our business could succeed was "for changes to take place in Washington." For our family to be happy "changes had to be made in Washington." We could never be "truly free or happy unless there were changes made in Washington." As you can well imagine there were neither changes made in Washington nor in our family life.

Maybe I'm old-fashioned, all right, I know I'm old fashioned, but I believe the only way to change anything is to take care of yourself first and your own family. Clean your own front steps and then if everyone on the block does the same, you'll have a very neat neighborhood.

The children are indeed our future; we must take care of them first. The family must be the number one priority if the neighborhood, the community, the state, the country, and the world are to survive. I believe in first things first. I wanted to change the world from the inside-out, while Stephen, seeing the "big picture," wanted to change the world from the outside-in.

The problem again between us was we spoke two different languages. We'd use the same words, but we had different meanings for those words. I wondered how we went round and round the same arguments over and over and still resolved nothing. I spent a lot of time thinking I was pretty stupid and wondering what was wrong with me. I blamed Stephen for a lot of our problems, but at the same time always felt if I were smarter or even less possessive or if I just knew how to communicate in a better way, we could solve our problems and "live happily ever after."

No, even I was not that naive anymore. I had grown

up believing I was responsible for everyone else, for their happiness or pain. I didn't connect the fact I was responsible for myself, for my own happiness and for my own pain. I did wonder however just who was responsible for me? What a revelation it was for me to learn it was me after all.

Poor Joshua at this time felt as if he had to be the father and the provider for the family. He was always thinking up grand schemes and plans to make a lot of money. For Joshua you see, it always had to be "a lot" of money. While he was in junior high school, Joshua became afraid of everything and everyone. We wouldn't learn until later just how afraid he was and what a burden it was for him every day just to go out of the house. The name for this is agoraphobia.

Noah and Gillian seemed to take care of themselves pretty well. Oh, they both still needed rides to dancing lessons, Noah twice a week to Portland and Gillian once a week in Kennebunk. I was always very happy Joshua never danced. He was more active with the school bands and the drama department.

How could they all be performers at heart? Then again how could they not be? During their early years they had all been surrounded by the theater in some way. The boys performed in front of audiences when they were five and three. They loved the laughter and the applause, and I suppose this always stayed in their minds. My sons still perform and compete.

Gillian just went on her way. Of course, she was lucky she was the youngest and the only girl. This status gave her benefits and advantages the boys had never experienced or enjoyed. Yet she was jealous of all the attention Noah got from his dancing. Somehow, we never spent the time encouraging

Gillian to pursue her dancing aspirations. We did encourage and foster her talent with the piano. Here she was truly gifted and special, and we hoped she would see the piano was her true vocation. Only she of the three children has this gift naturally.

I felt fortunate indeed to have three such clever, creative, and intelligent children. Yet, at the same time I felt as if they were all too much for me to handle, especially alone, as I thought I was.

The Libertarian candidate for President in 1980 was Ed Clark. Since Stephen was most active with the party at this time, he spoke out on many occasions to get "the word out," to raise votes, and raise the political consciousness of the state of Maine. His political activity became another source of conflict between us. I have never been a political person, but I am happy some people are. I know I could never have married a politician, probably the only thing worse than marrying an actor. Although Stephen never ran for a political office, he did everything else during this campaign. Mostly what he accomplished was to alienate many of our friends as he tried to show them the "truth." As if his politics didn't alienate enough of our friends, Stephen decided to sell Amway products. How to lose friends, easily and quickly, the Steve Hrehovcik way.

I love to vote. I suppose this is as far as any political involvement I get. If you don't vote, in my opinion, you have no right to complain about anything that goes on. I always made a very big deal over our privilege to vote whenever my children were old enough to vote. We always celebrated. I wanted to imbue in them the belief and faith in this country and just how grand it really was.

More than that I wanted them to know how lucky we are to be free to vote. I loved my year in Europe, but that year taught me this indeed is the best country in the world and how much most of us Americans take for granted. I feel fortunate to be a part of it and I wanted my children to feel the same, and I believe they do.

In spite of all Stephen's diligent efforts and work on behalf of the Libertarian party to elect Ed Clark, Ronald Reagan was elected President in 1980. Stephen, undaunted nevertheless, continued to work for the party even after the elections. While he was working on his political priorities, selling Amway products, my husband decides he and I need to do something together that is "fun." He wants us to act together in a local community theater group. This was his idea of "fun."

I didn't want to do it, of course, but Stephen pushed me into it with the idea that "it might be fun." He thought this would be something good for us to do together. I liked the "together" idea, but I do not have any "fun" with this group. I had long ago lost any need to perform and really didn't want to be involved with a theater in any way. The only involvement I craved was as part of an audience. He was insistent, and, in another effort to keep the peace, I agreed to take part in *the Haunting of Hill House*. It is a comical drama, at least I think it is; I admit I was never very sure.

Stephen was constantly struggling with his lines, and the director called me frequently to ask what "we" could do to help. He was blundering in his part almost all the time, forgetting lines and throwing off all the other actors. Stephen was screwing up and yet I was the one the director picked on during rehearsals. This was not a good experience for me since I had so little self-esteem to begin with.

Am I that bad, I wondered? To this day I really don't know the answer. Actually, I thought I was pretty funny. I was supposed to be the comic relief after all. When my children came to see the show, they felt embarrassed by their parents, especially when people laughed. It was ironic after all, since they were used to being on stage, even Gillian. We went to all their shows and were always supportive and encouraging. Yet when it was their parents, my children were embarrassed. I guess that is how most kids react to almost everything their parents do.

Since I felt humiliated myself, the kids might have picked something up from me. This was the last time I let my husband decide what was fun for me. Remember in our house fun was the F word. Years later, Stephen confessed to me he was wrong to assume we were of one mind about everything. To suppose I felt the same as he "was wrong," he said. I always told him I needed something to be mine alone, separate from him and the children.

I know my motivation to go along with him on all his schemes and ventures was to make him happy. If he were happy, I reasoned, then maybe I could be happy as well. Except for joining the Libertarian party, I gave almost everything else he wanted to do a try. All I ever wanted from this marriage was simple: I wanted to be with him and share our life together. Since he didn't seem to be interested in what I cared about, which was essentially the family, the children, and friendships, I went along with him and his interests and ideas.

Stephen is a very gifted man, a resourceful and intelligent person. One of his big failings, however, is his tendency to spread himself too thin. Never mind having your eggs in one basket, Stephen's problem was broken eggs and baskets all over the place. Many eggs hidden, empty, broken, but baskets aplenty and so many neglected. There simply was not enough time in the day or night to do all this man set out to do. Stephen believed he was a superman, a hero, check, and more than this he thought he knew all the answers and had to do everything alone.

Some of his many baskets at this time included the Libertarian party, the play, H&H, "Making a difference in the world," and the family. As Stephen was busy with all his busyness, his associate at the agency was actively pursuing his own plans. Hank's baskets were lined up in a neat little pile as he was planning to enlarge his pile and the size of his baskets by incorporating H&H without our knowledge or consent.

Stephen was no longer content with his association at H&H. Relations with Hank and the girls in the office were strained. We owed Hank a lot of money, were barely able to get by ourselves, and yet money was way down on Stephen's list of priorities. God, if money were ever important to my husband, we'd have been so rich! That at least would have been some compensation for his hard work and long hours, plus the many days and nights of isolation I felt.

Christmas at our house always brought a lot of pain and caused a major strain between Stephen and me. 1980 was no different and perhaps even a little worse than usual. Just when I thought things couldn't be worse than they'd been last year when his parents had been living with us, our situation did indeed get worse.

Maybe it is a good thing we can't know the future. How would we go on? It is also, I am discovering as I write this story, a wonderful ability our mind has to dim the past in our memory bank. I do not remember many details of this difficult period and refer only to my journals as a pathway to the past.

If I did not feel this story would be helpful to someone out there, even to one person, I would not venture backward. Remember we've talked about tenses, and I told you I am generally a present tense person. This journey back in time is not one I make easily.

The wonderful part is that it has passed, is in the past, not even a yesterday. I needed time to pass before I could tell this tale as I wanted so much to laugh at a lot of it. I wanted the time to see the humor and make jokes about it. Has anyone ever told you "You'll laugh about this years from now"? Don't believe it. At this point in my story I am still not laughing. I think because I know my sons especially are still suffering from so many of these memories.

Perhaps suffering is too strong a word. Recovering is the better word I am sure. I see now, more clearly than ever, how difficult these times were for them, how much we expected them to understand and be patient. Why do so many of us parents expect our children to be adults when we are having trouble being adults ourselves? I apologize all over again and hope my children have forgiven me and Stephen as we have forgiven ourselves.

We can't give them back these pieces from their childhood,

but hope they will use them to guide themselves to be better parents than we were. I hope, as well, they know they were loved always. I know now love is not enough; I thought it was, but I see it is not so.

Children need a sense of security as much as they need love. They desperately need to know and believe they will not be abandoned or stranded and alone. I am sad to admit Stephen and I were unable to provide our children with that sense of safety. How could we? We never had it for ourselves.

I recall with some regret a day when I actually did leave home. The boys were quarreling about underwear, of all things. I am not sure to this day exactly what it was about the underwear, but they were each tugging at it and screaming at each other. I went upstairs to their room, threw the underwear at them and shouted, "I'm leaving. I can't stand this anymore."

I ran down the stairs and out of the house and drove away with the tires screeching beneath me. Not thinking of what I was doing or where I was going or the impact my leaving would have on the three children, I knew only I needed to go, get out, run away. After all, running away was how I'd handled my conflicts in the past. Now as I approached the golf course, not even two miles from my house, I looked at the gas gauge in the car and pulled over to the side of the road.

"What am I doing? What's wrong with me? I have to go back." I turned the car around and went back home to face three hurt, confused, disillusioned, scared, and yes, abandoned children. I am not sure who was the most hurt or disappointed in me, the kids or myself. I asked Joshua if he had called Stephen, and he shook his head. "What good would it do?" I was saddened to hear his response and sat on the steps and hugged all three of them and cried and apologized. This incident is one I am sure none of them have forgotten, and may not have forgiven. I ran out on them. It may not have been for more than fifteen minutes, but I left them. I was scared, but that is no excuse.

I hope one day they may understand. That day was my worst. I felt out of control and I think out of my mind. I felt my life was hopeless. I was helpless, and I didn't have a clue what to do about it. I was alone with my rage. The depression I was feeling was becoming a huge hole, getting deeper and deeper and darker each day, each hour, each minute.

The week before Christmas 1980 and I had not gotten one gift, as usual. There were no checks forthcoming. I checked the mailbox sometimes twice a day, hoping there were some accounts receivable, but every day the box was empty. I didn't know where to go, where to turn or what to do. We were both working so hard and still we had no money. I talked to Stephen hoping he might have a solution. His answer: "We'll just tell the kids we have to postpone Christmas this year."

You tell me how you say to a kid there will be no Christmas this year? It was bad enough I had to fight with Stephen every year to have a Christmas, but now he actually wanted me to tell the kids we'd "postpone" it. "Perhaps," he went on to say, "we can get pictures of the things we'll get them when we have the money." After years of broken promises, did he actually think anyone would ever believe that?

Joshua still talks about that particular Christmas and always makes jokes about "postponing and pictures." Joshua remembers many Christmases when Stephen and I had what he calls our "annual Christmas fight." Yes, they were fights, not arguments or disagreements. We tried to have these fights in private, but the kids always knew. Even Gillian, who was only eight years old now, was afraid Stephen and I were getting a divorce. She was worried about everything and cried a lot.

One night she came into our bed and was crying so hard she told us how much she was afraid. I stroked her head and said very gently, "Poor Gillian, you have the weight of the world on your little shoulders. That is just too much for a little girl like you. I tell you what I'll do. I will take the weight of this part of the world off this shoulder. There. I will worry about Europe and Asia and Africa, and Daddy will worry about all the other places in the world. Now, from this shoulder," and I made a motion as if I were truly lifting a weight off from her tiny little shoulder, "we will take the worry of all of America and Maine and Kennebunkport. How does that feel now?" She nodded and smiled a little. "But," I continued, "we'll leave you Maplewood Drive. You can worry about that. Is that all right? Can you worry just about Maplewood Drive?"

I believe this little game helped her. She could visualize Maplewood Drive, the street where we lived. All the other places which she could only imagine were now literally lifted from her shoulders. Maplewood Drive was a "weight" she could carry. To have left her with no place of her own to be concerned for, would have made her feel more scared and alone, I think. I thought it was important for her to have a little place too. I knew she would worry anyhow, but now she knew exactly what she had to worry about.

Later when she came to me with some new fear, I'd simply remind her that it was my worry or Daddy's and not hers.

She'd go on her way then believing Mommy and Daddy would take care of it. I wish I had been as confident, yet I was happy I could relieve her of these burdens. I was not so fortunate with my sons.

Noah was working hard in high school and made the high honor roll his first semester there, even though he started three weeks late. I think in a way he was lucky to have the ability to bury himself in his schoolwork. That was at least one area over which he had control. He told us many years later he thought if he did well in school, we'd not only be proud of him but maybe Stephen and I wouldn't fight so much. This is another important piece of information for you, in case you don't know it already. Children feel responsible for adults' problems.

Joshua continued his music and dramatic interests and made friends with an older group of students. They were all nice boys, but I felt Joshua at fifteen was too young to have the privileges these eighteen-year-olds enjoyed. So, naturally Joshua and I were fighting a lot. One time, and of course he still gets mad at me for this one, I refused to let him go to a Pat Benatar concert in Boston. Since it was a school night, for me there was no issue. For Joshua it was a major issue. I see in hindsight I should have had more confidence in him and his friends and let him go. He wanted only to be one of the guys after all.

Stephen was unaware or unwilling to acknowledge anything was wrong at home. As far as he was concerned there were no problems between us or with any of the children. Any problems I had were "mine" and after all "kids will be kids." Since when did he know anything about kids or what it was like to be a kid? According to him, he was never one himself. More than that, I have always called Stephen's style of childrearing the "laissez faire" approach, that is to let the children do whatever they wanted. My husband couldn't discipline anyone because someone might not like him. Imagine! Stephen did not want to be perceived as anything but a "nice guy," even by his children.

Meanwhile I was worried I was turning into my mother: hard and cold and "tough." That is what my mother always believed she had to be: "tough." Because of the way she grew up and the rough Italian neighborhood where she lived in Rochester, New York as a child, she learned in order to survive in her family of seven brothers and sisters she had to be "tough." This one word sums up my mother's philosophy of life. I know she hung around her older brothers and cousins, one of whom was a professional boxer, and this didn't help promote any delicate image on her part. Perhaps because her own dreams of going to school to become a teacher were thwarted, she got even more "tough."

That was neither the kind of mother I wanted or wanted to be. I wanted to be the kind of mother I never had and always wanted; I wanted to be warm and gentle and loving. I knew somewhere inside myself this was my true nature. Sadly, just as my mother had to learn to be hard in order to survive, I believed I had to do the same. More than this, what really scared me was how cold I could be. I could be so cold to other people, I scared even myself. My own personality was suppressed and buried. No wonder I was losing my identity.

During this time, I had a recurring dream. In the dream I would lose my pocketbook and my wallet with all my identification in it. Frantically, when I went to recover it, the person in charge behind a desk would ask me my name and I couldn't remember. I'd recall my maiden name but not my name now. I was lost, confused and scared, even in my dreams.

The other dream I had over and over was of me driving a car. The car was out of control and would go neither forward nor back no matter what gear I used. Then the car would go only backward, out of control so I could neither steer nor stop it. The car stopped only when it ran into something like a tree or another car. Always out of control and always going backwards.

These same dreams in one or more variations, but always the same: loss of identity and going backward, were more real to me than my life. Hell, they were my life. I knew on a conscious level this was my life. I didn't know who I was aside from "Steve's wife" or somebody's "mother." No matter how hard I worked along with Stephen we could never get ahead or caught up.

We got only further and further behind. I couldn't believe or accept all our hard work was putting us more and more into debt. Never out of debt but always believing life would get better, we borrowed money and piled up more debt along the way. I was in a maze and felt like the laboratory rat, cornered with no way out, going faster and faster on the treadmill and getting nowhere. I was so lost and afraid; how could my children be anything but the same?

Still I believed I was doing my best to cover up. I thought I helped them live the lives of teenagers and a little girl. I believed everything was my responsibility: home, family, children, bills, money, the business. I tried to be everything to everyone – responsible, reliable, even fun. Of course, I could always be counted on to do "what I had to do." After all, I needed to be practical. "Good old Carol, you can always count on her." Everyone could count on me but me.

I yearned for someone to call me "Carol." I wanted to hear the sound of my name. I asked my husband, "Please call me Carol instead of honey all the time." I was "honey" or "Mommy" or "Mom" or Josh's mother, Noah's mother, or Gillian's mother. I was Mrs. Hrehovcik (even though they couldn't pronounce it) to the bill collectors. Where was Carol? Who was Carol? Was there any Carol left? Where did I go and how did I lose myself?

I wanted me back but had no idea where to go to look for myself. I was afraid I might not even like me if I found me. No, not in those days, not at this time, I might not have liked the Carol I found. I longed for a holiday, a vacation, a rest. I yearned for a time out from worry and stress and fear. I wanted a break from being a chauffeur, a good sport, a handy wife, a convenient sex partner. I was tired, tired, tired all the time. This busyness was not my style or personality and certainly not my choice of a way to live. The unfinished house, the failure at everything we tried and touched, this was not the woman I ever was or wanted to be. Something was very wrong, and naturally I believed it was me.

CHAPTER 19

Sacrifice, Struggle, Suffer – A Hrehovcik Marriage

1 981 and Stephen and I had been married sixteen years. We had long ago abandoned the April 10 wedding and "celebrated" the February 8 date only. I say celebrate in that we at least acknowledged this date to each other. Rarely did we go out for an actual celebration. We had so little money we felt anything like a dinner out was too extravagant. Also, we were not that happy together at this time.

Each year my hopes and dreams for a better life were shattered. Wondering if this was the way it would always be for us: no money, huge amounts of debt, angry, threatening phone calls, hard work with no rewards in sight, I lost faith in both my husband and myself.

I was afraid to answer the phone or read the mail. There were threats, often carried out, to turn off our lights, our phone, and once even our water. I ask you, how many people are ever threatened by the water company?

By now it was clear the agency was not going to make it, at least not with us in it. Stephen and I began to look for other ways to make a living. Stephen had always wanted to start his own theater and had this idea for an original production to be presented in the summer. Summer is the time of tourism in the Kennebunks, and the show was about Maine, so it seemed like a winner.

Stephen wrote an original musical for this summer production. He penned the clever lyrics and a series of sketches with comical characters one might encounter in the state of Maine. Once he found someone to write the music for him, the show came together, and we were set for auditions.

While he was writing the show, Stephen was drawing a map of the Kennebunks, a big job, full of detail and whimsy. It was a large, four color print map. He was working eighteen hours a day and there were days when he never went to sleep. Driven by the desire to make his show a success, he worked hard hoping to make enough money to leave H&H. Then we would be on our own again, and this would make us both happy.

While Stephen was working these hours, I was as usual working to keep the family together and carry on as if everything were quite normal. I'd go into the office, work on the business, assist him with his show, take the kids to their various lessons and wherever else they needed to go. Meanwhile we were trying to raise money for the production, find a location for the show and also come up with a cast, crew, musicians and a staff – besides me.

As if this weren't enough to keep any person fully occupied, Joshua was displaying serious problems that had us very concerned. I had been to the school guidance counselors several times because Joshua was having trouble in school. I thought the first step was to rule out the possibility of any physical problems. First, we took him to our regular doctor. He sent us to a heart specialist who in turn sent us to a neurologist. It was he who discovered the true problem with Joshua and with our family.

Joshua and I went alone to the neurologist as Stephen was so involved with all his work. I remember quite clearly when the doctor sat me down across from him at his desk and said, "Josh needs help. This is not a physical problem. This is an emotional problem and you need to take him to a psychiatrist."

I nodded and replied, "I've been thinking about it," and before I could finish my sentence, he spoke sternly to me.

"I am not telling you to think about it; I am telling you to do it. I know a good man who deals especially with adolescents. I'll call him now and make an appointment." There was no discussion, no arguing, no "we'll see." In fact, to tell you the truth, I was relieved that someone had finally made the decision for me. I could not bring myself to make the decision alone, and none of the school counselors had helped me decide this for myself and for Joshua. Finally, thank God, the decision was out of my hands.

This was one of those defining moments in a lifetime. From this day forward our lives would change; this was the beginning of a new beginning. Although there were still hard and painful years ahead, help was now available to us, and I breathed a sigh of relief that this moment had come at last.

Stephen and I were enough of an older generation to believe you handled your own problems. To do less would be admitting weakness. How foolish and quaint and stupid. I knew I was weak at this point anyhow and welcomed a hand to guide and help me up and out of the dark well I had fallen into. The valuable lesson we all learned was that help is available, and you have only to ask the questions to seek and find the answers.

For myself I was more relieved than afraid of what discoveries lay ahead for us. I would do anything to help my son, to help all my children, if that meant finding out I was a bad mother or was making mistakes I would do what I had to do to fix them. I had to make so many decisions about everything, and my life was so full of "should and have to," I couldn't make a decision about this very important person in my life. I have always thanked God that Joshua had enough subconscious desire to be better, that Joshua showed us the only way he could, by manifesting physical symptoms.

Joshua had been talking about suicide in ways that scared me enough I wouldn't leave him alone in the house. I even had Stephen remove the lock in his bedroom. Joshua said, "If there was a tall building in Kennebunk, I'd throw myself off it." Dr. Metzger, Joshua's psychiatrist, later said to us, "Be glad there were no tall buildings around. Anytime a person mentions suicide, no matter how he talks about it, you have to take it seriously."

In May, 1981 we began therapy with Dr. Metzger in Portland. The first meeting was with Stephen and me, next meeting was with Joshua, and the third week Stephen and I went to talk with him alone. This was the time of evaluation. I could see Dr. Metzger putting the pieces of a psychological puzzle together with the information he had gathered from his talks with all of us.

These initial meetings cost $100 each visit and the cost thereafter was $85, payable in cash for each of the weekly sessions. We had no insurance to pay for any of this, but Joshua's health was more important than any amount of money. How much would you pay to have a healthy child?

Our married life had not been easy in many ways, all right, not in any way. What I had imagined and hoped a marriage would be like was not anything I had in my own marriage. Even though Stephen and I never talked about it specifically, I believed marriage was something you shared, and I naturally just assumed he felt the same as I. Now sharing doesn't seem like a very difficult or complex concept to me, but I was definitely on a different plane with my dream of sharing. Isn't that what marriage is all about, to share with your mate the good and the bad, the hopes and the dreams, wishes and desires, sadness and joy and all the feelings in between? And Stephen? He was out there somewhere where most of the time I couldn't reach him.

All right, I confess right here I was in trouble before we even started. I think, you see, my husband is a genius, and I have often told him so. I frequently joke about Mrs. Edison (Edison lived in New Jersey too) and compare myself to her. I don't know anything about Mrs. Edison. Do you? But I am sure Mr. Edison did not know or care about the details that make up most of our ordinary, run of the mill lives. Who paid the bills I wonder? Who minded the kids? Who washed and cooked and cleaned so Mr. Edison was free to invent and become famous? Yes, I thought a lot about Mrs. Edison. Yet I knew she and I shared something more: we were never bored.

I for one would have welcomed boredom sometimes. There were times I longed for a sweet, ordinary guy who would pay attention to me and his family and let the world take care of itself. Ah...

I was always interested in psychology as a sort of hobby, but had no desire to make it an avocation, which it was soon becoming. I had no idea of the depths of the unconscious mind or how it can literally run and ruin a life. One of these people run by his unconscious or subconscious (what's the difference you may well ask) was my husband. The "interesting coincidences" became more remarkable as time went on. The road to discovery and recovery was exciting, painful and revealing of course. Yet it was more than that. We were like Columbus on a journey into and through a new world, only our small ship was our spirit and will to survive as a family, a couple and individuals. We were taking on a new world and hoping we were brave enough to meet the challenge.

If you are reading this book with the old fashioned belief that "people can't change," I tell you with complete honesty we can change, we do change and we must change not only to survive but to grow and to live better, more full and meaningful lives. I don't believe we change merely because we grow older. How many people do you know after all who are exactly the same as older people as they were when they were younger? My father, for example, is as he was, only more so, and not in a good way.

Perhaps someone in your family is someone you remember as a younger person and now as they are older you see qualities in them you either admired or disliked, but to a greater degree. As the shadow of their lives grows shorter, perhaps, they become more generous and kinder, if that was their personality to begin with. Or if they were always mean-spirited, self-involved and cheap, these traits become even more exaggerated. Such people cling to their material goods as they cling to life, as if by holding on to these things death somehow will elude them.

CHAPTER 20

Transition and the Road to Recovery

And so, the Hrehovciks of Maine were to embark on a journey of self-discovery and wellness. The desire to live healthier, happier, more fulfilling lives began with the awareness of Joshua's emotional problems, and that we, Stephen and I, were a big part of his problem and major contributors to it.

This was not easy for me to accept, especially at a time when I believed the only value in my life was my children. I also clung to the belief that I was a good mother. In spite of all my other failures I took refuge in the fact that "at least" I was a good mother. My children had always been the most important part of my life, my reason for being, for existing, for surviving. Now that illusion was gone, shattered along with all my other illusions. I had nothing left to believe in about myself. If I wasn't at least a good mother, what was I?

You see, it never occurred to me it was anyone's fault but

mine. Since I was the primary and often sole caretaker, I naturally assumed all the blame for Joshua's problems was mine. I believed I had failed as a mother and I had caused my son's emotional trauma. Imagine my shock, my utter surprise to discover it had something to do with my husband, with Stephen as well as with me. Hey, we were finally sharing something after all!

In fact, Joshua's problems had a lot to do with Stephen, with the kind of father he was and wasn't, and what Joshua needed him to be. Wow! I could feel a literal weight lift from my shoulders. Just as I had taken responsibility from Gillian, an objective person was telling me I was free from carrying the whole burden of blame. guilt and responsibility. Dr. Metzger told us it wasn't just me, or just Stephen, but both of us. Hallelujah.

We learned from Dr. Metzger that Joshua was suffering from anxiety disorder. Literally, suffering to the point of being paralyzed by the pain. We were told, much to our relief, this problem was treatable and curable. Joshua would need some medication for a while to help him immediately. At the same time, he would see Dr. Metzger every week for therapy.

I was so relieved to know the problem wasn't genetic, wasn't heredity, but a combination of Joshua's own personality, his position in the family, and the messages he received both directly and indirectly from both Stephen and me. Aha, that's where we parents came in: "the messages he received." Poor Joshua.

One of the first things Dr. Metzger told Stephen he must do was to insist Joshua stay in school. Dr. Metzger pointed directly at Stephen and said, "You have to do it. You have to tell him he has to stay in school." Since it had been Stephen who had previously agreed with Joshua that it was all right for him to quit school, now it was up to him as the father to tell his son he HAD to stay in school.

When Stephen first told me that he'd said to Joshua he could quit school, we had a huge fight. How could he agree to such a thing? I insisted Stephen finally put his foot down and give Joshua "a good kick in the ass." Naturally, what I thought made no difference to my husband, but now Dr. Metzger was telling him to do it. (Ha, I'd been right, so there.)

This may seem inconsequential to you, but believe me, I was very excited to know I still had some good instincts. After years of my opinions and views being ignored, I learned to mistrust my own ideas and instincts. Stephen had never listened to my ideas and disregarded my opinions and feelings. Naturally I felt I must be wrong all the time and not very smart. Of course, I reasoned, Stephen is the man and he must know more than I. At this time, I didn't know an instinct from a feeling from a thought.

That night when we got home from Dr. Metzger's office, Joshua was told he had to stay in school. Making this announcement was difficult for my husband to do as he had argued with the doctor about "going back on his word." Dr. Metzger got impatient with Stephen, who was a reluctant party to the entire idea of therapy to begin with and told him, "You are paying me good money for my advice. If you don't want to take my advice, then you'd better look for another doctor."

Joshua was furious and rode off on his bike, screaming at us the doctor was "dead wrong." We were so afraid of what he might do we called the doctor right away and told him what Joshua had said and threatened. So afraid were we that we might have sent our son on a suicide ride. Dr. Metzger assured us Joshua would be fine and was in his heart relieved that we had made the decision for him. I certainly understood the feeling of being relieved when someone else made a decision for you.

After all, the doctor reminded us, Joshua had been bringing home books, studying and even doing homework. Joshua had never brought books home from school and never did any schoolwork at home. Dr. Metzger guided us again. "Behavior is everything." he said. "If he really wanted to quit school, he wouldn't be studying and bringing his books home now." He was so right.

As Stephen and I and Noah and Gillian sat around scared and afraid and worried, not knowing where to go or what to do but pray the doctor was right, the phone rang. It was Joshua. He was at a friend's house in Kennebunk and they were ordering pizza. What a sigh of relief we all let out, and how our faith and trust grew for Dr. Metzger.

Stephen who had been skeptical all along about therapy, became a believer. Now my husband began to look inward, a part of himself he had avoided his entire life. For the first time Stephen was faced with himself and the realization that some of Joshua's problems were some of his own as well. Joshua began therapy in earnest that week.

We were blaming ourselves, Stephen and I, but happily we were not blaming each other. We knew enough that blame would not help Joshua. We had to be strong together, a unit, to help Joshua be well again. I was both relieved and dismayed upon hearing the problem. Relieved it wasn't an inherited disease and dismayed I had not realized how truly tormented Joshua had been and I hadn't helped him. I was concerned Joshua might not agree to therapy every week, but he wanted to be better and was willing to do his part in the process. What a brave, smart young man he was. Not quite sixteen, yet Joshua was so much more aware than his parents.

Naturally, at this point I didn't know how to behave. How would I treat my own son? What should I do differently? I surely did not want to continue to make the same mistakes over and over again. The doctor told me to go on as always since any drastic change in my behavior would only underline the condition.

That weekend we held the first auditions for Stephen's show, *Round 'Bout Maine*. God, talk about the eternal optimist. My heart wasn't in anything other than my son Joshua, his therapy and his getting well. My body went through the motions of doing what I had to do, but all I really wanted was some peace of mind. It would be many years before I would see that "piece of quiet."

I wish I could have spared Joshua from all his pain and torment. I would have given anything for my three children to have back a younger, more carefree childhood. I personally would have liked to have been spared the pain of losing all we had worked so hard for together. And Stephen, I can only give him credit for having the courage and the strength to change and grow and learn and question. Of all of us, somehow, I think the journey must have been the hardest on him.

My husband has never been afraid of hard work, but therapy is emotional work like no other. The most difficult self-help is to reach deep into your gut and pull out your inside. Even at this time, with so much passed and forgotten, to remember and recall all of it is painful, and except for this story, unnecessary. We forged ahead, survived, learned and somehow, a credit to our entire family, we came out on the other side, to a place of wellbeing.

Do I need to be more specific? I cannot. Suffice to say Joshua was in therapy all summer and part of the fall. Stephen and I met with Dr. Metzger once a month to learn what we had to do to help Joshua and ourselves. As Stephen and I learned more about Joshua's problems, we learned our own part in those problems

My rides back and forth with Joshua to the doctors were fraught with arguments, anger, silence and often tears. I wanted so much to know what he and the doctor talked about, but Joshua couldn't or wouldn't share with me. Now Stephen decided to follow Dr. Metzger's advice and go for therapy himself. Thus began the inward journey for Stephen and for me as well.

Later that summer our theater closed, Hank incorporated H&H and we were forced out of the business. We had no jobs, no income, and huge amounts of debt. As frightening as all that was, it mattered little beside the wonderful things that were happening within our family. I saw two of the most important men in my life getting help and getting better. I was happy for them but at the same time I knew I needed help for myself. Soon, I told myself.

At a time when we couldn't pay either our mortgage or our utility bills, we were paying $100 a week to Dr. Metzger (he'd raised his fee) and later $70 a week for Stephen's therapy.

There never was a question of spending the money for this very important part of our lives. This was an investment not only in Joshua's health but in his future, our future and the future of our family.

Almost everyone who knew us as a family thought we were such a special family. We were. We are. Was it because we were aware and willing to do something to make our life better? Or was it because all the kids were so gifted and so creative? Perhaps we were thought to be special because we were so close and generally loving and supportive of each other. We all paid a high price for our gifts.

That summer as Joshua was working hard to get better and live a healthy life, Stephen was working around the clock. He worked on his map and his show while trying to keep up some part in the agency. Our house was still not finished and now we had an unfinished addition beside it. The house became a symbol of lost dreams and broken promises, of all the unfinished business in our marriage and in our lives.

The house we had designed and built with such high hopes and expectations was a sham and a humiliation to all of us. Yes, I believe I was ashamed because I didn't know how to finish a house and to get things done. Everything was an uphill battle, and I felt as if I was always the loser. It wasn't because we didn't work hard; we were working all the time. I didn't understand how we could work so hard and still have so little, and then we had nothing.

By mid-summer the theater closed and we owed $20,000. Just for the theater! We owed another $10,000 personally for back bills at home and at the office. $30,000 in debt and I was overwhelmed. I couldn't even begin to imagine how we could survive. We had already used our house as collateral for a loan for the theater. Now it looked as if the only way out was to sell our house. There was so much love and promise built into that house, but little else.

Yet we vacillated, afraid to let go, while knowing in our hearts there was no alternative. Hank had taken over the agency and gave Stephen the chance to work for him, and I, of course, would be out. Stephen and I went to a lawyer who told us just to let go and get out. "Suing will eat up your whole life," he said, "and you."

Hank had taken our name and reputation and made it his, but we were advised simply to walk away and get on with our lives. We did, and that was the best advice anyone ever gave us. As hurt as I was by the pain and humiliation of losing yet another part of our lives, I was relieved too. I was glad another decision had been made for us. We were no longer an H of H&H.

That fall I took a job in downtown Kennebunkport. I was scooping ice cream and steaming hot dogs at a little stand by Dock Square. I ran the little shop by the cove all by myself and had no important decisions to make. I was a little embarrassed to be working there but happy I could at least contribute to the family finances. Stephen got a job with an ad agency in Portland, but still we couldn't make enough money to pay off all our debts.

My job was handy for me because I was close to home and the kids could either stop by the store after school or call me. It was more important than ever to me that I be available and accessible to the kids. I knew they needed me and the little stability my being there could offer.

I liked my little job at Aunt Marie's and met many nice, interesting people from all over the country. Most people like to talk and people on vacation are friendly and eager to talk about the area or where they have come from. There were many warm fall days when a lot of the kids from town would come in and buy an ice cream cone, and I was always happy to see them and talk with them.

There were other days, however, when I thought I would break down, just collapse and cry and cry and cry. A few times I had to call the boys to come and help me out. Some days were too hard for me to carry on. I was lost.

It was funny too, because during this time I met several people, all men by the way, who would come up to me and tell me how much they admired my husband. They said they would never have the "guts" to try something like Stephen had with the theater. These men admired his ability to take risks and follow his dream. How would they know risk-taking was like a disease with Stephen? I am sure they admired him for having a dream and trying to make his dream a reality.

I was usually unresponsive and wondered what kind of courage it takes to gamble your future and the future of your children and your family? Timing I believe is everything, and if you ask me, Stephen's timing was pretty lousy. Our children should have been free to be themselves. These were the years they should have been free to break away and follow their own dreams. They needed to make discoveries, try different paths, make their own mistakes and learn from them.

Instead my children had to be concerned with whether or not they'd have a house to live in, food on the table, electricity or a phone (and let's not forget water).

If we hadn't been living like this for most of our married life, perhaps I could have made a game out of it and laughed and smiled and carried on. But all the years of loss and failure had taken a toll on me. I could not pretend life was anything but what it was to me at the time: Grim.

By the end of the year we were doing our best to pick up the pieces. Stephen was still in therapy and his family wasn't talking to him. I think they were ashamed of him, after all, he'd gone to college, how could he fail? More than this I know his father didn't respect him and thought Stephen was weak. Stephen cried on the phone one day to his father after we had lost both the theater and the agency. His father's advice was to leave me and "come home to New Jersey." Thanks, Pop. I don't know but I guess Stephen was supposed to leave the kids too.

My family wasn't much better. My mother kept asking me how I could have been "so stupid?" (Of course.) Why did I "let" Stephen do such a "dumb thing?" "Let." As if I could ever stop him. She told me I should have screamed and hollered and put my foot down. Like she did, I guess, anytime my father had an idea or a dream or an ambition. I never wanted Stephen to turn on me in his old age as my father had done to my mother and accuse me of standing in his way.

To this day I don't know who was right or who was wrong. My mother was always afraid of change and eventually she made my father afraid too. I didn't want the same thing to happen to me. My parents grew old never moving again or changing in any way. I never heard them say "I'm sorry or maybe I made a mistake." Not to each other and certainly not to my brother or me.

Carol Hrehovcik

They gave up their friends one by one, abandoned their own families emotionally as well as physically. For the last twenty years of her life my mother's only companion was my father. They would venture out only within a very minimal radius.

Even driving to Maine, only an hour away, became more than they were willing to do. Mother's only interests were her books and reading, watching the news and the weather, oh yes, and playing cards. Whenever any of us had to travel, we'd call my mother. She always knew what the weather would be anywhere across the country.

When she died thirteen years ago, we thought for sure Dad would follow her. After all, he had no life of his own, other than what he shared with my mother. He was ninety-nine when he died. He stayed in his house and lived alone, mostly taking care of himself. He surprised us all.

While she was alive and I was struggling to survive, I gave up the idea of the mother I had hoped to be and the mother I never had. I wanted a mother who would always be there for me, who would encourage me, care about me and love me.

I was forty-four years old and I still yearned for my mother to love me, but all I got was criticism. No matter what I did, it wasn't good enough. More than that, as she always liked to remind me, I was stupid.

I believe all my life my goal was to do something to show my mother I was worth loving. I needed to prove to her I wasn't really stupid or lazy or bad. I wanted so much for her to see me the way I thought of myself – thoughtful, warm, loving and generous.

In the midst of all the turmoil in my life, I believed she

must be right. The image I had of myself must be an illusion. I wasn't nice or warm or generous and of course I must be stupid. I had no idea yet who I was, except I know I was feeling like the biggest failure in the entire world. I couldn't do anything right. Yes, I was a loser, a failure, and most of all I felt as if I were all alone.

Joshua ended his therapy in January of 1982. He was a different person, pleasant to have around and an active part of the family.

The money problems continued and there was no relief in sight. At the time I knew our lives were out of control as I continued my search for a better, well-paying job. No matter. We couldn't make money fast enough to satisfy our debts. The mortgage was so far behind that the bank threatened us with foreclosure.

Something good came out of all the turmoil and upheaval. While Joshua was in the midst of his anxiety problems, my parents became kind and supportive to me. Although I still felt anxiety whenever I called or went to see them, I was genuinely surprised by their new sense of good will toward me. I believe my mother's heart condition softened her in a way I had not seen before. One of the most loving memories of my mother came a few years before her death.

We were going to lunch in Haverhill, just the two of us, and she said out loud something very surprising. "I wish I had been gentler with you and your brother when you were growing up." It's a wonder I didn't steer the car into a ditch. I had always wanted my mother to be gentle and warm, and now she was confessing she was sorry she hadn't been. She went on to say, "But that is the way we were brought up and

I never learned anything except I had to be tough in order to survive. My mother waited on my father hand and foot and he even cheated on her. I swore I would never do that for any man."

And she didn't. Still my parents were together for nearly sixty years and managed to make their marriage work for them. Even though it was too late for mother to be different, it helped me to know she herself would have liked to be.

Sometimes in the years when she was sick, I would look at her and get tearful. I'd watch her walk away and know I would keep this picture of her in my mind. I wanted to remember her a little warmer and gentler than I had ever known her. Such memories are a great comfort and strength to me now.

Mother said her heart attack made her appreciate life in a new way. Things that used to be important to her just didn't seem to matter much anymore. She relaxed about her housekeeping, and I remembered all those terrible Fridays and weekends when we had to help out and she'd be on her hands and knees washing and waxing the floors. I remember how she insisted I never throw anything on the bedspread, and how she always wanted those damn hardwood floors dusted every day. That's why I never cared whether or not I have hardwood floors in my house. I'd rather vacuum than dust, and that sure isn't every other day.

At the same time Stephen was having more problems with his family, especially of course, his father. My father-in-law and my mother would have made quite a pair I thought. Kiddingly one time I said this to one of our therapists. He replied, "They did get married and here you are." Pointing to me and Stephen. What a shock! I could see just how right he was. Those two parents in us were our warring sides. I hadn't thought about it much before, but perhaps the other two parents in us were our peacemaker sides, but more than likely, knowing my father and Stephen's mother, our appeasing side.

Stephen and I discovered as we went on in various counseling sessions that many of our mistakes were caused by our desire to please the other person. To keep the peace, or so we thought, we denied our own feelings. We suppressed our own wants and kept quiet about our true desires. Needless to say, while our intentions were good, not to hurt each other, what we really did was hurt each other more.

Thus, they say the road to hell is paved with good intentions. I always knew Stephen would never hurt me or the kids consciously. The fact that he was so unconscious most of our early married years didn't help ease any of the family's pain or grief. He's writing his own book now and calls it *Rebel Without A Clue.* Oh, yes.

Stephen always said I felt "threatened" by his family. I always denied it until his father told him, "Divorce her and come home to New Jersey." Yes, then I did feel threatened. Stephen and I had been married for seventeen years by then, and yet his father wanted him to "come home."

While I gave Stephen comfort, holding him, sharing his tears and pain, his parents were home saying the rosary. I tell you it is a lot easier to say the rosary than it is to comfort and console the living here and now.

To listen, to seek to understand who you are, where you came from, why you are the kind of person you are, this journey of self-discovery takes courage. The big WHY, to ask and seek, is hard work, and takes more strength than saying any rosary, attending any mass, or reciting the Stations of the Cross. Some people manage to do both, and I admire them for that. But not my in-laws. I firmly believe God did not make us to suffer here on earth. I simply do not believe it. These people who professed this great need to suffer did not seem to me to be suffering at all.

CHAPTER 21

Survival of the Most Stubborn

Poor Mr. Hrehovcik did not count on the fact of me. Me, stubborn and proud, too proud to admit defeat in this marriage. My daughter-in-law once said to me, "Not many people hang on to their marriages like a pit bull the way you did." I rather like that image.

I may have been in pain, maybe I lost many battles, but I was determined not to lose at this marriage. I had too much invested in it: myself, my kids, my time, my energy, and yes, even my faith.

Damn it, I was not going to quit. I would not allow Stephen's father to "win." Not that there weren't plenty of times I would have surrendered. "You want him, you take him, he's yours." But somehow, for whatever reason, I hung on and so did Stephen. By some miracle, thank you God, so did my kids.

I'd love to say my kids hung on through faith, love, hope,

and charity, but hey, they were kids and that was all they wanted to be. Sadly, being kids was something they were not allowed to be. At the same time, I made sure I was always there for them. After school there would always be milk or tea and sometimes freshly baked cookies. I was the shoulder to lean on, ready to listen if they wanted to talk, or just be there when there was no talk.

And always I was the one who would slay dragons for them if I could. Sadly, of course, I couldn't always do that. As for Stephen, as addicted as he was to work, he was there for all their performances, recitals, band concerts, plays, little league games. He was there when he needed to show up.

That is the clue, "needed to show up." Stephen was not aware the children needed him not just for those special times, but all the time to know he was there, to be consistent and reliable. The children needed Stephen to be there to set boundaries, rules, guidelines. They wanted and needed a father, not a buddy, not a playmate. I know this was one of the hardest lessons for Stephen to accept. When the goal of your lifetime is to be the "nice guy," it is not a role you relinquish easily.

Of course, I would have loved to be the nice guy for a change. I would have loved it if he ever just once spoke up, hollered back at his father, disciplined the kids. Wouldn't I have enjoyed being the voice of reason and solicitude!

I would have said, "Now, Stephen, you have to understand your father's point of view." Or I'd have been happy to say, "Stephen, good for you; you took care of yourself and didn't let him push you around." Years later I did get the chance to say that when Stephen at last stood up to his father. Yet it was never easy or natural for him to do that.

I believe because his father was a bully, Stephen wanted to be totally different. Mr. Hrehovcik respected a man who would fight back. My husband is a gentle man, and so my father-in-law never respected him as either a man or his son. I am sure this awareness is as painful today for Stephen as it was hard to accept all those years ago. Like most men, Stephen wanted and needed his father's approval and respect. I, on the other hand, wanted my mother's love. Hey, were we made for each other or what?

Does it then follow we both came to our marriage with empty plates? We expected the other person to heap our plates full of all we required, needed and craved. Yet we never talked about these expectations, or our fears and doubts. There was no discussion about "what a marriage means to me." Needless to say, we never talked about money or children either. We were naive when we met and married and continued to live in the same blind alley for years and years afterward. It took the illness of our oldest son for us to face up to each other and to ourselves.

Stephen's father had a simpler solution for us, cheaper too. He told Stephen that all his troubles started when he left the church and turned away from God. (Well, at least it didn't start with me for a change, although I'm sure that was the implication.) Stephen needed only to go back to church, confess his sins (yes, he said that), and repent. When Stephen told his father he wasn't a sinner, his father did what he always did when faced with disagreement from Stephen, he hung up on him.

Stephen was working at an advertising agency in Portland

and finally free from H&H and even from Hank's persistent
phone calls looking for money. I think it finally dawned on
Hank there was no money to be had from the Hrehovciks
and he stopped calling at last. My job at the publishing house
sadly didn't work out for me. Not that my copy was bad, it
was a matter of money. I wanted more than they were willing
to pay and for the first time I didn't settle for less than what
I believed I was worth. Naturally, they found someone else
to do the job for the salary they wanted to pay. We creative
people are like that, don't you think? "Why, you'll pay us for
our ideas? How nice of you. Oh, no, anything will do." Not
this time for me, I decided, so I was out of work once again.
Now what?

Every day there were more threatening letters, more ugly
calls from bill collectors. Collection agencies were taking over
our delinquent bills. We were forced to face the inevitable
truth and put our house on the market. We put the house for
sale for $89,500 in February of 1982. Our realtor thought the
price somewhat in the high range, but was willing to give it
a try.

When I left the realtor's that morning after I'd signed the
papers, I had forty-five cents in my pocket. At home in the
refrigerator was one egg, a half a loaf of bread and a cup of
milk. I happened to meet our old associate, the other H, as
he was getting out of his car and I was crossing the street.
"Good morning, Carol." He even smiled at me. I was cold and
muttered something like a greeting, giving him my coldest,
most hateful look, indignant he even had the nerve to speak
to me. Yes, if looks could kill...

It would be many years later before I could understand

and even forgive Hank for his behavior toward Stephen and me. He was doing what he knew how to do best, just like the rest of us. And God, we were ripe for the picking, except they were mighty slim pickings.

At this time, I wrote in my journal, "there's never been a rest from despair, fear, anxiety and dread." My parents see me in such misery, they join the "leave him" club. They blame Stephen for everything, pretty much the same as Stephen's parents blame me, except of course, my parents blame me for being "stupid," as usual, and for building "that mausoleum."

If I left my husband my parents would let me and the kids have their third floor apartment. How could I refuse an offer like that? I could stay in Kennebunkport and be miserable on my own or return to my parents' house, be called names, and still be miserable on my own. "Let me weigh my options."

I had my answer one night soon after. Our wonderful old neighbor up the hill died suddenly. Mr. Hamilton was our friend and adopted grandfather. Although we all loved and adored him, Gillian was the closest to him. At a mere ten years of age, she felt his loss more deeply than the rest of us.

She came into our bed in the middle of the night because she was having a bad dream. When she felt better, she asked her Daddy to carry her back to her bed. Stephen got up, lifted her and carried her back to her room. As the two of them left the room, a sort of light around them from the night light I suppose, she said, "I love you, Daddy." And he replied, "I love you, Gillian." Suddenly I had the answer to what I had been asking myself.

I had been searching and searching for some clue, and now I knew I would stay with Stephen no matter what. As long as we were together, all of us, I knew that was the most important part of my life. I told him, "I will stay with you as long as I live, for richer or for poorer, for better or for worse, in sickness and in health." At this moment I truly believed everything was going to work out all right. I felt a sense of peace and my own sense of priorities was back in place.

I often remember and reflect on this particular moment, and still see Stephen lifting and carrying our precious Gillian. I can see the light that surrounded them in our bedroom on Maplewood Drive. Gillian saved me once again. I believe she saved me with her utter simplicity, honesty, faith, and love.

The boys have saved me over the years in other ways. When life was so bleak for us financially, Noah applied to Interlochen Arts Academy for his junior year of high school. Josh had been accepted into the National Honor Society at the high school. Teachers were telling me how special and unique my sons were, and more than their cleverness, intelligence, and abilities, the teachers remarked on the quality of their characters. As one of their teachers predicted, "They will do wonderful things in large proportion."

The most important part of all of this was Joshua feeling good about himself for the first time in years. I was no longer afraid he would harm himself. Noah was beginning to think about his future and plan for it. Yes, I felt blessed and smart at the same time. I was proud of both of my sons, and yes of Stephen and myself. We faced, along with Joshua, many unpleasant truths and were willing to work together to make a better life for all of us.

After my bitter disappointment with the publishing firm in Portland, I decided once again to get back to what I yearned to do more than anything else. I wanted to write and so I began to write this story. That was 1982.

I had no idea so many years ago the long road that lay ahead of us still. Children grew up and as we grew older too, life became more complicated and went from bad to worse to a little better. Finally, there were more days of sunshine than rain for us, when tears weren't the hallmark of each moment and fear wasn't my constant companion. How many turning points are there in a life?

If you are looking for one decisive moment, one major breakthrough, one gigantic revelation, a thunderbolt of clarity, then this is not the story for you. Yes, I had that moment, a glimmer of clarity and vision, a moment of seeing into my soul and knowing a truth. But moments come and moments go, and even visions fade with time. Ah, but the soul! The soul holds on and clings and won't let go of what it knows: the truth, your own individual, personal truth.

CHAPTER 22

Count Your Blessings

During this time, I was afraid still of everything and everyone. If I didn't see a bill collector lurking around every corner, I saw Stephen's family ready to pounce on me, or my own family. There was no money and almost never any food in the house. Stephen was very unhappy with his job at the agency in Portland. I tried my best to console him, cheer him up, but I was so afraid myself that all I really wanted was for someone to take care of me.

Who consoles the consoler? I felt shy and timid, anxious, fearful, insecure and unloved. Joshua and I fought a lot as he gained his newly found self-confidence. He even had a girlfriend. Noah was accepted to Interlochen and while we wanted him to have the privilege of attending, without a full scholarship, how would he go?

My niece, Lorrie, left her husband, took her baby, and moved back to my brother's house. My mother tells Louis to adopt the baby. How right she was; she saw then so clearly what most of us wouldn't see for years. I'm sorry, mother, I didn't give you half the credit you deserved. I couldn't see past my own pain and unhappiness at the time.

No one had come to look at our house, so there were no offers. We picked one of the worst times in the history of real estate to sell our house! The bank would remortgage the house for a short time but was influencing us to "sell fast." So many balls in the air and I felt as if I were the only one running to pick them up.

Stephen was always busy but not happy. Along with his old arrogance, he'd lost his self-confidence and wasn't sure who he was anymore. He was sending out resumes, but along with the real estate market, the job market in Maine was also suffering. Why did we hang on there? Why did we continue to cling to the past and even more to the present? We had picked up whatever roots we had before and set out for a better life. What stopped us now?

I think it was our children. I believe we couldn't complicate their lives anymore by moving away. Even though our situation was bleak right now, somewhere inside us, both Stephen and I felt hope for our future. We either had an inner strength or an incredible stupidity. It wouldn't be the first time. I believe somehow, we still had faith in each other.

Stephen must have had an enormous amount of faith in me. To think I could or would hold on to this last plank in our sinking ship was a gigantic leap of faith on his part. What was the motivation for me to stay? Was it love? Stupidity? Courage? Strength? Faith? Or was it just being plain old stubborn? My unwillingness to give in to defeat, to say I had failed. I think it may have been a combination of all these qualities, not one more or less, or even in particular.

I know too it was my children who were the force that kept me going. At this time, I certainly would not have won any mother of the year award. Yet both Stephen and I were holding on to whatever thread of love that was left between us. We wanted to make our life better not only for ourselves but most especially for our children.

I think it is important for them to know they were the source of any strength I had left. Each of them, Joshua, Noah and Gillian were my lifeline and support in ways they will never know or understand, until they become parents themselves.

This was a difficult time for me personally and I made a big mistake of wanting and needing understanding from my kids. What a fool I was. I did not realize they were kids and the problems of adults must not become the problems of children. I confess I was not able to make any kind of a sound judgment or decision. I was lucky to be alive. Just getting out of bed every day was a major accomplishment for me at the time. What got me out of bed I know was faith and my three children.

Let's talk about faith. I have been accused from time to time of not being a very holy or religious person. People have expressed doubt in my faith and belief in God. I have never been loyal to any kind of organized religion, but I have always maintained a very personal relationship with God. I don't feel it necessary to share this with anyone particularly as it is between me and God. I could ask myself whether I was right or wrong, but I choose rather not to second guess myself in this regard. I have over the years given almost every part of me away, now no one is going to get his hands on my life with

God. More than anything I require one aspect of myself that is mine alone, and if that meant not sharing my own faith and love of God with anyone else, well that was the way it was and still is for me.

How many parts of our lives are we able to keep to ourselves? In these times when privacy has become a rare commodity even to the most common person among us, I cherish mine and always will. Too bad more people don't feel this way. I mean, who really cares who you have sex with or what you do in the "privacy" of your own home? It seems people welcome the opportunity to talk about the most intimate details of their lives in front of millions and millions of strangers. I don't want to know all your secrets and I won't let you know all of mine. Even in the writing of this book, I find I cannot share totally out of a sense of modesty on one hand and on the other who really cares?

This of course is all beside the point as we are talking about a marriage and how this one marriage survived. How in God's (yes, God) name did Stephen and I survive together and come out on the other side? Surely it was not because of any support from either of our families, both waiting for us to admit we'd made a mistake, eager in fact to shout, "I told you so."

Stephen's family wanted him back "home" under their control, to return to church and "repent" all his sins. I was never sure if Stephen's father meant "God the Father" would forgive Stephen or if it was more "Mike the father" who would forgive his son once he repented those damn sins of his. One of which, I'm sure, perhaps even the most predominant sin being that he married me.

My family, on the other hand, wanted me to leave my husband so that I could get on with my life, make some money and take care of my kids. My parents were, after all, pragmatic. I confess to believing this was a logical and, on the surface, a sensible solution. The flaw with that kind of thinking is that life is more than money and providing material comforts to your family.

Whether you are a single parent or a part of a pair, the loving and nurturing of children is more important to their wholesome well-being. I knew I could surely take care of their bodies and minds, but I wasn't sure I was equipped to take care of their spirits. I don't mean a spirituality. I thought that to deprive a child of living with his father was not a step to take lightly. Was Stephen totally useless? No, of course not. Was he worthless? No. I was clinging to some feeling inside myself, not love, really not love, but the feeling I knew somewhere inside him was the man who could and would make me happy to be his wife. One day I was sure I would be glad once again I had chosen him, and he had chosen me. I told you in the beginning this was not a love story, but I see now that it truly is just that, an indefinable love story.

Aside from the love we both were searching for in each other, we needed the love and approval of our parents. But more important and significant for each of us was the need to discover self-love. In order to accept and love each other, we first had to look inside ourselves and learn to love and accept our own Self. The hardest lesson I learned was I am responsible for my own happiness. Not Stephen, not my mother or father, not my children, but me. Only Carol can make Carol happy. I am responsible for my own happiness.

This truth was a shock to me. I was so sure Stephen was supposed to make me happy. He'd made me unhappy enough. So? What a great lesson! Like most lessons it sounds easier than it is.

"I am responsible for my own happiness. I choose to be happy. I love myself and accept myself as I am, for who I am. I do not expect myself to be perfect. There is no perfection in this world. Perfect is an illusion."

I had to learn all of this. I, who had always sought, needed, and desired freedom, found it at last in this litany of affirmations. Yet these are beyond affirmations. This is truth beyond philosophy, beyond reason or logic or mind-bending ideology. I hope you recognize the power of these truths. I hope you can say them to yourself and mean every word you say. Feel them inside yourself, way down in the deepest part of you. "I am responsible for my own happiness. I choose to be happy. I love myself and I accept myself as I am, for who I am."

I did not, I confess, make this discovery overnight. Not only that, I deluded myself enough to think I really did love myself and of course I wanted to be happy. Didn't everyone? "No, Carol, apparently not." Yes, I wanted to be happy, but I wanted Stephen to make me happy. You see, I had some work to do.

I was confused in this regard for many years. I had a lot of questions but no answers. How would I know now what was right for me? I'd spent most of my life trying to please everyone else. Who would give me permission to please myself? Me? I needed permission from a higher authority, whoever that was. After all, wasn't I supposed to be perfect?

Not just good, you see, or even good enough, I thought I must be perfect, had to be perfect. A perfect lady, a perfect daughter, a perfect wife, a perfect mother, and a perfect worker no matter where I was working or what I was doing.

If work was Stephen's God, then the need and constant quest for perfection was mine. I was not conscious of it, and yet there it was. When I learned that it was all right not to be perfect and even impossible to be so, I was free. Not only was I free, I knew then life could be more fun. Giving up my quest for perfection, knowing it was all right since perfection does not exist on this earth, the doors to joy opened for me.

All right, here we go again, more philosophical meandering. What fun! Let's talk about perfection. As in "I can type this letter perfectly." "My resume must be perfect in its presentation." There are of course areas where perfect must occur: lines of an engineering drawing must be perfect, two and two must add up to four, and the accounting of all numbers must balance. Aha, but in the realm of body, mind, soul, spirit, a relationship, a feeling, an inspiration, a creation, there is no perfection.

There is no perfect play, movie, novel, painting, marriage, child, mother, father, aunt, uncle, or friend. You can make your own list, and yes, you may even disagree with me. However, let me point out to you if there is perfection there would be no disagreement or discussion about it, would there? It simply would just be, wouldn't it?

I needed very much to think about this. I had to give myself permission NOT to be perfect. I knew I did not have the perfect house. I did not have to make perfect cookies, cakes, dinners. I could make mistakes and shrug my shoulders and say it's all right; it's only a cake or a meatloaf or a chicken. I could even throw it away and I'd still be Carol, still be myself. Hey, I might even like myself better because this was more me, playful and forgiving.

Ha! Me forgiving! I found I could forgive myself for making a mistake. When I learned to forgive myself, then I learned I could forgive other people too. For in the past I wanted perfection not only in and for myself, but I wanted and required it from others as well. I used to shout inside myself, "Hey, you guys, don't you know you are supposed to be perfect? Who told you it was all right not to be perfect? And how did you find it out before I did?"

For me words have always been playful. Shall I put this word here or there? Does it make more sense here or does it sound better there? I can go merrily on my way or merrily I go on my way to wherever, here or there again.

Play. Aha! Yes, another aha. Stephen and I were in more trouble because we had so little sense of play in our lives together. I loved to play. That was my life as a child and what I thought all children had to do. I know it was a good thing that I had children, so I had someone to play with. I love to play, and I really don't care how you define play for yourself. Remember yourself as a child, or if that doesn't help you, go watch children at play somewhere. To play is to laugh, to laugh is to delight in or with. There is no sense to play, hence, nonsense.

You may be thinking about now this is nonsense. See. I am playing with you. I had fun, how about you?

It is interesting to note that I include the section on play and lack of perfection at this particular point in the story. Yet, when I think about it, it makes perfect sense (oh, oh) as there was no joy for me and very little play at this point in my life or marriage. Had I forgotten how to laugh? Was I afraid to be playful? We'd been married for seventeen years and had only one vacation in all that time. The few holidays we had over the years were spent visiting with Stephen's family, and that sure was no holiday for me.

There is so much information and knowledge available to you now. I know you are making wiser, more informed decisions than we did. I also have the sense it didn't take you seventeen or twenty years to figure it out. However, if you are part of a couple, no matter if you've been together or married five months, five years, fifteen years or even fifty years, you know there are always questions, doubts, insecurities, anxieties. How do you handle these issues? Do you talk with each other? Are you open and honest with each other? Is one of you in denial about something, perhaps, or everything?

I used to think everyone else was so much smarter than I, and smarter than Stephen and me together. Now I am thinking this is not necessarily true. Technology is smarter of course, but we as human beings are the same as we always were. People and human nature don't advance as fast as the technology.

No, I think human nature and its development take time. And time seems to be the one precious commodity we can't control. Time very often is not on our side. While we may work harder, faster, get more information quicker and more efficiently, most of us seem to be content or even complacent about our relationships. The most important people in our lives frequently are also the most overlooked aspect in our lives.

To Love and To Cherish

It is not a question of which came first, the proverbial chicken or egg. It is rather knowing who and what is most important to you and your life. What gives your life meaning? Who gives your life meaning? Do you let those people know they come before work or football or golf? Are your priorities in line with your family and friends? Or do you have another set of priorities totally separate from the people you love and care about? What does your life say about you? What would people say about you if you died right this minute, right here in the middle of this sente...? Oh, look. I am playing with you again.

Speaking of priorities, I have certainly strayed from mine as I recollect the reason, I am writing this book. I want to encourage you to hang on in your marriage, to fight for it, to be brave and yes, even tough. I want to encourage you to make your family the number one priority in your life. While you may not be able to take the rewards you gain to the bank, no bank could ever give you the interest payable as your children get older and become your friends.

The future is truly with and in our children. The peace of the world begins with the strength and peace of your family. Each family is unique and important. There is no one out there more important than you are to yourself, your companion for life, and your children.

We owe our children. We brought them into the world, and we owe them our love and devotion. We don't owe them our lives, nor do they owe us anything in return except respect (if we have earned it). The most we can hope for with our children, I believe, is they will make a better life for themselves and their children, if they choose to have children.

Each generation we hope will be better than the last, smarter and more sensitive to the present and to the future.

Back to the Hrehovciks, meanwhile, and how not to do it and at the same time hope that you can do it, that is keep your marriage and your family together through the bad times and the good times too.

The summer of 1982 and Stephen lost his job at the advertising agency in Portland. He was out of work for six weeks that summer and we had more fun than we'd had in all the years since we'd moved to Maine. We couldn't pay our bills of course, but for the first time I could remember Stephen was able to relax and not feel guilty. He was spending time with me and the kids and we all seemed to thrive on it. Noah had been accepted to Interlochen School for the Arts, and money was coming in from several generous, local people.

Stephen and Noah had flown to Michigan to see the school and for Noah to audition. My father had cashed in a mutual fund and given both Louis and me a thousand dollars. We spent a large portion of that money on the trip to Michigan. Looking back now, that was probably not the smartest choice to make, but we felt Noah was so gifted we wanted him to have the opportunity to make the most of his abilities. This was not a happy or easy decision for me. At the time Noah was my rock. He was steady, still temperamental, but steady. He had his goal and was intent on succeeding and doing what he felt he needed to do.

Sadly, Stephen and I did not feel the same. Our goal, or at least I thought our goal, was to get out of debt, but at the same time we did not want to deny our children their future. We tried to protect the kids in whatever way we could, but did that include pretending Noah could go to an elitist private school? And how would this affect the rest of the family?

We hadn't told the kids Stephen had lost his job. Naturally they wondered why he was home so much. He told them he was working on some special projects. Of course, looking back now, I can say once again how stupid (that word) and how wrong we were. Our children knew our family was in financial trouble, but they were still children after all, and my natural inclination was to protect them. This backfired on me. Once again may I remind you this was long before I knew anything about codependency-dependency and enabling. I could have written the book, or more likely the book was written for me. Isn't hindsight wonderful? Or is it awful do you think?

Meanwhile I kept going on job interviews, but I know now I sent out vibrations that I really didn't want the job, whatever it was. I loved being home with my children, especially in the summer. Noah was taking a driving course; Gillian and I took long walks into town and rode our bikes together to her piano lessons. Joshua was working at an inn in Kennebunkport and was looking at college brochures. He was seventeen that summer, and as usual we had a great birthday party for him. Our family was lucky at this time to have many good and supportive friends, even though we had lost others along the way.

Yet this year, 1982, with all its losses and insecurities, was better than what we had experienced the year before. Surely, I thought, we were on the road to recovery. The road to recovery was a long journey and it continues still. For me, the most difficult decision I ever made was to call for help, to reach out for professional help from a psychiatrist whose name I had carried in my wallet for more than two years. That phone call was one of the most difficult calls I ever made and the most important, as that call was the beginning of a new life for me.

In spite of my background and education there was still something inside me that believed I had to do "it" myself. I had to help myself and I believed I had to make myself better. With so many bad things happening at once and yet at the same time some good things beginning to happen as well, I knew I had to make some changes. I had to change some part of myself, but I didn't have a clue where or how to start. At the same time, I was plagued by fear this depression of mine was genetic and I would never be better. Perhaps, I thought, depression was an inherited disease and there was nothing I could do about it.

I was so afraid of this kind of a diagnosis that it was more than two years before I was brave enough to make the phone call to Dr. Collins. As with most unknown parts of life, the anxiety turned out to be far worse than any reality. I had been paralyzed by this fear. I thought how much better Joshua was doing and how a psychiatrist had helped him. Stephen too was getting better in so many ways. He had gotten a new job at last. He became a design engineer for Weyerhaeuser in November of that year.

Since Stephen was seeing Dr. Goodman and now Joshua had completed his treatment with Dr. Metzger, I thought this was a good time for me to get some help for myself. I also knew enough to know I had to be the one to make the changes in my life. I wanted to be happier and I knew I was the only one who could make that happen.

Why is it that many of us will do anything to help our children, but hesitate to give ourselves the same benefit? At least that is the way it was for me; I'd give or do anything for my kids, had done almost everything for and with Stephen. I still tried to please my parents, and appease Stephen's family, yet I put myself way down on the list. Not because someone asked me to, I just did it. I took on the role of martyr and then was mad as hell I did it. I couldn't stop myself; I didn't know any other way to be.

Making that call was so difficult, making an appointment and actually taking the first step to say I needed help. I knew I wanted to be better and most of all I wanted to be happy. Curiously, after I hung up the phone, I felt much better, relieved and almost lighthearted. I recall thinking, "Hey look at me; I'm all right. I really have things under control, and I can take care of myself." I almost called back and cancelled the appointment, but now that I'd made the decision to ask for help, I was eager to get started.

The first of three appointments was scheduled for the next week for a half hour. I would have liked to have an hour to get started, but I appreciated this evaluation was a way to get some people talking. I understand others might be reluctant or shy about opening up their minds and hearts. Not me. Once I made the decision to go for help, I wanted it fast; I was more than ready and willing.

Nevertheless, this was a wonderful way for me to begin, and I discovered I had an immediate rapport with Dr. Collins. I felt lucky to have had him recommended to me and of course "stupid" that I had waited so long to call. But here I was at last, and anxious to know what was wrong with me. Of all the therapy that was to follow, I still find the decision to call the first time was the most difficult of all. I knew many of my problems were indeed my very own problems. I didn't know exactly what they were, but I knew enough if I wanted a better life, I would have to make some changes.

You should not go to therapy if you are unwilling to make changes, or if you are unable to hear things about yourself you are reluctant to face. My goal was simple. I would do whatever I had to do to achieve that goal. The goal was to be happy and have a better life. To me it was not an impossible dream and I was willing to work for it.

I discovered the most important truth for me was I had not inherited a predisposition to depression. I was not destined to be depressed the rest of my life. I had to make some changes in myself and face many unwelcome revelations about myself. I learned I needed to change my behavior if I ever expected to see any changes in my marriage and my life.

I loved the learning that took place in those hours of therapy with Dr. Collins. I listened and responded and shared and wrote most of it in my journals. Even now when I get stuck in some of my old patterns, I go back to those notes and feel as if I've had a session all over again. Then I am reminded what is important for me to do and I know I am all right. There is no real end to therapy you see. Although I wanted to "finish" in the regard of being on my own, and living what I had learned, I knew there would be times I would also need to go back for help, and I have.

The bank decided in December to foreclose on our house. The only way we could stop it from happening now was to declare bankruptcy. Since we hadn't been able to sell the house and since neither Stephen nor I felt bankruptcy was an honorable way out for us, we chose to deed the house back to the bank and walk away.

I was so glad I had Dr. Collins to share my feelings with. He helped me let go of the past, take care of the present and look toward the future. The future, he reassured me, would be better for me because both Stephen and I were looking for answers. Especially now that Stephen had a wonderful, new job and got paid every two weeks, I was optimistic about our future.

Yet there would be many hard financial problems yet to face. But, my God, Stephen was getting paid every two weeks. People still called demanding money, money we didn't have, but at least now we didn't have to sell furniture in order to eat. First things first. Soon I was able to make up a chart of pay schedules and who would get paid when. Now whenever anyone called demanding money, I could say to them, "I can't pay you this week, but I'll be able to send you x amount on this date." Generally, people responded all right to that; they just needed to know something.

We learned the best way to deal with late or delinquent payments was to call the person and confront the issue head on rather than wait for them to come after you and perhaps take more drastic measures. This is easy to say now, but I was so overwhelmed at the time, all I wanted to do was run away and bury my head in the sand. I didn't believe this was "just business." I thought it was personal and I was a bad person because I couldn't pay the bills.

I had been working on my resume and knew one of the

answers to improving our financial situation was for me to get a job. Nevertheless, I was paralyzed. I felt I had always been the one bailing us out of our financial leaky boat by running out and taking the first job I could find. Now I wanted to work at something I enjoyed.

I wondered what it would be like to look forward to work each day and not wish I were anyplace else on earth but there. My wings had been clipped so many times before. I was still lost, confused and angrier than I realized. I was determined to rediscover Carol before I jumped and took just any old job. There was nothing I could do fast enough to get us out of the money mess we were already in. I wanted to get better myself as fast as I could so I wouldn't make the same mistakes all over again.

What a wonderful journey of self-discovery therapy was for me. I was an eager and excited patient. For the first time in years I began to know myself again. I was Carol Dispenza Hrehovcik. I discovered I was intelligent. Me. I, who had been told my whole life I was stupid was now told I was intelligent. I didn't believe it at first. I thought, "Well, I've got him fooled." But little by little I began to believe "yes, indeed I am smart," had been smart most of my life and it was all right for me to be smart.

This was the number one lesson I learned and for me the most important. I needed once more to learn to listen to and trust my own instincts. I'd lost my ability over the years to recognize an instinct from a wish or a fear. I had to reprogram my brain, my heart and my gut to listen, to trust myself and my natural, good instincts.

So far, I had learned two terrific things about myself: I

was smart and I had good instincts. Wow! I was really on to something. I just had to re-learn what was inside me all the time that I had mistrusted and neglected. Another major validation for me was to learn I was not a bad person and my feelings were okay. My feelings were all right and I wasn't a bad person even when I was angry or depressed or lonely or sad or even happy sometimes. "You mean, Carol, it is all right to be happy and to have feelings?" Not only was it all right but it was "normal." Wow!

I was learning a lot about myself and who I was and what I had let myself become. "What I had let myself become." This was an important acknowledgement for me. I was the one responsible for my own happiness and inevitably my own unhappiness. I would have loved to blame Stephen totally, and did on many occasions, but even before therapy I knew that was not true. The old adage that it "takes two people" to make or break a marriage I discovered to be oh so true.

I was not happy to hear some truths about myself of course. I had such a strong desire to have a better, happier life I was willing to listen and accept what was difficult to hear about me. I had a lot of anger inside me I had to get rid of somehow. I wasn't sure how to do this and asked for guidance. There was no real answer then, but I know for me the biggest cure was time, time and talking about it with someone objective who made me feel safe.

Intellectually I knew some answers and understood them in my mind. However, it wasn't until these answers reached my gut – that part inside myself where I physically felt the truth – that I could finally be better. Then I could rid myself of the anger and the rage I had let fester deep inside myself for so many years. I had been taught to be a "good girl," to be polite and not make people angry. Naturally then I turned the anger inside myself and this was the root of my depression. I believe I was in a state of true depression for more than nine years. I knew there had to be a better way.

I had such a marvelous experience with therapy I wanted to shout and declare to everyone, "Hey, you know what you should do?" I wanted everyone I knew to have this new power. This power was unleashed inside of me, and I wanted to share it with everyone. Fortunately, one of the other big truths I learned in therapy was I was not responsible for everyone else. I was shocked. At the same time, I was relieved. "You mean I am not responsible for everyone and everything? I just have to take care of myself? How do I do that?"

I always thought I was independent and self-reliant, but I learned I hadn't a clue how to take care of myself. I was good at taking care of everyone else but me. There is of course a name for this: Codependent. I was a major codependent. Even though the word dysfunctional may be overused at this time, when I learned about it, I felt as if all the pieces to a giant puzzle were finally fitting together.

I know I would never have been able to make these changes on my own, no matter how much reading I did. I needed the one on one therapy. I have never been a joiner of groups anyhow, and although I read a lot, what helps me the most is to talk. I need someone to listen to my thoughts, feelings, and ideas. Then perhaps I come to an "Aha" moment when even I understand myself. I needed the talking and the guidance. I was eager to learn and listen and be led gently into this world of self-discovery. I needed help.

Once again, our family had reached a turning point. Through this journey of self-discovery, I was able to help not only myself but my husband and my children. I knew I needed help and I give myself credit because I sought it, found it and embraced it. When you have been feeling so bad for so long and then start to feel good, you know you don't ever want to go back to feeling bad again. The longer you feel good, the less tolerance you have for feeling bad. Try it, you'll like it.

If you are one of those fortunate people who can heal and help yourself, I admire and applaud you. Please know however, if you do need some help from time to time, there is help out there, available to you. No one cares or rewards you for doing it by yourself. There are no penalties and no bonus points either way. Ask yourself where you want to be and how you could get there. Only you have the answer to those questions. The decision of course is yours alone to make in your own way and in your own time. However, if you are on the brink of saying I need help but I should do it myself, I would encourage you to get the help. That is a brave move on your part, very brave and I think very smart. Whatever way you choose to go, good for you.

Wouldn't I love to tell you I went for therapy, discovered all my problems, fixed them and then went merrily on my way, the road to happiness stretched out before me. Alas, little did I realize the hard work that was still to come. There is no substitute for time, and I couldn't wish myself or my family to be happy and all well now because I was ready. No, "now" was my timetable. Sadly, we all needed more time to heal, recover and uncover, to cry and fall and stumble our way through the quicksand of life to the clearing I knew now was out there.

To say that life goes on isn't saying it quite completely enough. Life doesn't just go on; life continues to be and we deal with it the best we can. How lucky I was at last to have some tools to help me cut my way through the jungle and lift me up and out of the mire. I learned many skills and was equipped with new tools to guide me on a new path in my life. Although there was still a lot of groping going on, I clung; I grew stronger; and as Nietzche put it: "That which doesn't kill you, makes you strong."

Did I mention I wanted to be a bimbo? I always joke about this, but here I assure you I like being smart much better. I don't mean smart in any way like education or book smart; I mean knowledgeable about life and people. This is an emotional intelligence that we used to call common sense. I note with some degree of sadness, common sense seems to be a commodity low on the ability scale of too many people. Are we born with it, do you think, or do we learn it as a skill handed down from one generation to another?

In observing my three children, myself and my husband, too, I have come to think of it as a combination of the two. I believe we are born with a predisposition to common sense but also it is a skill that must be nurtured and developed. I feel I was lucky to be born with the ability to put two and two together and figure out what may happen next. Joshua has it, Gillian has it, and Noah has developed it far beyond my capacity. As for my husband, I think I must give up on his ever reaching this level of awareness. Remember though, I said I thought he was a genius. What else could I expect from my resident genius?

Here again I owe my parents an apology. I have in the past been reluctant to give them credit for anything as I could see only the pain they caused me. When I saw them treat my children the same as they had me, I grew only more intense in my anger and my dismissal of them. I saw them only as the people who bore and raised me, but I wanted to distance myself from them in every other way, both physically and emotionally. I no longer wanted them to be in a position of hurting or insulting either me or my family. I could never do anything right in their eyes, and even when I did something that wasn't wrong, it was never enough or good enough.

Naturally I wasn't too keen on the idea they might have done something right either. To be fair, I did learn many very valuable life skills from them. I learned about problem solving and what happens next. I learned if you work hard, life gets better. I learned the value of money and common sense, and to treat people as individuals. I learned from my mother to appreciate beauty, and from my father to expect to be rewarded for your work.

Other valuable traits I learned elsewhere or in spite of my parents. I surely did learn survival skills from my mom and dad. I believe I also learned my sense of martydom from my parents. I recall my mother would do without a new winter coat so Louis and I could have one. I was always well dressed and used to having nice things around me. Even though my mother was always "saving them" for whatever she deemed was a special occasion. When she was older, she wondered why she saved them.

I think I learned more from taking the opposite view of my parents about most things. To me my father was the cheapest man I ever knew. My regard for money therefore was high but I enjoyed spending it. Naturally, I never became the saver Dad was. I saw it as hoarding, and I am still trying to learn the balance between saving and enjoying. I confess at this point I may never find that balance no matter how much I endeavor.

My mother, whose love of reading was surely passed on to both my brother and me, had an awareness of money and liked the best of things. Yet I would say she was frugal for most of her life. She had a great love of flowers and I treasure the memory of the pleasure they gave her. Unlike me however, my mother seemed obsessed with the "oh, sure, they are pretty now, but (a) you should have seen them yesterday or (b) they're going to die tomorrow." Is it any wonder then I became a present tense person? To mother the sun may be shining now BUT "they are talking about rain or snow or sleet or hail or something awful for tomorrow." And no day of course was ever as nice as the day before.

I think my dad was the adventurer in the family, and in his early days was both spontaneous and brave. My mother's fear of the future and change held my father back from doing something special with his life. Mother held dad back, and he let her, and so theirs was a match like most of us, good and bad.

My brother and I have a good sense of humor and manage even at the worst of times to find something to laugh about. I admit I wasn't laughing a lot for many years, and yet I still found some joy in life and living. Louis and I are both puzzled by this piece of our personalities, but grateful we enjoy a healthy sense of humor. I know this contributes to our survival.

When I started the book, I began with where I came from and how Stephen's early years influenced and shaped him as well. Before I went for help, I attributed most of my problems to my parents. I had a long list of past injuries and was not ready until much later to pay them any respect or give them their due. I was not happy to face this particular part of my therapy. I couldn't blame my parents for all my problems. Damn!

When I was at last willing to face my own part in my problems, I was able to forgive them for theirs, and by this time I saw no need to confront them with any of my discoveries. What would be the point of it now, I thought. I needed to learn to deal with issues as they arose. I couldn't allow myself to run away all the time, as this had been my coping mechanism in the past. Nevertheless, I was not going to confront my parents with the past and their part in it. It was enough for me to know and to understand.

I will tell you I still had a long way to go before I could give them credit for anything good. On the one hand I could forgive them, but still I checked the debit column and found them owing. As far as I was concerned the ledger was overdrawn by them and there were almost no assets on the credit side.

Only as I have grown older and able to look back with some objectivity have I been aware of some of the good values they passed on to me. I learned a lot about my mother when she was sick and dying in the hospital. I admired her strength and her willingness to fight and not go "quietly into the night." She held on to life for fourteen years after her first heart attack. I think at the end she was too exhausted and simply, finally let go. I admired her courage. I hope I have the same kind of courage and dignity and spirit to go when it is my turn. Somehow, I believe I will.

I realized too that when I gave my parents credit for something good, it did not take anything away from me. I thought if I gave them any value I would therefore be of less value. Lord knows I needed all the pluses I could gather. Now I am comfortable enough with myself to look and say, "Oh, yes, I learned this from them and thank you." Why do you think it takes us so long to grow up? Well, thankfully, most of us do, eventually. Do you think there is a universal age when that happens? No, I don't think so either. Growing up occurs any time, early, late, or never.

I remember bemoaning the prospect whether or not my children would ever grow up. Would they ever be responsible, mature adults? A good friend consoled me with these words: "Just when you think they'll never grow up, they do." She was right.

Isn't life just the most wonderful thing? Don't you think it's a book we write for ourselves and it's a page turner? We don't know how it will end, but let's enjoy every page we write!

And so, for me, therapy changed my outlook and the way I had been living my life. Stephen and I would have continued to destroy each other if he and I hadn't made changes. As there was still some love there deep inside for him, I charted a new course for Carol. I knew who I used to be, and since she and I were old friends, I decided to seek her out. Armed with new knowledge, I would take Carol=me, where I had always wanted to go but been afraid to try. I had been afraid, yes, but when I hadn't let the fear paralyze me, I took chances. I had gone to Germany myself and later to graduate school in Washington. I'd even married bravely, all right, perhaps foolishly. Nonetheless, I had shown I could be a "contender." I had spunk after all.

I knew I could make decisions and be responsible for myself. My children whom I had taught to be independent and think for themselves seemed to be doing well. Perhaps I could do as well for myself. The teacher then became the learner and from whom better to learn than my own children? They had never asked me to be a martyr, and I am sure they did not see it as an attractive quality. What did that teach them? I had scoffed at the concept of martyrs, and yet had embraced it as a way of life for myself.

The first order of business then was to shed my martyr's shroud and reward myself with something, anything at all. I had to do something for myself. Easy, I hear you say. Not for me, not at the time. I laugh about it now, but I recall to this day how difficult this assignment was for me. Yes, it was an "assignment."

Remember at this time we had little money, piles of debts, threatening letters and phone calls, the bank in the process of foreclosing on our house and more liens on our property than the tower of Pisa, and yet I had to, mind you HAD TO buy something for myself.

I have been an obedient girl, person, for most of my life, but more than that was my goal and desire to be better. I knew this was an important step toward that goal. I was willing to do whatever was needed for me to have a better life, so off

I went one day to buy myself something. I didn't have any money to spare, but I took ten dollars to spend and went to Bradlees Department Store in Westbrook.

Some of you may remember Bradlees, one of a chain of discount stores that has since disappeared. It featured both personal and household items. I wasn't to buy anything for the house or the children or Stephen, just for me. Well, even in 1983, ten dollars did not buy much. What on earth could I possibly buy? Where would I even begin to look? When you have done without for so long, as I had, you learn to do without to a point where you feel there is nothing you really need; you can get along without most things. I walked up, down and across all the aisles, trying hard to focus on one thing that would inspire me to take care of myself. Lingerie? No, I didn't "need" that after all. I, who had been completely color coordinated in my single days with all matching lingerie now walked by the department thinking lingerie would be "frivolous." Skirt? Blouse? I didn't like my body so why would I buy anything like that? When your self-esteem is so low, there is nothing you can buy that will make you feel better about yourself. At last I found myself in the shoe department.

Ah, the shoe department! Aside from lingerie another old passion of mine was shoes. Maybe it was because my father always worked in the shoe industry, but I loved shoes and never had enough, until now, of course. Standing there in that shoe department reminded me of my old self, an old self who used to shop in the better department stores, bought six or seven pairs of shoes during one of Filene's basement sale days. Finally, I knew where I would start to help myself back on the road to recovery. In the shoe department of Bradlees!

Finally, I was inspired. I liked to take walks and I sure could use a new pair of sneakers. Aha, I thought, a perfect blend of practicality and usefulness and still at the same time it would be something just for me, something I was sure I would have done without had I not had this "assignment."

I found a pair of white canvas sneakers with red trim for ten dollars. Ten dollars! The amount I had budgeted for myself. I remembered owning red shoes, yellow shoes, and even a neat pair of green suede with black trim, and now I was almost thrilled to get this pair of sneakers. The red trim I thought was a playful touch that would cheer me up.

On my next visit with Dr. Collins, I proudly wore my new sneakers and pointed to them as a giant step (so to speak) in my recovery. He looked and smiled, and I laughed at myself. "It's a start," I said. And it was.

I kept those sneakers for years after as a reminder to myself that I was worth something. I remembered it was all right for me to take care of myself. Those sneakers were a symbol to me of where I had been and how far I'd come. I was able to throw them away at last when we moved into our new house in 1993. After ten years I felt strong enough inside myself to throw away the sneakers that had started me on my path to recovery, self-awareness, and greater self-esteem. Now that I think of it, perhaps a new pair of sneakers was more appropriate for me in more ways than one.

Here I was in the doctor's office, flashing my new sneakers and laughing at myself. Perhaps the Carol I used to know and like was not so lost after all. Oh, sure, I was off the track and unsteady on my new course, but now I knew for sure I was going to be all right.

There's a quote I like. "Life is a tragedy to those who feel, but a comedy to those who think." If I were to sum up my marriage to Stephen, I know it would be a combination of tragedy and comedy. In the past I had felt too much and had no safe outlet to express those feelings. Until I went to see Dr. Collins, I thought life was meant to be a tragedy for me. I could laugh at some of it, but honestly even now I cannot laugh about it all. People who tell you, "You'll look back on this and laugh one day," don't really know what they are talking about. There are simply some things in life you can't ever laugh about.

My therapy with my good doctor was the beginning of my awakening. I came to understand my parents, my brother, my in-laws, my husband and myself. The knowledge that my life was truly in my own hands was news to me, and exciting and frightening at the same time.

All my life I wanted someone to take care of me, not because I couldn't and hadn't done it, only because there was still a little girl inside me who wanted to come out. A little girl I believe who exists in most women but who is generally not allowed to appear. There is also a saying, there is more little boy in a man than there is little girl in a woman. Why do you suppose that is? I can think of lots of reasons and I am sure there are sociological as well as personal reasons for us all.

Perhaps for me I was the younger child who needed to prove herself. I know I desperately wanted my parents' approval. Did that mean I had to be "tough" like my mother? I didn't want to be tough at all. I was full of conflicting needs and desires. I wanted to be taken care of, and yet I yearned for control of my own life. I can honestly say I had no desire at all to control my husband, as if that were ever possible; I just never thought about it.

I wanted to know my life was on a course I could manage, that was as much as I could handle. I wanted my dreams, my desires, my wants to count for something and not just be cast aside as they had been all through our marriage. I know this was my biggest resentment in my marriage, the fact it was always Stephen's dreams and never mine. Sometimes we still have a problem with that.

I was eager to learn and to get better as quickly as I could, I would do whatever I had to do to make that happen. Even though Dr. Collins and I would disagree from time to time about an issue, I always had my goal in mind. That goal was to have a fuller, happier life for myself and my children. What about Stephen? Yes, I wanted a better marriage.

Dr. Collins and I disagreed about the reason I hadn't left Stephen. After all, if I had been so miserable, why didn't I leave him? "For the children." I told him. He shook his head no "It is fear of abandonment." I totally disagreed, but I didn't understand the meaning of abandonment until years later.

I know now Dr. Collins was right. He and I would go back and forth on this issue and I wondered what difference it made whether it was the kids or fear of abandonment that kept me in my marriage. I always thought it was more a stubbornness issue myself. I did know more than anything that I really wanted our marriage to work. Just how to do that without losing myself completely as I had these past years was the problem for me. I had allowed the marriage, Stephen, and my children to swallow me up. It was time for me to stand up for myself and on my own two feet, with or without Stephen.

Now that Stephen had a good job it was time for me to take care of myself. Where to start, I wondered. What did I want to do with my life and what could I do? I needed a job.

I was as always willing to do my share but not at the expense of my own integrity. I decided I was no longer willing to be the bail master. I wasn't going to work at just any job to make money as I had in the past. At this time, I wasn't sure what I wanted to do or even could do. I knew I didn't want to go back for my teaching certificate. I had been cured of teaching for a while.

At Dr. Collins' suggestion, I went for vocational assistance with a woman from the department of human services in the state of Maine. I sat in the office in Biddeford, Maine and waited and watched many different kinds of people going in and out. Some of these looked rather seedy to me and even unkempt. I wondered what I was doing there. I knew I was out of my element and I wanted to get up and run out of there as fast as I could.

I had gone to state employment offices before and received wonderful assistance, but this was something totally different. I wanted desperately to leave. Still I stayed and waited my turn because I wanted more desperately to get better. If this woman could help me, I was willing to sit there and wait and be uncomfortable for a while. I would endure the embarrassment of sitting in this office to get the help I craved so urgently. I have always been very proud of myself and grateful too that I had the courage to follow through on this other voyage of self-discovery. I think my curiosity is an asset to my personality. Once again, I wanted to know what was on the other side of the mountain, or as in this case, behind the door.

Susan had a smile for me, and I could see she was intelligent and very capable. She turned out to be compassionate but tough. She never let me get away with anything or give the easy answer. Susan was a quadriplegic because of some early childhood disease but could write with a pencil in her mouth. I felt so ashamed of myself for my whining when I saw Susan and how she was obviously overcoming such physical barriers while maintaining a very helpful life.

What the heck was wrong with me? I had this tendency to compare myself to everyone else and empathize with their problems and then found myself angry with myself for thinking I even had a problem. So, big deal, I thought, I am suffering from low self-esteem, somehow that didn't seem like such a big deal. However, it was important to me and I had to live with myself. Whatever problems I had, big or small, I was here to get help, and so I tried to focus on that.

Now for someone like me, the self-appointed martyr, to focus on herself was a challenge. Susan's first suggestion to me was that I take an aptitude test the next week. It was being given right there in the office for a couple of other people as well. Although Susan wouldn't be administering the test herself, she thought this would be the place for us to get started. I enjoyed taking tests and for some silly reason I thought an aptitude test was one of those things we used to do in school. Multiple choice, silly questions like, "Would you rather milk a cow or go to a symphony?"

There were of course no such questions; it was by far a more intellectual challenge than that. Fortunately, I was beginning to believe I was smart, thanks in large part to Dr. Collins, so I wasn't afraid to take this test. That is until we got to the part for manual dexterity.

Oh, brother. I had no manual dexterity at all. If they had only asked me, I could have saved us all a lot of time and for me a lot of embarrassment. I wouldn't say I am totally clumsy with my hands, but there is no gift in these hands at all. They can do dishes and lift stuff, but other than that I'm in trouble. And I was in trouble that morning because I took what seemed like forever to me to get those damn pegs back into their particular place.

Meanwhile the other two people testing with me had finished this part of the test rather quickly and adroitly I thought. Now they had to stand back and wait and watch me. What the hell, I couldn't run away, so I kept going as best as I could. I thought the examiner would call time any second. But instead of calling time, he waited until I finished the whole darn pegboard.

I was saying to myself "I'll never do this; what am I going to do? Oh, my God, we'll be here forever." (I just love making those gross generalizations, don't you?) Somehow, I finally finished with the pegs and then breezed right through the rest of the tests. All the while chuckling to myself. "Well I know I can't be a carpenter or a seamstress, but what can I be?'

The discoveries uncovered from this test were so amazing to me and mind opening. My self-esteem went up several major points. This however was only the beginning. Susan made me follow through with research on every subject I might be even remotely interested in. She never let me get away with vagueness or hedging of any kind. She forced me to be specific and follow through, but more importantly she forced me to be honest, with her and more so with myself. The only true disappointment I had was the discovery I would probably not have had a successful dancing career.

I pursued the choices I made and with her guidance and support, I began my own ghostwriting business. This was perfect for me as I could work out of my house so I could be home for my kids, which was still important to me. This would allow me to write at my own pace and choose the jobs I was interested in writing about.

To prove I was capable of actually writing, I had to give Susan some of my work, samples from the newspaper and also some of my poetry. Allowing her to read my poetry was a major hurdle for me as I had not shared my poetry with anyone since college. I had always been particularly sensitive about my poetry. For me, allowing others to read my poetry was like letting someone look into my soul. I didn't want anyone to say, "Aha," as if now they knew the secret about me. What would be worse was for someone to read the poems and not like them, then of course I would feel rejected as a person. But I let Susan read them. I trusted her and valued her opinion. She liked them and smiled at me "Yes," she said, "you can do this." I felt proud.

CHAPTER 23

Letting Go and Looking Ahead

While all that was going on for me personally, the financial house of Hrehovcik had collapsed. We let the house on Maplewood Drive go, deeded it back to the bank in March of 1983. I was miserable and relieved at the same time. Looking back now I know we could have salvaged the house, held on and held out, but the fight was out of me and I guess with Stephen as well. To me this house represented failure, lost dreams, broken promises and everything bad and wrong in our marriage. There was nothing finished in the house after eleven years. There was just a lot of unfinished business. The house in so many ways had become an albatross around our throats. I didn't want to fight for it any longer.

The bank agreed to let us stay in the house until June. By then Noah would be back from Interlochen and Josh would graduate from high school. The person in the family who took this loss the hardest was Gillian.

This was the only home she'd really known. She was still in school at the consolidated school and didn't want to transfer away from all her friends. All she loved and cherished so much was in Kennebunkport. Josh, Noah and now Gillian had lost the security that all children so desperately needed. It would be many years before we would discover just how big a toll this turbulent time was to take on all of our children as well as ourselves.

In June of 1983 we and began to pack our household belongings in earnest. Noah was home from Interlochen and would be attending Kennebunk High School for his senior year. Joshua had graduated from high school and had been accepted at the University of Bridgeport in Connecticut for the fall semester.

The afternoon we signed the papers at the bank, Stephen and I were licking our wounds, although Stephen was never as big a "wound licker" as I. Nevertheless, we decided to visit one of our local realtors. I was so distraught and discouraged I didn't even bother to go into the office. Stephen came out with his face beaming. "Jack thinks he might have a house for us to rent right here in Kennebunk."

I personally have always considered Kennebunk and Kennebunkport pretty much the same place. I later learned they are not. The people in Kennebunkport are very rigorous in their promotion of the fact they live in "the Port." I wanted at that time both for myself and more especially for Gillian to continue to live in Kennebunkport; I just couldn't imagine living anywhere else. I wanted Gillian at least to have some continuity with both her friends and her school.

Stephen on the other hand, was just as adamant about leaving Kennebunkport and moving closer to the turnpike and his job in Westbrook. He said Gillian would be in Junior

High School in Kennebunk within a year and both Joshua and Noah would both be off to college soon. He reasoned, and rightly so, our lives were changing, and it made more sense for us to be closer to the turnpike and the access it provided.

We were lucky then to find this wonderful house close to the turnpike in a lovely neighborhood, with a paved town road. OH, BOY! This meant the town plowed the street, and we would no longer have to worry about having the road paved or repaired. To me this was like heaven, one less arrangement I had to worry about or take care of. The only thing that could possibly be better than this would be to be on a sewer line and not ever be concerned with a faulty leach field or smelly septic tank.

Jack told us the location of the house and I fell in love with it from the moment we drove by. I had the same feelings as I had when we drove up to the red house so many years before. I loved the cream color house, the pine trees surrounding it, the proximity of the turnpike and the high school and the fact it would be a year-round rental – a home. There was a sidewalk around the corner where I could walk to town safely or ride my bike. We'd be safe there.

I knew I would love the inside as well, and of course I did. Although there were only two bedrooms with an unfinished upstairs area, I was confident we could all be comfortable there. This house was picture perfect to me. There was a fireplace, a washer and dryer in the basement, a formal dining room with two built-in corner cabinets, a huge living room, and two bathrooms. I adored it and thought "We could be happy here."

On the day we were moving out of Maplewood Drive, my

husband announced he "had to work." This left me, Joshua, Noah and poor little Gillian to pack everything and move it downstairs. We had a lot of "stuff," but not a lot of furniture. We'd sold most of it to eat during those very lean times.

There were boxes of books, boxes of papers we'd written, boxes of business papers and many more boxes of toys and games and dolls. I couldn't bring myself to sell all the toys and children's furniture. I was sure my children would want to pass some things on to their children, and so I packed with the future in mind. It took us four days to move out of the old house into the newer, finished, smaller house. It was a lot of hard work and we worked hard at it. Stephen eventually showed up later in the afternoon with a truck from work and Stanley to help us. Nevertheless, it was a four-day job.

After more than eighteen years of marriage, there was little in the way of material goods to show for it. So much for my theory of work hard and things get better. Where had we gone wrong? Could it be at last we were on the right track to financial recovery and reward? Stephen had a good job; he was paid every two weeks; we could pay the rent and I was starting my own business. Although we had no money and were in overwhelming debt, I was optimistic.

Since we had decided not to declare bankruptcy, even after we were advised by two lawyers to do so, there were many difficult years ahead. Years with poor credit, little cash, and a need to parcel out money to all our creditors. Our so called "honor" took a great toll on our children. If I knew how adversely our decision was going to affect them, I would have reconsidered bankruptcy.

Meanwhile we sought the help of a credit counselor.

Stephen refused this kind of help, but I was eager for assistance. We didn't do it, but I would advise any of you who may be in financial trouble to go for help. Let someone help you. We didn't because to my husband felt a sense of "shame" that he couldn't do it himself. Was this some displaced "macho" thing? I don't know; all I do know is he and I were in total disagreement on this issue. I believe not taking advantage of this credit counseling service was more of a mistake than not declaring bankruptcy. Why wasn't I strong enough to stand up to him and say, "We will do this. This is the right thing to do."

I'm sure many of you women reading this understand even better than I. You know there are times when your husband, boyfriend, "significant other" will not change his position. No argument, no logic makes any difference. This was one of those times for us.

We struggled, fought, alienated each other and some of our friends, hurt our children in the process, and were generally unhappy. Yet after many years of hardship and deprivation, we paid off all debts but one. There was one woman we couldn't pay. We owed her ten thousand dollars for her investment in Stephen's theater. I was ashamed and thought I was a bad person.

I was foolish enough to think once we got out of the house on Maplewood Drive life for the Hrehovcik family in Maine was going to be better. After all I was in therapy, Stephen had gone for counseling, Joshua was better, and both Gillian and Noah seemed to have bounced back from all our upheaval and uprooting. I tell you, sometimes I am so naive even I can't believe myself. For someone who prides herself on her acceptance of reality and her ability to deal with herself and issues honestly, I sure can kid myself, can't I?

I don't want to say Stephen has a short memory, but I believe the only way he has survived is to deny the facts of our experiences and the pain they caused our family. I think if he ever admitted this to himself (never mind to me or anyone else), the pain would be more than he could bear. I believe this is one of the reasons Stephen never completed any therapy. As soon as he was close to uncovering a truth he couldn't face, he'd find a reason to quit that therapist and stop all together.

At first, I was concerned about this. I also didn't understand. I knew I had to complete therapy; I needed to finish. This finishing is of course called closure. But as I think about it today, it makes perfect sense. Stephen wouldn't complete his therapy because to finish was simply not in his vocabulary. What seemed to be most important to him was to start and make a big fuss and then stop. He never finished our house, did he? He never finished a room or a project, no, that's not fair. He finished some projects, the fireplace, for example. Sometimes I find it hard to be fair, even after all these years. Has that ever happened to you?

At last I accepted the fact that Stephen had gone about as far as he could go in therapy. After all, when I look at his family, I see what a miracle it is that he has changed as much as he has. He had the courage to ask hard questions of himself and to change what he could. When you have denied your feelings all your life, how do you learn about feelings when you are a grown, mature man?

I give my husband so much credit for this, for his courage and his bravery and for his willingness to face some harsh truths. No matter he quit therapy whenever he was too close to some truth he was either unable or unwilling to face. After all, who am I to say to him, "Hey, go face that pain and get on with it." I have problems enough of my own.

When I did have a problem that was more than I could handle, and I knew I needed objective help, I'd go back to Dr. Collins who always set me back on track. Now he's retired, but I've been lucky enough to find a strong woman therapist who helps me find my way. What a disservice it is to call psychiatrists "shrinks," when in fact what they truly do is help you expand your mind, your heart, and your soul. If you allow it.

I was getting back to my old self, my identity, Carol, and so I set up an office in the sunroom of the yellow house on Oak Bluff Drive. My logo was very clever and catchy enough to get me a feature article in the Portland paper. "The Write Spirit" was launched. I loved the cartoon ghost Stephen drew with his tongue sticking out at the corner of his mouth.

My business was not a great success, but I did get work doing copy for brochures, which I enjoyed, a business newsletter which was fun and a learning experience, and I also got to do a lot of resumes which I didn't especially like to do. I confess I wasn't very aggressive about going out to look for work. I was still shy and afraid of rejection.

That year Joshua started and finished one semester at Bridgeport. I was furious when he quit school, which was a waste of energy on my part. Then he got a job as a salesman at a local radio station selling advertising. He was a natural salesman, but he quit that after three months. I think I was angrier about that than I was his quitting school.

What I did not know was Joshua was suffering from agoraphobia, a fear of being in an open space, outside and facing the unknown. I didn't know he was suffering still from this form of anxiety, that every day was a challenge for him to go out the door. I didn't know and didn't understand until many years later. I apologize, Joshua.

Funny, too, because I remember being afraid myself when we were living on Maplewood Drive. After we lost the business and when we knew we'd have to give up the house, I was afraid to see people or meet anyone on the street. I would turn around if I saw people when I was walking. I was afraid to walk down Wildes District Road; I really thought I would get run over and die. I was afraid the same way Joshua explained he was afraid, and yet I never knew this fear had a name.

Noah was unable to attend Interlochen for his last year of high school. This was just as well, for not only could we not afford it, but I still believed he was too young to be away from home. When we had gone to pick him up that spring, he was lost and confused. I was sorry I had not listened to my instincts, which had said, "Turn around and take him home. Don't leave him there." But when you have a child as talented and gifted as Noah, you want to give him every opportunity to succeed.

So, Noah would be attending the local high school which was within walking distance of our house on Oak Bluff Drive. He was a senior now and resumed dancing with his teachers in Portland. There was an article about him and his dancing in the local paper that year. Since he'd attended Interlochen, Noah was more serious than ever about making dance his career.

My dreams for him to go to Harvard were soon dashed as he was adamant in his decision to attend the Boston Conservatory. I had to defend his choice even though I personally was not excited about it. I knew how smart he was, his love of learning and his need to be intellectually challenged, but Noah had made up his mind and there was nothing I could do but support his decision.

At least I felt as if I had no choice. I thought it was the right thing to do at the time. How do parents get their children to listen and take their advice? Then again how does anyone know what is truly best for anyone else? It wasn't as if Stephen and I had made such a great success of our lives after all. I know what really influenced both of us to be supportive of Noah in his creative quest, was our not being supported ourselves by our parents. In other words, we gave him what we had most wanted for ourselves.

Gillian was serious now also about ballet, but it was more than I could deal with then. One dancer in the family was more than enough, so poor Gillian got the short end of the stick. In a way it was ironic because Gillian was a more talented dancer than Noah. She had a natural ability that shined across the stage, whereas Noah had to work at it ever so diligently. It wasn't a case of one being more talented than the other, just one had the natural ability and the other had the perseverance. Also, because Noah was the older of the two, I thought he ought to be first.

I was weak and too blind to see Gillian's needs at this time. I apologize to you, Gillian.

On the other hand, I don't need be overly harsh on myself as I believed Gillian's talents were better suited toward a musical pursuit. Her unique gift was the piano. She composed her own songs from the time she was seven years old. Later her piano teacher wanted her to get advanced training and enter competitions. But at the age of twelve, my willful, headstrong daughter decided to stop playing the piano and concentrate on ballet.

Once again, my dreams for one of my children would go unrealized. At this point, having been defeated by all three of my children, I gave up all my dreams for any of them. "The die was cast." Now they could all make their own decisions and go their own way, their way – not mine. Phooey.

I look back now and realize how foolish I allowed myself to be. I am sure many of you have similar stories you could tell about you and your children. Because I was the disciplinarian in the family, I felt defeated and such a failure. I didn't trust myself or my judgment. If I didn't listen to myself, how could I expect anyone else to listen to me?

In September of 1984, Stephen's father died suddenly. His heart finally quit on him. Since his surgery, Mr. Hrehovcik hadn't been doing all he should to take care of himself, and so he died as he had lived, his way. I ought to be ashamed to admit it here, but I smiled when I heard the news. I didn't plan it and was shocked at myself for my reaction; it just happened. Of course, I had to stifle my true feelings and be sympathetic and supportive of Stephen. However, in my own heart and mind I was relieved the man was dead. I felt Stephen had grieved him already and that his death wouldn't affect us much now.

Wrong again! I thought Mr. Hrehovcik's dying would be a good thing for Stephen and me; my husband was finally free. I continue to astonish myself even in retrospect – how foolish can a girl be?

More painful for me at this same time was the news we would have to leave the lovely house on Oak Bluff Drive. Just as I was beginning to feel more secure, more comfortable and daring to dream of the future once more, the yellow house sold, and we had to move again. Naturally I cried when the sign went up. This was news I could not smile about.

Still first things first. The funeral in New Jersey.

I wrote in my journal: "Steve's father died yesterday sometime in the late afternoon, Sept. 9, 1984. Mike called about 8 P.M. Stephen took it very well, reacted in a realistic way, I thought, sad, of course, but didn't suddenly make his father some archangel. We talked about how he had gone through his grieving process already when he was seeing Dr. Goodman. Perhaps that helps a little."

"We made up Saturday, which I feel good about now. So many thoughts and reactions, only a short time ago I wished for it, and now it's here. It is a surprise and my initial reaction is one of relief."

I called my folks and my Dad said, "You sound happy." I'd have to be careful because I didn't want people to know how I really felt. Is it possible – obviously it is – to loathe someone so much you are glad he's dead? I hope I never feel that way about another person ever again.

I hadn't called Noah yet, but Josh's reaction was curious. He worried about Steve and didn't want to see him get hurt again. I know looking back now I was foolish, unrealistic but oh so hopeful. I was worried about Steve. I felt he would be all right. I believed his father's death would free him at last. I felt no guilt and hoped he didn't either.

Josh worried about a scene and the "big show." I decided I would simply leave if anyone was unpleasant. Also, Josh brought up "the will" and asked his Dad, "Will you fight?" Steve insisted his family "would never do that." Josh and I believe they had and would. My plan then becomes first to see Dr. Collins, and then our lawyer, Earle Patterson. I was determined my father-in-law would not win from his grave too. I wouldn't let him. I felt good and knew I was stronger than before.

Of course, the very funny, ironic issue was that we had no money to eat that week, let alone travel to New Jersey. In my refrigerator were four hot dogs, some hamburger, rolls and milk. Both pantries had been empty for two days – no soup, no nothing. But guess what? I was not worried because I know I didn't care if/when we had to go down there. I didn't care about any of it. God, how I will not smile... I hope the last laugh isn't on me. God, I want to win one I want to come out on top – I got excited just thinking about it...

CHAPTER 24

It Ain't Over Till the Fat Lady Sings

At any rate, the illusion of family was there. Baba of course was telling everyone "not to cry" because she couldn't, and hey, now she even had center stage with no one bossing her around. She'd probably live for another fifteen years. It would be more than interesting to see what developed.

My old-fashioned upbringing tried to make me feel bad about feeling good. Surely, a lot of it was anxiety about actually, physically going down and facing them all. Some people in New Jersey had never met me, and I could only imagine what they'd heard. The important thing for me to remember was that I was strong, and I was my own person. I had no allegiance to any of them. I didn't have to do what I didn't want to do. I wouldn't try to please Stephen or appease my mother-in-law. In fact, the more I thought about it, the more of a farce it was. Why was I going? All right, I was going to be supportive of Stephen. That was it.

His father's death could make a man of my husband or it could set him back. I was mostly confident Stephen would be all right. He had received professional help after all and he could get more if he needed it. I knew I needed it. Well, Carol, happy birthday.

The question was, had his father cut him out of the will as he had always threatened to do? What happened now? Mike and Anne were in charge of everything and Steve was left out just like always. "This bloody show will end up costing us money and we'll be in trouble again. Oh, God, I know it. I feel it in my bones." Oh, me of little faith.

But hey, it was my birthday and here I was going to the place I hated the most, to see people I didn't like or care about and I think I had a right to be depressed. Then I thought about it in another way. This was a birthday present in some deluded fashion. My sense of humor said that I would win yet. Wherever the old man was in the spirit world, I was stronger than he was. Memories don't always fade with time, as I can still see my mother-in-law take me by the hand to "look at Pop." "We like you. God says we have to love everyone." God, I can see it still.

September 17, 1984. Right after I wrote in my journal, Noah called to say Happy Birthday. He could not attend the funeral as he had a performance at the Conservatory. I was glad someone in our family wouldn't be there for the show. Then my mother called to tell me to keep my mouth "shut" and to "ignore" everything.

About 11:30 a check arrived from the family in New Jersey. Because Stephen was already there, I cashed the check and then I bought myself panty hose, makeup and some treats for the trip. Joshua, Gillian, and I packed the car and left home about 2 p.m. We stopped for lunch at the Weathervane. I had wine, cherrystone clams, and a lobster roll. I was good to myself on my birthday.

Josh drove all the way; we took his Trans Am. It was a lovely day, and the three of us had a good trip. Josh and I talked a lot – mostly Josh.

We crossed the Tappan Zee Bridge and it was early. I knew we would be there very soon. I started to feel anxious and afraid and not as strong as I thought I was. We passed the Linden exit. We took many wrong turns. It was still early. We went to the house in Linden and no one was there. We went back to the funeral home. I got out but couldn't get in, so, we rode around some more. Finally, Josh and Gillian went into the funeral home and Stephen came out to get me. I started to cry, "I can't go in."

"Yes, you can" he said. "Everyone is asking for you. I'll stay with you."

He took me by my arm, and we met Kresna, Setka, and Mary Hilla as they came out of the funeral parlor. They all smiled, hugged me and kissed me, and said they were glad I came. I was relieved because I thought they would be mad at me for not liking the old man and for not visiting. I felt a little better.

Inside the first person to come over to me was Andrea, Mickey's wife, and then Mickey and Stephen and Mark Savka. (Karen, I was relieved wasn't there). Mark Hrehovcik and Maryellen did not come to speak to me for a long time. Mark, in fact, walked away from me and so did Maryellen. My sister-in-law Lee came to speak to me as I made my way across the room. Stephen lead me to speak to his brother, Mike, his sister, Anne, and his mother, who we all called Baba, which was grandmother in Slovak. We then went to the casket to look at Mr. Hrehovcik. My mother-in-law took my hand as I knew she would, but I would not kneel by the casket. Gillian said a little prayer as she kneeled by the casket.

I was relieved when the visiting hours were over. My family and I left together, got in the car and Gillian bursted into tears. She didn't understand the emotions of a wake. "First there's crying then people are laughing." She said Maryellen hardly spoke to her and when she did, all she said was, "Oh, you're here." Gillian was so excited to show her how grown up she'd become and was confused by Maryellen's behavior.

I no longer felt hurt because now I was mad. My plan then became to ignore the family and watch my own. I stayed especially close to Gillian. There was much confusion about sleeping arrangements, but we stayed at my mother-in-law's. I was relieved once more because I did not want to stay at Lee's.

I had a sense that Mike was genuinely glad I came, but Lee seemed to put on a show and her kids' rudeness to me reflected her feelings. Because of their behavior toward me, I ignored Mark and Maryellen, but I watched them. Gillian then said she wanted to stay with Auntie Lee and Maryellen. I told her no, but she said, "I want to prove how strong I am." She left with them for the night. But at the funeral the next day she said she shouldn't have, and she and I stayed close together most of the day. I insisted she ride with me in the car for the entire funeral.

Josh was a pall bearer. Mike asked Josh, and then told Anne's two boys, "You guys are pall bearers, right." It was a very long morning. The closing of the casket with the family present was catharsis for Anne and Setka. There was religious stuff at the funeral home – a one and a half hour mass. The cemetery was refreshingly brief. I got a rose with thorns – appropriate I thought. I wanted to throw it or give it away but I placed it on the casket. In the car, John Savka, Anne's husband, says "Well, it's finally over."

"Perhaps it has just begun" I said.

John, Lee, Gillian and I rode in the ---casket--- (Freudian slip) car together. I wouldn't be surprised if John had some of the same feelings as me. I noticed Mark Savka and Steve Savka never cried, neither did Josh. Stephen cried at church.

My feelings fascinated me. First of all, I didn't expect to feel the way I did at the funeral parlor. I felt complete indifference to the man as he lay there. I said to myself as I looked at him (for the benefit of the audience), "I hated you, you old bastard, while you were alive and I don't hate you any the less now that you are dead. You made my life miserable while you were alive and I'm glad you are gone." But I felt really untouched emotionally by his death or any of the rituals. Usually I feel sad when I see anyone else sad and crying, but I didn't feel any of it. I felt indifferent. I was pleased by that and thought I must be over the deep anger I'd had for him. But I knew it was because he was dead and couldn't hurt me anymore.

I ignored Maryellen and Mark when I would have liked to comfort them, but I did not reach out. Mary Ann Hilla, one of Stephen's cousins, sat next to me in church and I noticed she didn't go to communion either. At the end of the mass there was the kissing of the cross. I did not believe in that, but I did it anyway. Josh and Gillian went to communion along with their father.

After the funeral we all went to the "hall." This is a tradition in this part of Linden. There is a big sit-down dinner for more than 150 people, and when the bar is open it's more like a wedding than a funeral. Gillian and I "stuck together." Lee announced, "We only have food for 100 people; the family can't eat."

I replied, "Gillian and I will eat," and we did. As expected, there was plenty of food for everyone and leftovers besides.

When everyone got back to the house, there were many exhausted people and crying, cranky babies. Mark's wife, Diane, was dealing with four fussy babies; her Jessica was especially crabby that day. Josh and Stephen noticed Mark's impatience with the baby. I did not note this until the next day.

Mary Hilla gave Gillian a pillow especially for her and took her out for the afternoon. I walked here and there and ate and talked to some people. It had been a long, emotionally draining day.

That night we took Gillian to Mike's to pick up her clothes. Lee was cordial but reserved. So was I. Maryellen sat across the room and the evening was pleasant enough and very interesting."

There is much more in the journal about this time and information we gather from Mary Hilla and Setka and Kresna. We learned about the financing Maryellen and Mark got from the Malenich family, from the Hrehovciks and Father Steve. I felt sick and depressed about this as I discovered these people didn't ever have to go to a bank to get money.

The biggest news to us was what we learned from the Hilla family and most especially from my father-in-law's own sister who told us about him: "Since he was a little boy, he made me cry, and he could still make me cry." Setka said sometimes she wouldn't talk to him for six months. "If there were 100 people in a room, he'd manage to insult someone and make someone cry."

Kresna had heard him holler at his wife for talking to Stephen. That was why she had to sneak phone calls to Stephen. They all realized he was mean to Stephen but didn't know we had lost our house. They all agreed if we had lived in New Jersey that never would have happened.

Kresna particularly understood my father-in-law wanted us to lose our house so we would move back to New Jersey, or at least so Stephen would. I know he didn't care whether or not I came back with him, in fact I know he would have been pleased if Stephen left me altogether. He even told him that on more than one occasion.

The biggest, most important news to me was "they all liked me and knew what he was really like and that he had always been mean to Stephen." I felt validated and relieved. That half hour of honest revelation made the whole trip worthwhile. Not only did it relieve any residue guilt I may have felt, but now I had the knowledge that other people knew the truth about Mr. Hrehovcik. His own sister said he was a bully and a mean man. They all felt sorry for his wife, and me and Stephen as well, but they couldn't say anything to us. I'm not sure why. After that I didn't care about the will because someone knew the truth. That truth was more important to me than money. I'd always said, sometimes in jest, "I just want him to pay for all our therapy bills." Meanwhile my own family in Massachusetts "had been worried about me." It made me feel good that they cared, so I called to reassure them I was all right, because now I really was.

When we returned from New Jersey, Noah was sick at school and later admitted he felt guilty about not attending his grandfather's funeral. I take responsibility for that error in judgment. He'd had a performance at the Conservatory, and I thought since his grandfather had caused us nothing but pain, Noah's attending would be some kind of a statement. Karen, Anne's daughter, wasn't there either, so it wasn't as if Noah were the only missing relative.

Because of what Stephen's aunt and godmother revealed to us, I felt better than I had in all the years of our marriage. I cannot express what it was like for me to know that someone knew the truth about the kind of man my father-in-law was. I recalled his own sister revealing her brother was "always a mean" man, as well as Kresna being stunned to learn we had lost our house. She had said, "It would never have been allowed to happen if it were the other guy."

She meant Stephen's brother, but we understood Mike played the game. He played by the Hrehovcik rules as set down by his father and so was rewarded with what he needed. We, of course, had to be "punished" for not being part of the circle, for daring to lead our own lives, away from the family. Independence was not rewarded.

Now that his father was gone, poor Mike would be set adrift for a while to carry on and take charge – the price of "playing the game." Both Stephen and I felt the price was too high and not one we wanted to pay. Although on the surface it did not seem as if Stephen and I had a lot in common, when it came to the very core of who we are, we shared the same important values. Integrity, for example, and the desperate need to survive away from our families, and to live life on our terms.

I wish I could say our life became easier now and we drew closer together. Sadly, this did not happen for several years. Yes, it did happen after many years of struggling and working very hard. The journey was long and often wearisome, and I wondered if it was possible for us ever to have a healthy, meaningful life together.

Soon after the funeral in New Jersey we were forced to move again. I was sad to leave our pretty yellow house. I was also sad when I had to break a promise I'd made to Gillian. It was a promise I did not make lightly and was sure I'd be able to keep. If we had been able to rent another house close to the school, I would have been able to keep my promise. Unfortunately, this house was rented to another couple with an even sadder story than ours. So, Gillian was forced to ride the school bus again; I had hoped we would continue to live close to the junior high she was attending so she could walk to school. Alas, not to be.

CHAPTER 25

Alone Again, Naturally

As disappointed as I was about another move to a house I didn't like, (in fact the day we moved I ended up flat on my back with a major migraine headache) some good things happened too. I met a wonderful man with whom I enjoyed a good friendship. His name was Steve too.

The funny thing was the way we met. I was hanging laundry in the backyard and so was he! We started to talk and discovered we had a lot to share and much in common. He was recently married after having been a bachelor for 32 years. His wife had just had their first baby, a boy, plus they had another boy from his wife's first marriage.

This Steve enjoyed being a father and a husband. He did most of the cooking and the housework as well as maintain the most beautiful yard and gardens in the neighborhood. We both loved the summer and spent many an enjoyable evening on his patio enjoying our gin and tonic and long talks about nothing and everything. What fun it was for me to be "so suburban," as my Joshua used to say.

Nevertheless, these years at Ridgewood Circle were not happy years for me and most of my family. Joshua chose to live in the basement; "the bat cave" he called it. He and his wife now enjoy their own beautiful home, and I can't think of anyone who deserves it more. Noah was away most of the time at school in Boston and Gillian was entering junior high school. Stephen continued to work at Weyerhaeuser in Westbrook. With everyone growing up and becoming their own selves, I decided it was time for me to get another job.

My income from my own business was not enough to make a difference financially for us. The "Write Spirit" had lost her spirit again. Even though I had finished my therapy with Dr. Collins and had learned once more to like and value myself as my own person, I still had a way to go. This last move was a backwards step for me, but I was determined nonetheless to rediscover the Carol I had once been and to make her an even better, stronger model than the previous one.

Life seemed to have a rhythm of its own now, and slowly, slowly because of a steady paycheck, we were paying back a lot of the money we owed. To do this, however, we all had to deprive ourselves. More bad financial news was yet to come when the bank sued us for repayment of the money we had borrowed for Stephen's theater.

Once more I felt betrayed, confused and angry. How on earth could we pay them back, sue us or not? Again, I felt like a failure and a bad person. Somehow, we made an agreement with the bank and the matter was settled, at least to their satisfaction. Should we have declared bankruptcy as we had been advised by two lawyers? I often think if I knew how much my kids were going to have to suffer for our folly, I would have agreed to it in an instant. I have had doubts about our choice over the years. Stephen, on the other hand, has never doubted we did the right thing by avoiding bankruptcy.

Would there ever be any peace of mind for me? I knew I needed that as well as emotional and financial security. Now I also knew something more. I knew I would have to take care of myself; I was responsible for me. If I wanted "things" then I had to be the person to get them.

I applied for and got a job at one of the local banks. I would sell an electronic device that verified credit card approval. The industry at that time was not sophisticated. In the mid-eighties, computers were still new and not in widespread use. As impossible as this may sound now, it was of course true. This would be a challenging part-time job for me, but most importantly it meant that I would still be home when I was needed.

Selling was not something I would have tried earlier. The old me would have taken any rejection of the product as a rejection of me. I think I wanted to test myself to see just how far I had come and also selling meant being out of the office. I needed that freedom; I couldn't be closed in all day.

I had the most wonderful boss I have ever known. If I got nothing else out of my job at the bank, I discovered there were a lot of good people out there who took pride in their work. My boss wanted me to succeed and encouraged me in every way. I liked her very much and wanted to do a good job simply because I admired her so much. The hours were just right for me and the promise of a good life seemed once more to loom on my horizon.

I remember when I had the first customer turn me down.

I was driving away and caught myself smiling and thinking, "Look at me. I'm alive. I'm all right. I am still the same person, no worse and maybe even better. I'll live. Wow." This was so intensely revealing to me because I knew, at last, I was healed. I was in fact, just fine, "Thank you very much."

When the position at the bank turned to full time, I decided this was no longer the job for me. I was nearly fifty years old and I didn't want a career, at least not that kind of a career. I knew I didn't want to work so hard or put in the longer hours. Work was never fulfilling for me. No, to me work was something you had to do in order to make money to live. I believed life was about more than work. Since Stephen was still not home at any decent hour, I felt it was my responsibility to be there for my family, especially now for Gillian. Someone had to be the chauffeur, the cook, the emotional supporter, and the watch dog.

It wasn't long before I started another new job, part-time again, as a library aide in the local high school. In fact, it turned out Gillian and I started high school together. Naturally, like most teenagers, she wasn't thrilled to have me working in her environment. However, she soon got over that and came (almost) to enjoy seeing me in the library every day. It certainly was convenient when she needed money, for example.

I discovered I was doing all my work at home before I left for my paying job. Moreover I maintained all my other jobs as well: chauffeur, cook, maid, food shopper, cheerleader and emotional support team leader. In other words, all I had really done was add another job to the long list of jobs I already had.

Yet I loved working in the school library. I enjoyed the high school kids; I liked the teachers and I liked the work, being surrounded by books and magazines and newspapers. Later I learned to use some of the media machines, although I admit I was a reluctant learner. Mostly I enjoyed being my own person with my own identity.

People called me Carol, kids called me "Mrs. Herocheck," and once they got to know me, I believe most of them liked and respected me as I did them. I treated them in a fair way, respected them and so expected respect in return. This was the way I brought up my own children, and I believe most people, teenagers included, respond to this in a welcome manner. I believe respect is an underrated commodity today, yet I know this trait is key to any learning or exchange. More than that, respect is the necessary element in all relationships.

As with all jobs in education, the bonus was to have summers off. I believed everything was working out just great for me now. What I missed and didn't see happening were the problems Gillian was experiencing. Not too late, fortunately, but late enough to frighten me to action. This was a shocking reminder to me I was still and would always be first and foremost a mother. A role it seems I was ready to relinquish too early.

At the same time, I was unaware of the problem with Gillian, Noah decided to leave the Conservatory to dance professionally with the Hartford Ballet. Although we were disappointed with Noah's decision to leave school, we felt we must be supportive. Because of the manner in which Noah chose to withdraw, Stephen was opposed. Nevertheless, we helped Noah leave the Conservatory late one night. With no word to anyone except his roommate, Noah packed up his belongings, and with our help, left for Hartford, Connecticut.

In retrospect I see how foolish and shortsighted I was not to question his motives and to accept this behavior as acceptable. In this case Stephen's instincts were better than mine, but I wouldn't listen. Later he had to handle all the awkward and embarrassing financial difficulties with the Conservatory.

Meanwhile Gillian was taking her ballet very seriously. She was playing the flute in the high school band, but sadly had given up her piano. As much as Gillian was always a joy and delight, she also was a strong-minded, willful, independent person. Once she made up her mind to do something or not do it, there was no wavering in her decision.

However, I will admit once she makes a mistake, she learns her lesson and does not make the same mistake again. How many of us can say that about ourselves? If you are anything like me, you often make the same mistake over and over, until one day you finally learn something, if you are lucky.

As unhappy as we were, she had given up her piano and was now concentrating on the ballet, Stephen and I believed the ballet in the end, of course, would give her poise and grace. It did this and more.

Ballet gave her something else indeed: the desire to be thin, to be very thin, to be frighteningly, dangerously and life-threateningly thin. Funny isn't it, when you see your children growing and emerging into young adults, you sometimes don't SEE them. I knew Gillian was conscientious about her weight. I knew also unlike her brothers she did not share her father's trait of a fast-burning metabolism. Gillian was more like me with a slow burning body chemistry. However, she was a careful eater and not one prone to eating junk food.

So, when some of her teachers at school and some of her friends talked to me about their concerns for Gillian's change in her body weight, I told them she was just fine and there was no problem. I reassured them all I was aware of her diet and eating habits and was even proud of what she had been able to accomplish with her diet in such a short time.

Since I also had to watch my weight and was very aware of any food I ate or cooked, I was conscious of preparing well-balanced and healthful meals. Gillian was younger and more active, so it made sense to me she would naturally burn her calories faster than I.

I tell you the anorexic is a clever person. People with this eating disorder are so preoccupied with food they begin to cook for you and prepare meals for the family. I welcomed her new recipes and her interest in cooking. I was totally fooled; I believed she was eating as well as preparing meals. I was pleased to see her looking so good and happy with herself.

When I did look more closely at her, I would sit down with her and talk about her weight loss. I suggested on more than one occasion she had lost enough weight now and did not need to be so concerned with her diet. She would always agree with me, and I foolishly thought the matter was settled. Still, I had my eye on her. Again, I had warnings from other teachers at the high school and her friends. "We've talked about it," I told them. "Don't worry, I know what's going on." What I did not know was the extent of her excessive exercise regimen.

During this time, a teenage girl in Portland, about Gillian's age, died from anorexia. The horrified parents discovered it wasn't merely the fact of their daughter's diet that made her so thin, but the girl had been over-exercising. One of the women I worked with pointed this fact out to me and suggested "perhaps" this was what Gillian was doing.

True, Gillian was teaching a water aerobics class two times a week and taking ballet lessons three times a week. I considered this a very real possibility. What else was she doing I didn't know about? Now I was looking at her with new and wary eyes. I noticed she was always wearing heavy, bulky sweaters and sweatshirts. Each day she looked thinner and thinner and suddenly I was worried too.

However, it wasn't until she and I went shopping for a new dress that I knew absolutely my lovely Gillian was sick. Gillian went into the dressing room and sent me to find a different, smaller size dress she liked. When I returned to the dressing room with the dress, I surprised her because she had no time to cover up her by now emaciated body. I was shocked and sickened to see the bones in her chest, rib cage and neck. All I could think of were the pictures I had seen of Holocaust survivors. This is what Gillian looked like to me standing there in that dressing room waiting to try on a dress I never gave her. "We're going home," I said. She knew her secret was exposed.

Why we stopped to eat after that, I don't know, as if I could resolve this horrible illness with one meal. By the time we got home later that day, both Gillian and I ended up in bed. I threw up, then she was sick, we both cried and poor Stephen was running between the bathroom and our bedrooms, not knowing who to comfort first or even how. What used to be one of my favorite restaurants, I cannot pass without remembering this day; we've never eaten there again. As helpful as Stephen tried to be, he did not see the sickness in Gillian. Even now I know Stephen has no idea of the impact this disease had on both Gillian and me.

But for me that day I had to face the truth: this disease was out of control. I chastised myself for being blind. However, I knew blaming myself was not going to help my daughter, and we needed help now.

Because of the discovery of the appalling nature of her body at this time, and the news of the girl's death in Portland, I needed to act at once. I knew Gillian could not help herself. It was up to me to get her the help she needed to get better. Faced with the unthinkable truth that Gillian might die, I could not run away or wait for someone else to make a decision. There was no escape from my responsibility to save my daughter.

I did the hardest thing I've ever had to do in my life. I sat her down and faced her with the truth. "Gillian, I think you are sick, and you need help. You are so dangerously thin I'm afraid if we don't get help now you will die, just like that girl in Portland."

I did not say this calmly; I cried the whole time I talked to her. I was so afraid and yet I was determined to make her understand and accept the truth of what I was saying. I was more afraid of her dying than any anger she might express toward me. She cried too and said to me, "At last."

Gillian knew she was sick but told me, "I didn't know what to do about it. I was waiting for you." She was waiting for me and Stephen to "notice" and help her. The next day Gillian and I met with her high school guidance counselor. She gave us the name of a woman who worked especially with young girls suffering from eating disorders.

The first thing we had to do was get Gillian to a doctor and check on her physical condition. How much harm had she done to her body during this time? Stephen came with us to encourage and support Gillian during this difficult visit. Gillian cried and cried and cried the entire trip to Portland, at the doctor's office and most of the way home after that.

At first Dr. Pachta was impatient and angry with Gillian. Gillian, who has always needed a gentle hand, was resistant to go back to the doctor. When Gillian accepted the fact that what she was doing was committing slow suicide, she understood a doctor didn't have a lot of patience with someone who would choose to destroy her body and her health. At this point Gillian would have liked to back away and out of what was happening to her.

Getting better was not going to be easy for any of us, but of course, especially for Gillian. However, she knew we were determined she get well and were ready to do whatever needed to be done to help her. If this meant she had to suffer some embarrassment, it was better that than death. It was horrible for me to see her hurting so, and soon she began her counseling. Together with counseling and regular checkups with the doctor, Gillian began her long, difficult road to recovery.

Naturally this involved Stephen and me. We learned Gillian was not anorexic simply because she wanted to be a ballerina. No. She felt Stephen and I were headed for divorce or worse, and she needed to feel in control of something. So, she chose this diet and exercise regimen. Moreover, Gillian's counselor said she would not take Gillian as a client unless Stephen and I went for counseling as well. We agreed.

Of course, Stephen and I had been for counseling many times in the past five or six years. Obviously, it hadn't helped our family situation. We made an appointment to talk with a marriage counselor she recommended. Gary turned out to be not only her associate but her husband as well. Still we decided to try. After all, if we didn't like him, we would find someone else.

Looking back now I would say this was highly irregular and perhaps not especially ethical. I don't know and I really don't care because as it turned out, Gary was very helpful to us. More importantly than that, he was someone Stephen liked (at last) and listened to. Stephen liked Gary right away; I wasn't as positive, but I was willing to put my feelings on hold.

I also put my feelings aside with Gillian's counselor. I was fairly certain I didn't like her, but Gillian seemed to respond to her and build a good rapport with her. That was more important than any negative reactions I had.

Since I had worked on my own problems with Dr. Collins, tried my hand at my own business, and had a job I was happy with, I finally had a pretty good sense of myself. My self-esteem was high at this time. Although naturally I was devastated by Gillian's sickness, I had found after all the courage to do what I needed to do. I welcomed counseling at this point and hoped it would benefit all of us.

I'd better warn you. You cannot enter therapy or counseling

thinking you are going to like or agree with everything your therapist tells you. You are sure to hear some things you either don't agree with, or more likely, things you may not want to admit.

Stephen and I heard many issues we didn't agree with or want to accept. However, our priority was to help Gillian in any way we could. Also, by the way, it would be nice for us to help ourselves. Wouldn't we just love to get along better after so many years of quarreling and quibbling? There were too many years of vacillating between love, hate and indifference.

How do you talk about your therapy? What did we learn, and did it help us get along better? Was there an easy cure all? Would Stephen and I suddenly be loving and warm with each other? No. But therapy this time did bring us one step closer to self-discovery and deeper understanding of the other person.

There is no magic in therapy. In fact, I found I could not understand or accept some revelations until years later. At least that is the way it was for me. Intellectually I could acknowledge "perhaps" this or that was true. But the big "Aha" came over time. Then I knew in my gut what was true, and I understood emotionally the truth of something I was unable previously to accept or understand.

Every step along the way was one step closer to Stephen's and my relationship getting better, improving, and seeing our love for each other grow again. As we got closer, Gillian began to feel more secure. The clue to helping Gillian recover from her disease was to work together as a family and as a couple. Once again it seemed to take the illness of one of our children to bring Stephen and me together.

Of all we've learned over the years, the most important issue is to give ourselves credit. We would only see what we hadn't done, how we had failed, or what we had not achieved. Gary especially, reminded us to give ourselves credit, to look instead at all we had accomplished. After all, he reminded us we were still together after all these years, 23 at that time. For whatever reason, and in spite of all the odds being against us from the very beginning, Stephen and I remained married. Very formidable odds indeed: our two families, religion, my pregnancy, Stephen's denial about his feelings and his negation of mine, yet here we are today, 42 years later.

I don't believe my husband was unusual when he used denial as his primary source of dealing with problems. This is referred to as "repress and deny." Now, I know several people who manage to live what seems to me a pretty good life employing the old "repress and deny" syndrome. This method says, "I don't have to solve this problem because there is no problem." By denying any such problem exists, one is free from having to come up with a solution. It must be nice to live problem free. I don't know many women who employ this method very successfully.

Stephen was forced by our children to admit the reality of our marriage and the problems that existed within it. First there was Josh's anxiety and now Gillian's anorexia. He may have been able to deny his own feelings and even mine, but now he could see for the first time that feelings were an important part of all our lives. In fact, feelings gave our lives meaning and validity.

The question became how does a man learn about his feelings when he'd been taught to ignore them? Or even more, he learned feelings do not exist. How does such a man learn to feel again? Over time, my husband re-educated himself. He learned about feelings and how to express himself. He deserves much credit, since I can't imagine learning something so elementary at such a late age. But he did it; he's done it, and sometimes, I laugh, I believe we may have created a "monster." But I wouldn't have him any other way. Thank you, Stephen.

At this time Stephen believed if he couldn't or didn't feel the emotions, then it followed, at least in his mind, that I didn't feel them either. He would always argue with me about my feelings and ask "why" did I feel that way? I grew up with parents who would never let me have my feelings. All I ever heard from them was "You shouldn't feel that way," "Don't feel that way," and "Why do you feel that way?" My God, did I marry my parents?

In childhood I learned but did not accept what my parents told me. For example, I was taught it was "bad" to feel angry, that it was "bad" to be jealous of my brother or anyone else, that I had to be the "better" person. Better than who, I wondered. Anyone else, I guess. I was constantly reminded of what I "should" feel or not feel. I know now anytime I feel I SHOULD do something, more than likely it is not something I WANT to do.

How many of us really want to do something simply because we should? Yes, of course there are certain niceties of etiquette which speak of a well-bred, civilized person. I'm sure you do those things or say those words not to offend or hurt someone. But given the choice of hurting yourself or someone else, whom do you choose? I often chose to hurt myself and not the other guy. However, I have made the most startling discovery. I can't tell you where it came from, perhaps in reading or therapy, but mostly I believe it was trial and error, and I might add, a lot of error.

I have learned when I have doubt about what to do in some particular circumstance, I do not ask myself what "should" I do, but ask instead "What do I want to do?" As soon as I ask this very simple question, I know the answer instinctively. In fact, it is so happily simple I wonder why more of us don't employ this method. I do not offer it to you as a "feel good, me only" approach. More I believe this is an honest approach to an honest dilemma. "What do I want to do?" By removing the "should" your path becomes clear.

I learned from Dr. Collins to get rid of the should's, the ifs, the wishes in my vocabulary. I am still working on the wishes. Which of course brings us straight into the realm of codependency. Remember that codependency was a new issue in the early eighties. Talking with friends about Stephen's workaholic tendencies, or more accurately his work-addiction, was like talking in a foreign language.

Especially today it is like a badge of honor to be a workaholic. You see, Stephen was ahead of his time! I did not understand why Stephen was compulsive about work, and worse why he chose to work and not make money. Years later I learned work can be like a drug; in excess it has the same effect as liquor to an alcoholic. Gary used to call work "Steve's drug of choice."

I did not understand, and I do not think Stephen quite understands or accepts even now his work is an addiction. Like a drunk who can be sober for months but will go on a "bender" when something is wrong or unsettling in his life, so does Stephen go on what I call a work-bender. Sometimes I can see it coming and other times I don't see it coming at all, and most of the time I won't know what caused it to be in the first place. I have further read that a work addict is never cured. But then how could he be?

CHAPTER 26

The Good News and the Bad News

We thought with Gillian's anorexia, perhaps we had faced the last big hurdle in our family life. Still there was more to come. Our son, Noah, was at this time in California with aspirations of becoming an actor. Indeed, when he first arrived in Los Angeles he appeared on "Concentration" and won a trip to Hawaii. We were thrilled for him. "Wow, a trip to Hawaii." However, Noah was disappointed with himself because he hadn't won a car. He saw this experience as a disappointment and a failure. Here was a sign of more bad times to come.

Noah also was getting work as an extra in some TV shows and even a movie. We thought perhaps Noah at last had found his calling, to be an actor. As he later confessed, he'd never been happy in the ballet. Still he had managed to make a professional career in dance. Noah had gone to LA with his girlfriend of the time, and I was glad he wasn't alone.

But as time went on and Noah became unsure of himself and his goals, he found getting work more and more difficult. The temporary jobs hardly lasted a month. Work as an extra was more sporadic. While he was wallowing in self-doubt, his girlfriend, Nancy, was getting on with her life and her career. Finally, as could only be expected, she left him for another man and Noah was now alone.

Stephen had to go to California on business and managed to spend some time with Noah when Noah was working at Disney. Noah told his father he had never walked around the lot until that day with Stephen. By now, of course, it was abundantly clear to us Noah did not want to be an actor. Noah did not seem to know what it was he wanted, but he was surely running away from something.

After his breakup with Nancy, he sent me a very angry letter, accusing me of being responsible for all his problems with women. He further requested I not write or talk to him until he got in touch with me. I was not very surprised and yet at the same time I was shocked by his accusations. The whole matter seemed like a cliché, and yet funny at the same time. "Blame your mother" was very popular at the time. Maybe it's always been the "mother."

I was more hurt than angry. I knew how hurt and disappointed he must feel about his breakup with Nancy, but I did not believe it was my fault. At the same time, I remembered something I had written in my journal years before, that I knew it would be Noah who would give me the most pain, and that he of all three children would be the one to turn on me.

I believe instinctively I knew the one child you do the most for is often the one who turns on you in the end. I had sensed this years ago and now it had come true. I read Noah's letter only once as I didn't want to let it in too deeply in my mind or heart. After a short time, I sent him an amusing card with a short note. I thought everyone gets angry, even mad, but how long do you stay angry?

Apparently, Noah felt he had to stay angry with me for a very long time and we hardly spoke for several years after that. At least he was talking to Stephen and so he was in touch still with the family. I was jealous of their new closeness. I had always been Noah's champion and defended him not only against the world, but often against his father, as Stephen treated Noah frequently in a less kind way than he did Gillian or Joshua.

I felt I had to take better care of Noah to make up for his father's lack of affection and awareness of what a good person Noah really was. Perhaps because Noah was so brilliant and so strong-willed, or maybe it was because Stephen could never control Noah, their relationship in the past had always been rocky, until now. Suddenly I was the bad guy and the one left out. Noah saw Stephen as some kind of victim of my terrible temperament and anger.

I have always had a theory about this sudden turn on me. I believe Nancy had told Noah he was too close to his family and especially too close to me. Noah and I often had the same feelings at the same time, even miles apart, and we would share these extra-sensory connections and wonder about them. I believe he had to prove Nancy wrong, and show her, even after she left him, he was in fact not a "momma's boy." The truth was Noah was never a "momma's boy." Even though he and I shared a close bond, Noah was always his own person.

Oh, sure, I took care of him, defended his right to choose his path to dance, act, or leave school, even when I didn't agree with him. And I often didn't agree with him. My first choice, my dream for him was always for him to go to Harvard or some other Ivy League school where I felt he would flourish in the world of academia.

However, the reason I went against my own desires for him and my instincts in what I believed would be right for him was because I felt I had to make up for Stephen. Because Stephen was so unflinching in his attitude toward Noah so much of the time, I thought by giving Noah extra attention and devotion, I could make up for his father. How wrong I was! To me my intentions were reasonable enough, but very wrong indeed.

I could never understand how or why Stephen felt the way he did about one of his own children. I also believed Noah was so gifted he needed all the support and encouragement we could give him as parents. I wanted Noah to have the opportunities Stephen and I never had. More than that, I wanted him to have the love, support and encouragement from us that we never had from our parents. I believed so strongly Noah would be a success in whatever path he chose, and it was up to us to help him along the way.

Soon Noah wasn't calling the family at all. Whenever Stephen and I called we always got the answering machine. Because we knew he was out of work and had been very despondent and lonely, we got scared of what he might do. When we were afraid for Joshua, at least we were here to help him. But with Noah three thousand miles away, we felt helpless.

Until one night. Stephen and I talked and faced the very real possibility Noah may indeed be suicidal. To say these words out loud, to express the fear is a horrible acknowledgement and one of course neither one of us wanted to admit. Stephen decided to call the police in Los Angeles. I was so proud of him when he made that decision and relieved, too. I was too afraid and felt so helpless I needed Stephen to be the strong one now.

As Stephen talked to the officer on duty and told him the circumstances, the officer asked, "When we get there, what might we expect?" The question was candid, and Stephen was honest in his reply. "We know he's been very depressed lately, and we haven't been able to get in touch with him for weeks. We just don't know what's going on."

It was about 8:00 p.m. California time on a Saturday night when two policemen knocked on Noah's door. Happily, Noah answered the door. He told us later how shocked and astonished he was to see two policemen at his door, and even more shocked to discover his father had called them. The policemen and Noah spoke briefly and then one of the officers said simply to Noah, "Call your father." Much to our relief, he did. Noah later did confess to us he had indeed been contemplating suicide. Knowing we would go so far as to send the police to his door, I think helped him to change his mind. Whatever the reason, I thank God and my husband, too.

If there is a message here, I think it would be to trust your own instincts. You know your children and even when you think you cannot do something or face what seems too awful a situation to deal with, you can, and you will, and you'll be grateful you did. After all, who knows your children better than you?

Soon after this incident, Noah came home for two occasions, my mother's funeral in August, and then again for Thanksgiving. Shortly upon returning to LA that year, he decided to come back to live in Maine. Noah was coming home.

Noah arrived home in April of 1993. Gillian was a junior in college in Ohio, and Joshua was living at home again. He'd been engaged for a short time that summer, but soon ended it and moved back home. This summer we were to be a family of five again. It was a difficult transition for all of us.

CHAPTER 27

Adult Children

Stephen and I didn't have much time alone, and during the time we did have, he was working more and more hours. To me, it was like the old days, when I was alone and lonely so much of the time. Since I had left my job at the high school and everyone was living back home, I was a full-time mother again. In some ways I didn't mind; in others, of course I did.

For example, my two sons have always been competitive and of totally different temperaments. Now relations between the two boys were even more strained and volatile. Joshua, who rarely lost his temper, blew up at Noah on more than one occasion. One time, Joshua was so angry with his brother he put his foot through the wall where he kicked it instead of kicking Noah. When Gillian arrived home for the summer things got worse as both Gillian and Joshua had problems with Noah. For whatever reason, our home that summer was filled not so much with love as intense tension. It was a painful time for the whole family.

At the same time, Stephen and I were looking for land to

build another house. We decided to build after looking at so many houses in Kennebunk and the surrounding area. We learned many lessons from our first building experience and knew we would be smarter this time. We were determined to do it right this time. We made an offer on a piece of land in Kennebunk, on Kimball Hill. We would be the third family in a development of only ten houses.

My friend Steve Baird introduced us to this piece of land, and both Stephen and I fell in love with it. The land sat high on a hill overlooking the Mousam River and was surrounded by woods on one side and a tree-lined border on the other. There was a field across the way and the land below had previously been a working farm. The man who originally owned the land was not only a farmer but a community spirited, generous soul. He had installed a ski tow on the very land where we hoped to build and there was a skating pond at the foot of the hill. There was an area for sliding and a little shack where the kids would stop in for hot chocolate or hot cider. Both the shack and the homemade rig for the ski tow were still on the property. Those who had grown up in the town all remembered Kimball Hill with a great fondness. This warmth of generosity and good feeling made Stephen and me determined this was where we would live.

I wasn't sure how all this family tension and dynamics would affect our dream project. We had, after all, lived in the house on Ridgewood Circle for nearly nine years, and not happily. Now the house we hoped to build was not planned for five people, and yet here we were. Oh, dear.

We assumed Noah would be off on his own again somewhere, thinking his stop at home was merely transitional.

We couldn't be sure about Joshua, as he worked right here in town, perhaps he'd like to live at home for a while. Gillian had one more year of college. She'd be going to Austria for one semester, then she had one more semester in Ohio before graduation. We naturally assumed she would choose to live elsewhere as she had been away from home for most of her growing up years.

Since these were unanswered questions that seemed out of my control, I concentrated on doing my part to make our dream a reality. I thought everything else would work itself out in whatever way was to be. I was learning to let go, especially to let go of my children. No one prepares you for the "letting go" part of being a parent. At least I know I wasn't ready. Were you? I was now anxious and even eager for them all to live and lead their own lives. I was having enough problems with my own life.

I am not particularly well-equipped at dealing with more than one major crisis at a time. I need to take events or issues one at a time and then move on. I am very capable of juggling multiple tasks, but I have a problem when dealing with multiple emotional issues. In my family, it seemed as if that was all I was doing.

At this time, my husband surprised me again in a very wonderful way. Since his father's death and my mother-in-law's move to Pennsylvania to live with her daughter, there had been some talk about either selling the house in Linden or at least re-mortgaging it to get some money. This house was a big cash cow sitting there but not producing any interest. Of course, it did provide my mother-in-law with a sizable income, so financially she was not a burden for Anne or any of her family. There is, of course, much to be said for this.

Stephen had previously introduced the idea with no success, and had, in the light of such fierce resistance from his sister, let it go. Now we would figure another way to make our dream come true. One thing we learned through all the trials and errors over the years was there was always a way. To be sure, we knew it wouldn't be easy, but between us we would figure it out.

To our surprise and delight, and it seemed not only out of the blue but also out of character, Stephen's sister brought up the idea herself of taking a small mortgage on the house in Linden, enough so all three siblings would get some money. My husband, excited and eager to make a reality out of the talk, took charge of this situation in his family. I don't believe either Mike or Anne was prepared for Stephen's determination. He was determined to make it happen, to get the money not only for us but for his brother and sister as well. I mean who can't use $30,000? Much to my utter amazement, Stephen did indeed "make it happen," and we had our down payment. How sweet it was!

CHAPTER 28

Building an Almost Dream House

Building our second house was an almost perfect experience. There were no horrible discoveries, no major problems, and no terrible setbacks. I often say it takes building two houses to get it right. Fortunately, we learned valuable lessons from our first experience and now nearly everything involved with building our second home went smoothly. Well, almost everything went smoothly. I am married to a Hrehovcik after all.

After we had all the plans and blueprints ready to go, we were given the standard builder's contract to sign. Have you ever read one of these contracts? Stephen did. He tore the contract apart, piece by piece, spent an entire weekend rewriting it, and even went so far as to consult a lawyer about the validity of it all. Then Stephen went to the builder and presented the revised and better-written contract, at least in his mind. Needless to say, the builder was not happy. In fact, he was so angry, his salesman called me at home and told me I had better talk to Stephen or the whole deal would fall through. Our only choice at this point was to sign the damn contract and get on with it.

Now, I am often a slow learner, I admit, but when I do learn something, I feel secure with it. One thing I did learn in all the years of living and struggling with my husband is to let him do whatever it is he feels he has to do, and then we can "get on with it". Personally, the contract was meaningless to me. I knew there would be no problem with the contract, the house, the building or any of it, but if re-writing the whole damn thing made Stephen feel better, it was no big deal to me. Now he had done his thing and it was time to move on.

Scott, the salesman, gave Stephen the names of other buyers the builder had contracted with and told Stephen to call them for references. The references were glowing, and now armed with a renewed confidence and no need to self-sabotage, we signed the original contract. I always believed this was my husband's last gasp at fear of commitment. From then on, the building of our house went smoothly and without major incident.

There was one factor in the building process that was important to me. I wanted to be sure we had people with good vibrations and no negativity. This may sound silly to you, but I am sure you have encountered both positive and negative people in your lives. The positive people are more fun to be around. Don't you like them better? I didn't want anyone working on our house who was nasty, mean-spirited or worse, incompetent. Lord knows we had enough of those people.

Everyone who worked on our house was wonderful, good-natured, and professional. Not only did these people take pride in their work, but they also found pleasure in their jobs. For most of the men who worked on our house, I would say they genuinely liked what they did for a living. Isn't that a wonderful declaration for any of us?

From the very beginning, from the concept of a classic cape design, to the work with the firm's architect, to the actual building, our house became what we had envisioned. Not the dreams of grandeur we had once planned, but a comfortable, warm house that would be a home to live and work in, and one day retire in.

Stephen and the architect got along very well, a fact for which I was very grateful. And here is more unsolicited advice: if you ever plan to build a home, work with an architect. An architect will assist you to achieve the plan you have in your mind. In other words, he can produce the vision of what you may only be able to envision. Also, he knows all the codes and what will work and won't work. Stephen and I both had some ideas and Fred, our architect, either made them a reality in the most efficient way or said no, you can't do that.

Because of our work with Fred, we made only two changes in the house as it was being built. This saved us any major costs above what we'd budgeted. We knew from experience any changes you make as the house is being built means more money, and by the end of it, those changes could be very expensive.

Because the blueprints were so exact, the two changes we made came only after we stood in what would be the kitchen. First, we enlarged the kitchen window and then we moved a wall over to allow for more sunlight and open space when I'd be working in the kitchen. As I stood there and placed myself working at the island that was to be there, I imagined what it would be like to look at a wall. I knew I wanted to have an open view, and I do.

The most important aspect of our new house for both Stephen and I was to have lots of windows and sun. We had designed the house to have a southern exposure and planned the garage on the north side. When the time came to put the stakes in the ground for the exact location of the house, Dwane, our supervisor for the building project, advised us for economy's sake to turn the house around. He said it would be more efficient to flip the plan and have what was to be the southern exposure be the northern exposure. The cost to do it the way we planned because of the slope of the land would be more than we could afford because we'd need too much fill.

More unsolicited advice: Make sure you and your architect walk around the land so your design will fit in with whatever exposures you want. Perhaps a southern exposure isn't that important to you. It was to me. I was so distraught by the prospect of turning the house around, I sat on the hill and cried. I tried not to, but I couldn't help myself. We had been living in such a dark house for nearly nine years, I needed the sunlight. I wanted the sun to follow me around the house all day, and now the sun would be hidden behind walls. I was very unhappy. Poor Dwane did his best to reassure me there would still be plenty of light, and he pointed out now we would have the better view of the surrounding hills and the river as well.

It turned out he was right, of course. Now whenever I come down my stairs in the morning, I have the most beautiful picture of the woods across the hill. Every day and every season is like a painting from our bay window facing north. Sigh. At the same time, there are other days when I am in my kitchen and I almost want to smash the wall that blocks the sunlight from me.

Yet, I love this house. I love the openness and the daylight as it pours in from all sides. We have yet to build our garage or to finish our decorating, but basically the house is warm, friendly, inviting, warm and safe. All I wanted it to be. I feel comfortable, snug and safe, and friends and family who come to visit feel welcome and comfortable. Your vision may be entirely different from ours, and I hope you achieve what you set out to express.

For us to have this house at last, to have found this "piece of peace," as Noah used to say, was worth the wait and even the previous pain. I am very grateful to God, to my husband, to Stephen's family who made it possible for us to build once again, and to my children and yes, even to myself. I had a dream, a plan, and faith. Perhaps, oh no, more than perhaps, I know there were times I had given up hope and faith and trust, but now I welcomed it in our lives. I was able to give myself and us credit for all we had done and what we accomplished. So often we see only what we haven't done, what we haven't accomplished, instead of giving ourselves credit for our successes.

The building of this house is a significant place to end this book. Not to say our life has continued with no further problems, pains, or pleasures. We have, like most of you, had our share of setbacks, disappointments, incidents. At the same time, again as most of you, our lives continue in a pleasing pattern as we grow older and our children are now adults. This alone is a whole other story, but one I find wonderful to observe and even be part of from time to time as their adult lives continue to unfold.

The significance of the building of this house is symbolic of the difference in our lives. This house represents in a very real way the positive changes Stephen and I made. The growth we accomplished and the lessons we learned along the way are all reflected in this, our second, and we hope last home.

Just as the house on Maplewood Drive became a symbol for everything that was missing and wrong with our marriage, our house on Kimball Hill reflects what is right. This house has put Maplewood Drive out of our minds and hearts. Stephen and I look forward and not back. Those two people from that time and that place do not exist anymore. Oh sure, Stephen and I still have our setbacks, regressions, disillusionments with ourselves and each other, but we are two other people now. We have forgiven ourselves and each other for the past. We have learned and we have grown from our mistakes.

We hope our children, particularly our sons, have forgiven us too, and have learned sooner than we ever did how to move on and have a good life. Our adult children give us much pleasure and joy. We are friends and share in each other's lives.

Joshua is married and living in Massachusetts only an hour away. The biggest irony of this is he and his wife live less than two miles away from the house where I grew up. Joshua works hard I know at being a good husband, and fortunately he has a wife who appreciates the gentle qualities in him.

Noah returned to college when he was twenty-seven, but then dropped out again after a brief marriage and divorce. He recently started his own business, and we are all anticipating he will make a success in whatever path he has chosen. Since his personal journey through a short-lived marriage, Noah has made his peace with our family and I believe his rebellion is all behind him.

Gillian graduated from college and has been living and working in Maine ever since. She continues to surprise and delight us with her steady approach in her career path and her life. And whoever thinks God doesn't have a sense of humor must know Gillian is one of the most devout Catholics one would ever meet. I find that humorous indeed.

I am enjoying watching these three wonderful adult children develop their own stories and am curious to see how well their lives unfold. So far, of course, they are way ahead of Stephen and me. Our deepest wish for our children is they do not suffer all the trials and storms we passed, and they will learn and grow sooner and younger and smarter than Stephen and I ever did. So far, all the indications point that way.

When I look at my life as I frequently do now at the age of sixty, I ask myself where have I been? What do I have to show for 60 years? Where am I going now? I have taken a wonderful journey which I hope to continue for many more years to come. In spite of the hardships and the anguish I am happy to be where I am now with my husband. I am grateful to be friends with all my children. Mostly what I have to show for my life so far is the gift to the world of my three children. I believe Stephen and I have given the world three very special and wonderful people: Joshua, Noah and Gillian make this world a better place just by their being in it.

They are my legacy. I know others have attained a bigger and more impressive legacy, but I personally cannot think of any accomplishment more meaningful or fulfilling to me than my life as a parent. I can look back with pleasure and pride with all three of my children knowing I did something right. I can also look ahead with the knowledge Stephen and I have made an important contribution to the future. I think this is a very good legacy indeed.

CPSIA information can be obtained
at www.ICGtesting.com
Printed in the USA
LVHW091918130320
650003LV00005B/28

9 781950 381418